THE COMPLETE IDIOT'S GUIDE® TO

RVing

Third Edition

by Brent Peterson and April Maher

ALPHA

A member of Penguin Group (USA) Inc.

ALPHA BOOKS

Published by Penguin Group (USA) Inc.

Penguin Group (USA) Inc., 375 Hudson Street, New York, New York 10014, USA • Penguin Group (Canada), 90 Eglinton Avenue East, Suite 700, Toronto, Ontario M4P 2Y3, Canada (a division of Pearson Penguin Canada Inc.) • Penguin Books Ltd., 80 Strand, London WC2R 0RL, England • Penguin Ireland, 25 St. Stephen's Green, Dublin 2, Ireland (a division of Penguin Books Ltd.) • Penguin Group (Australia), 250 Camberwell Road, Camberwell, Victoria 3124, Australia (a division of Pearson Australia Group Pty. Ltd.) • Penguin Books India Pvt. Ltd., 11 Community Centre, Panchsheel Park, New Delhi—110 017, India • Penguin Group (NZ), 67 Apollo Drive, Rosedale, North Shore, Auckland 1311, New Zealand (a division of Pearson New Zealand Ltd.) • Penguin Books (South Africa) (Pty.) Ltd., 24 Sturdee Avenue, Rosebank, Johannesburg 2196, South Africa • Penguin Books Ltd., Registered Offices: 80 Strand, London WC2R 0RL, England

International Standard Book Number: 978-1-61564-189-5
Library of Congress Catalog Card Number: 2011941056

17 16 15   8   7

Interpretation of the printing code: The rightmost number of the first series of numbers is the year of the book's printing; the rightmost number of the second series of numbers is the number of the book's printing. For example, a printing code of 12-1 shows that the first printing occurred in 2012.

Printed in the United States of America

Note: This publication contains the opinions and ideas of its authors. It is intended to provide helpful and informative material on the subject matter covered. It is sold with the understanding that the authors and publisher are not engaged in rendering professional services in the book. If the reader requires personal assistance or advice, a competent professional should be consulted.

The authors and publisher specifically disclaim any responsibility for any liability, loss, or risk, personal or otherwise, which is incurred as a consequence, directly or indirectly, of the use and application of any of the contents of this book.

Most Alpha books are available at special quantity discounts for bulk purchases for sales promotions, premiums, fund-raising, or educational use. Special books, or book excerpts, can also be created to fit specific needs. For details, write: Special Markets, Alpha Books, 375 Hudson Street, New York, NY 10014.

Publisher: *Marie Butler-Knight*

Associate Publisher: *Mike Sanders*

Executive Managing Editor: *Billy Fields*

Executive Acquisitions Editor: *Lori Cates Hand*

Development Editor: *Mark Reddin*

Senior Production Editor: *Kayla Dugger*

Copy Editor: *Krista Hansing Editorial Services, Inc.*

Cover Designer: *Kurt Owens*

Book Designers: *William Thomas, Rebecca Batchelor*

Indexer: *Tonya Heard*

Layout: *Ayanna Lacey*

Proofreader: *John Etchison*

Contents

Introduction

Now in our third edition, *The Complete Idiot's Guide to RVing* was designed to take the novice fumblings out of RVing. Sadly, most RV dealers don't take the time to properly tutor newbies in the hows and whys of owning and traveling in a recreational vehicle. As such, lessons are usually learned the hard way, through sometimes difficult trial and error. Although some consider this steep learning curve a rite of passage, I say malarkey to all that. An informed consumer is more likely to enjoy and benefit from his or her RVing adventures—and more likely to stay and thrive in this pastime.

RVs are amazing creations and one thing is certain—they are not designed to sit. In one big way, this book helps my personal crusade to keep RV enthusiasts behind the wheel. If I could arrange it, I would have a "No Parking" sign tucked inside every owner's manual as a tongue-in-cheek reminder that RVs are meant to be used, not parked by the side of the garage.

Long after the owner's manual is put in the glove box and the "Welcome to RVing" video is played, this book will be around to answer your questions. After three generations of camping, my family and I have been there, done that when it comes to RVing. This book is chock-full of support information to get you out of the weekday box and into new life adventures. It will help your RV trips go smoothly with easy-to-read, practical advice. And by traveling smoothly, where you went—and not what went wrong—will be the focus of your memories.

For me, such memories are priceless. All the beautiful places I have been were first experienced from the front seat of an RV. Imagine awakening in your favorite state park—Henderson Beach State Park on the Emerald Coast of Florida, anyone? Or being the one to replenish the campfire and share stories of the day while visiting Chequamegon-Nicolet National Forest near Eagle River, Wisconsin—the possibilities are endless.

Because I have been fortunate enough to see the beauty of Banff National Park in Alberta, Canada, burned my share of s'mores at family reunions lakeside in Wisconsin, and been chilled with patriotism at the sight of Mount Rushmore and the towering redwoods in Muir Woods National Monument in California, I have an inkling of what lies ahead for you. One summer we made it to the Iowa State Fair, just to see the Butter Cow. I'm not kidding. There's fun to be had out there in an RV. Get going!

How This Book Is Organized

Part 1, Choosing the Right RV, pares the field of the countless recreational vehicles available to the one that best suits you.

Part 2, Buying or Renting an RV, takes you through every step of the buying process, from test-drives to livability tests, from finding the right seller to finding insurance, and all those little extras.

Part 3, Operating and Maintaining Your RV, is a comprehensive look at what a recreational vehicle can do and how things work.

Part 4, Start Your Engines, details RV driving and towing, the importance of weights, and how to set up when you get there.

Part 5, Hit the Road, explains everything you need to know to plan that perfect trip; stay in touch as you go; and overcome such trip-busters as bad weather, accidents, and breakdowns.

Extras

As you read through the book, you'll notice sidebars that contain definitions, tips, warnings, and miscellaneous information to help you better understand RVing.

ROAD SCHOLAR

With all the complexities of a house and a vehicle, RVing presents many challenges. Fortunately, we've included lots of tips to help you through them.

RVOCABULARY

If you're gonna walk the RV walk, you've gotta talk the RV talk. These sidebars contain important lingo to help you sound like a pro.

PULL OVER

Travel is not without its share of possible dangers. Don't worry—I guide the way with a list of things to look out for as you go.

ONE FOR THE ROAD

Ranging from the trivial to the practical, this sidebar helps make sure you stay in the know.

Acknowledgments

From Brent Peterson: Writing can indeed be a lonely profession, but it still takes many people to get a project like this going. I'd like to thank my wonderfully supportive editor, Randy Ladenheim-Gil, for her support and recognition of this subject matter as book-worthy. Credit should be given to the entire Alpha Books team for making my words look so good. The contributions of "The RV Doctor," Gary Bunzer, were many and monumental. Not only did he review the text to make sure no one blows up, but his ideas, insights, and numerous photographs vibrate throughout the pages.

I have learned a great many lessons from so many talented RV writers along the way. Joe and Vicki Kieva, the first family of RV travel, helped a young editor learn the industry, while the late, great Bill Farlow taught me how to stand up. More thanks to Ann Emerson for giving me my first job in this industry, and Bill Brophy for hiring a confused kid right out of college and setting him on a course of journalism. Credit should also be paid to veteran newspaperman Terry Shelton, writer Robert Dana, and a host of amazing teachers who helped me discover my skills. I can't forget my mom, who pushed me to write. On the home front, my life simply doesn't go without my strong, beautiful wife, Anne. The profound joy and satisfaction I feel for my two boys, Parker and Maddux, continues to amaze me. To borrow a line from Jack, they make me want to be a better man. And there is simply no greater office mate than the ever-mellow Daisy the Beagle, loud snoring and all. Special thanks go to Aline Fiedorowicz, Eric Schieber, and my perpetual sounding board, Joby Gardner, for easing the hard times, as well as my terrific network of friends and family. How one guy got so blessed, I just don't know. Thank you, God. Finally and most sincerely, my deepest appreciation goes to everyone who purchased this book. Without you, I'm just a guy with a laptop.

From April Maher: Kudos to Brent Peterson for writing an eminently readable and practical guide to RV life. Gaining knowledge as well as seeing the humor in the pitfalls of RVing is a refreshing reality. In the years between the second and third editions, RVing continued to evolve and change. There is more concern about the environment, as the new trends chapter explores. And I added a chapter on renting an RV, as this is a fun alternative to owning.

I hope you keep this book onboard for every RV adventure you take and that you dog-ear the pages and refer to them often. I also hope that, as you flip through the book, you think of ten other people you can give it to as a gift.

My intro into RVing happened early in my marriage. My husband and I were lucky enough to take a trip of a lifetime and drove the Alaska (ALCAN) Highway to Alaska in an S-10 Chevy Blazer towing a Jayco pop-up camper. Along the way, we explored the majesty of the U.S. and Canadian landscapes, reveled in the history, and seized the opportunity to share space with the great outdoors in two countries. Armed with our "rig" (and our *Chicago* and *John Denver* cassettes), we fearlessly headed out for a month-long adventure. We had the time of our lives.

For this edition, thanks to my technical and hands-on RV experts, Mark and Dawn Polk, owners of RV Education 101, producers of RV training videos on how to use and maintain RVs, for your kindness and expertise when I reached out. Also thanks to Kevin Broom of the Recreational Vehicle Industry Association, who knows or can find the answer to any RV question posed. Thanks, too, to Lori Hand, Kayla Dugger, and Mark Reddin at Alpha/Penguin Books for walking me through the process, keeping me on track, and making it way better than I could do alone. And thanks to Marilyn Allen, simply the best literary agent a person could have. A special thanks to Anita, Keith, Diane, Linda, Renny, and Mary Lu, who each had "good catches," which is the highest compliment a writer can give.

To my family and friends who inspire and support me in ways too many to mention here, I thank you from the bottom of my heart. Especially to Tom, who fanned the flames of my wanderlust early on. He has taken me to more beautiful places to camp than a person has a right to see in a lifetime. To my son, Brian (Go U.S.A.F.!), who willingly hit the road with us, either smushed in the back of a Ford Mustang or ensconced in the family van (without complaint) and, as a result, has a love of nature and travel all his own—a loving thanks from Mom for all the joyful memories you've given me.

Special Thanks to the Technical Reviewers

The Complete Idiot's Guide to RVing was reviewed in earlier editions by two experts who double-checked the accuracy of the text. Their efforts on this book were absolutely invaluable. Thank you, thank you, thank you, Gary Bunzer (a.k.a. "The RV Doctor"), for your huge, technical brain, and Shelley Zoellick, a terrific writer and researcher. You guys are flat-out awesome.

Trademarks

All terms mentioned in this book that are known to be or are suspected of being trademarks or service marks have been appropriately capitalized. Alpha Books and Penguin Group (USA) Inc. cannot attest to the accuracy of this information. Use of a term in this book should not be regarded as affecting the validity of any trademark or service mark.

Choosing the Right RV

Now's the time to start thinking about what kind of recreational vehicle is best for you and yours. Choosing the ideal RV requires careful consideration as to what you'll use it for, who's coming along, where you're going, and for how long you'll be gone. Decisions, decisions! Don't worry—I'm here to guide you. Remember, to a certain extent, this choice will dictate the kinds of trips you take, for better or for worse. Will your travels take you across the country or just to the local state park? Do you want to rough it by camping far removed from civilization, or is a lazy weekend at a plush RV resort more your speed? Is this vehicle suited for the whole family—the kids, the cat, and your next-door neighbor—or is this just for weeklong trips with friends? Let's figure it out.

The ABCs of RVs

In This Chapter

- Why RV?
- What exactly is an RV?
- The types of recreational vehicles
- Unique advantages to RVing

Traveling RV style is like owning a separate vacation home in every place you would ever want to visit. You see, RV travel is all about freedom. It's just you and a wide-open itinerary. Take the family on an extended trip out West or simply down the road for a weekend at your favorite state park. If you want to stay longer, you can. Don't like the weather? Hop aboard and head off in pursuit of golden sunsets. Eat out or cook meals in your very own kitchen. And best of all, everyone has his or her own stuff, place to sleep, and comfortable way to get from here to there—and everywhere. Flexible travel means everyone's happy. You can visit an amusement park one day, a sunny beach the next, and a baseball game after that. It's living life on the go—or on the slow. The choice is yours.

If you're like me and you've always wanted to see where Elvis lived, there's nothing stopping you—not with an RV in the driveway and a willing crew. And that's just one great reason RVing is so popular. Here are a few more.

Togetherness: Spending time with family and friends is probably the reason cavemen started vacationing in the first place. It's a time to reconnect with your cave family and friends—not to mention getting a much-needed break from the ho-hum of the whole hunting-and-gathering routine. The same is true with

RVing: whether you're sitting around a campfire feeling groovy or having a jam-packed day at the Jam Festival, in the end, it's about being together.

The Great Outdoors: Sure, the Discovery Channel is nice, but there's simply no substitute for seeing the real thing—nature in all its splendor. No, not even the mighty internet can do justice to the profound impact of Colorado's Rocky Mountain National Park or the breathtaking views of the Grand Canyon like camping there in an RV. RVing gives you a front-row seat to many varieties of wondrous trees and the sound of chirping birds, a spring-fed stream filled with elusive fish, and mountains and valleys void of development.

Low Cost: Besides the fact that you're going to have to buy or rent some kind of RV, over time, the savings can be dramatic. No need to pony up the money for pricey hotels, rental cars, cab rides, or three restaurant meals a day, not to mention taxes and tips. Instead, find a free or inexpensive campsite and fix a fresh meal in the comforts of your home on wheels, with all your must-haves at your fingertips. And the only tip you'll need to provide is how you want your burger cooked!

Less Hassle: Trains, planes, buses, and cruise ships depart on *their* schedules, not yours. One of the great advantages of traveling by RV is that you control your own agenda, an impossibility in the busy world of commercial travel. RVing is about going where you want, when you want. In an RV, you are the captain of your ship, your own pilot, the boss of the applesauce.

Smaller Carbon Footprint: According to the Recreational Vehicle Industry Association (RVIA), families of four who take an RV trip generate less CO_2 than those who fly, rent a car, and stay in a hotel. So leave the Dreamliner behind and climb aboard your RV dream machine.

Variety Is the Spice of Life

Simply put, an RV combines transportation and living accommodations in one mobile package. Of course, that's a pretty loose definition. After all, my family never considered my parents' station wagon to be a "recreational vehicle," but we sure ate and slept in it enough during our epic family trips up north. Just think of the battles my brother and I could have avoided if we'd only had the roominess of a 40-foot motorhome to divvy up instead of the ongoing turf wars in the back seat. But I digress.

No matter how plush the family wagon or minivan is, neither merits RV status. To qualify as an RV, a vehicle must provide a place to sleep, basic cooking functions, and livable space. Sleeping on the floor of your sport-utility vehicle and dining on stale pretzels doesn't count. Legally, an RV must not exceed 400 square feet when on the road. But RVs usually go well beyond that simple definition, because most are loaded with many of the comforts of home. In fact, for many people, RVing means pretty much life as usual, only with changing scenery.

RVing is not exactly roughin' it. Life onboard an RV is similar to that at home. Lounge about on your couch watching game seven of the NBA Finals. Prepare an ambitious meal in a kitchen equipped with running water, gas stove, oven, microwave, and counterspace. Work on your computer, play games, or chat around the dinner table. Feeling chilly? Adjust the thermostat (or put on a sweater). A tad warm? Flip on the air conditioner and cool down in no time. Thirsty? Grab a beverage from the refrigerator or a glass of water from the kitchen faucet. Sleepy? Retreat to the master bedroom (if so equipped) or pull out the sleeper sofa or convertible dinette into a comfy nook. RVers shower in their very own shower. They enjoy free use of their very own bathroom. And because we're talking about some serious leisure time here, there should always be ample time—and storage—for one's golf clubs or fishing poles (tell me you didn't forget those)!

PULL OVER

Throughout the course of this book, the term RV is used somewhat generically. Numerous types of RVs exist, in varying sizes, weights, methods of propulsion, room configurations, number of passengers they can accommodate, sleeping arrangements, onboard amenities, self-contained camping features, and cost. It's not uncommon for an RV brand to come in more than a dozen floorplans, with options designed to transform an inexpensive model into a costlier one, or a modestly appointed RV into a luxurious version.

Moreover, many deluxe RV models boast a list of entertaining options that would make Donald Trump giddy. Rooms called "slide-outs" slide in and out at the touch of a button, providing extra living space. Global Positioning Systems (GPS) track your latest moves and can tell you how to get from point A to point B—you can even pick the voice you like best, like the one named Aussie Karen. Satellite television systems make sure you never miss your favorite show. Multiple flat-screen televisions, DVD players, surround sound, and cable TV hook-ups keep you and the family entertained all the way to Grandma's house.

As I'll cover in upcoming chapters, RVs come in all shapes, sizes, and budgets. Floorplans and sleeping capacities vary from model to model and from one type of vehicle to the next. Some kinds are suitable to live in full time, a way of life enjoyed by hundreds of thousands of people all across the country. Other RVs are better utilized for shorter getaways, outfitted with everything for taking memorable trips with your crew. No matter what your lifestyle is, where you plan to go, or who's coming with you, there's a recreational vehicle built for you.

ONE FOR THE ROAD

The first versions of today's recreational vehicles were created in the early 1900s by those dissatisfied with—what else?—the state of commercial travel. Early models were essentially camping paraphernalia laden or pulled by horses. With the invention of the automobile, homemade tent trailers and car tents were created, adding free mobility to these rudimentary designs.

Different Strokes, Different Folks

To understand whether RVing is right for you, it's crucial to first understand what RVs are and how they function. The best way to answer that question is to examine each type of recreational vehicle and its unique capabilities. Because RVing combines many of the accommodations of a small home, there's no shortage of available choices.

RVs come in two basic categories: motorized and towable. The major difference between these two groups is, you guessed it, that one has an engine (motorized) and the other requires some help getting around (towable).

Motorized RVs

From the smallest, most entry-level unit to the most grandiose example in the lineup, every motorized RV comes equipped with its very own method for getting around—an engine. It might be a diesel engine or a gasoline version, located in either the front or the back of the unit, but by golly, the only things motorized RVs require to get going are a turn of the key, the right kind of fuel, and a willing soul behind the wheel.

Motorized RVs (a.k.a. motorhomes) offer the noteworthy advantage of having all living and driving functions under one roof, in one vehicle. Unlike towable owners, those in the motorized camp, so to speak, need never hitch up to another vehicle. This, of course, also means never having to unhitch themselves when they reach their destination. This is doubly validating when it's raining outside. And because motorhomers are piloting only a single vehicle, many drivers find motorized vehicles much easier to navigate than when towing a trailer. That doesn't mean a motorhome can't tow a secondary vehicle. With an appropriately rated hitch (more on this later) and a knowledge of tow ratings and vehicle weights, motorized enthusiasts may have the option of towing anything from a car, to a boat, to a trailer full of motorcycles. A vehicle towed behind a motorhome is often referred to as a *dinghy*.

 RVOCABULARY

A **dinghy** vehicle is a term borrowed from the boating world, used to describe a car or truck pulled behind a motorhome through the use of a tow bar, dolly, or smaller trailer. It is also sometimes referred to as an auxiliary vehicle or toad vehicle.

There are five types, or classes, of motorized RVs: converted buses, Class A motorhomes, Class B motorhomes, Class C motorhomes, and truck campers.

All these RVs possess an engine, but after that, differences abound. Factors such as the number of passengers each can sleep and transport, the types of onboard amenities, floorplan styles, overall sizes and weights, and, of course, costs usually vary dramatically within the motorized category. The difference between an entry-level truck camper and an extravagant converted bus is as different as choosing between a condo and a stately mansion—the basic living necessities are present, but in varying degrees. However, all such motorized vehicles meet our working definition of a recreational vehicle, with, at the very least, a place to sleep, cook, and congregate. But rest assured, life onboard is far more interesting than that, as you'll see when we explore each motorized RV at length in Chapter 2. For now, here's a brief look at each.

Converted Buses

Remember that boring old Greyhound you took back and forth to college? Well, now picture that same bus, only with the full rock star treatment. Converted buses are the absolute top of the line—usually custom built and equipped with anything an owner's pocketbook can stand. The sky's the limit. In addition to the usual RVs that are full of beds, kitchens, bathrooms, and living rooms, bus owners are usually looking for a lot of unique extras, such as wildly expensive entertainment systems boasting the latest gadgetry, Jacuzzis, plush interior features (think lots of leather), slate or ceramic tiling, premium fabrics, and basically the best of everything. Lengths usually start at 40 feet, making them the mac daddies of the motorized world.

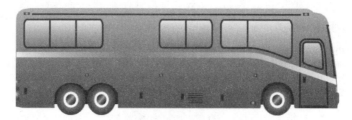

A customized bus.
(Courtesy of RVIA)

Class A Motorhomes

The most common RVs in the motorhome group, Class As are the best of the mass-produced bunch. For those unwilling to shell out seven figures for a converted bus, a gasoline- or diesel-powered Class A motorhome is the next best thing. Floorplans might include a master bedroom in a room all its own in the rear of the coach, a large kitchen full of cooking appliances and storage for all your foodstuffs and appliances, a private bathroom and bathtub/shower, a living area with lots of furnishings, and a cockpit, where the driver and co-pilot sit.

A conventional Class A motorhome.
(Courtesy of RVIA)

Like magic, at the touch of a button, out comes a room. It's common now to see many models with two, three, even four slide-outs spread throughout the coach. This adds living space and makes the RV much more roomy. Additional sleeping areas are enabled through convertible sofa beds, and dinette tables and benches can often unfold to form additional bedding. Some Class As can accommodate up to eight passengers, with overall lengths ranging from 20 to 40 feet.

Class B Motorhomes

A van in RV's clothing, Class Bs look like an inflated version of the family mini-van, with one major exception—complete livability. These motorhomes might offer a standard queen-size bed or a dinette area that converts into a sleeping area come nighttime. Some models sleep up to four in relative comfort, though a willingness to snuggle often helps raise these sleep counts. A small kitchen, storage areas, bathroom and/or shower, and cockpit take up the rest of the usable space.

A Class B motorhome, also known as a camper van.
(Courtesy of RVIA)

The most versatile offerings in the motorhome class, camper vans, as they are sometimes called, also serve as a reliable everyday vehicle, with sizes averaging approximately 15 to 20 feet in length.

Class C Motorhomes

Although alphabetically the last of the three classes of motorhomes, Cs are bigger than Bs and, despite their larger dimensions, are often less expensive. Their hallmark feature is the boxy nook residing over the cockpit area, which is often used for a sleeping area. Otherwise, these motorhomes are more or less condensed versions of larger motorhomes, with most everything onboard that the big boys have.

A Class C motorhome, also known as a mini-motorhome.
(Courtesy of RVIA)

Class C sizes range from 20 to 32 feet, usually built on a conventional truck chassis with an attached cockpit area. Known also as mini-motorhomes, they have a sleeping capacity that can sometimes reach up to eight passengers and slide-out rooms that are fairly standard.

Truck Campers

The least expensive member of the group, truck campers are not bought as much as they are built. Start with a typical pickup truck (maybe even your existing one), add a hard-sided camper shell, and voilà, you have a truck camper. The camper portion, or shell, can be removed when not in use or left affixed to the truck bed for spontaneous getaways. Long the favorite of outdoor types for their go-anywhere attitude, truck campers usually sleep two to four passengers and come complete with a small cooking area, dinette, storage space, and bathroom and/or shower. With the camper attachment, overall size may be only several feet longer than your standard pickup truck.

A typical truck camper.
(Courtesy of RVIA)

Towable RVs

The major difference between motorized and towable RVs, of course, is that towables have no …? That's right, no engine. Believe me, I've looked, and there isn't an engine anyplace. Thusly (how many times do you get to say *thusly*, anyway?), towables require a tow vehicle to move them around. Without a tow vehicle, a towable RV is about as useful for sightseeing and touring as your first apartment. Thankfully, the towing process is fairly simple, as we'll explore in Chapter 13. And as is the case with motorized RVs, each of the five towable types offers a different set of onboard features and sleeping capacities, sizes, and weights, from less than 700 pounds for a little Kamparoo to over 20,000 pounds for a Fifth Wheel.

Although towable RVs (a.k.a. trailers) require the aid of a tow vehicle to get them from one place to another, not just any kind of truck or automobile is up to the task. Tow vehicles must be of a certain size and equipped with an engine and a hitch/receiver powerful enough for the job. The same family sedan capable of pulling a small fold-down camper couldn't budge a 20,000-pound fifth-wheel trailer, no matter how hard it tried. Larger vehicles can tow smaller towables with no problem. (More on this in Chapter 13.)

Towable RVs enjoy the same levels of popularity as their motorhome brethren do, and many buyers find the lack of self-propulsion (okay, an engine) the most alluring feature. After all, no engine, no engine trouble. Break down in a motorhome, and you experience the double unpleasantness of finding both your home and your vehicle stuck in the repair shop. Better still, towables are cheaper than similarly sized and equipped motorized versions. Moreover, the absence of a cockpit opens up more usable space for storage, a larger bedroom, or added furnishings. Because many folks already own a vehicle suitable for towing (I'll explain matching up an existing car or truck with a towable in Chapter 13), you might already have the perfect tow vehicle in place. Furthermore, after you've reached your destination, towable owners may simply unhitch and head out to explore the area in their go-anywhere second vehicle.

There are five choices in the world of towables: fifth-wheel trailers, conventional travel trailers, sport-utility trailers, lightweight/hybrid travel trailers, and fold-down campers.

Although the manner in which they get to and fro is radically different than in their motorhome counterparts, life onboard a towable unit is pretty much the same, depending on the type you choose. Fifth-wheels can reach 40 feet in length and outshine most condominiums in terms of luxury appointments, while fold-down campers, the smallest in the group, offer a relatively inexpensive entry into the RV lifestyle, with all the basic features. We'll examine towable RVs more closely when they take center stage in Chapter 5. The following is a brief introduction to each member of the towable family.

Fifth-Wheel Trailers

Fifth-wheel trailers, or fifth-wheels, are the biggest, most expensive, and most well appointed of all available factory-built trailers. In fact, they are the only RVs with two separate living levels, with the bedroom area stationed in the bi-level *gooseneck* area, which affixes to the cargo bed of large pickup trucks or conversion vehicles. Several steps separate the upstairs bedroom from the main living area.

RVOCABULARY

The area of a fifth-wheel trailer that hitches into the bed of a pickup truck or conversion vehicle to make a connection for towing is called a **gooseneck.** Inside, the gooseneck area is raised from the rest of the interior, reached by stairs, and almost always used as the master bedroom.

Typical fifth-wheels come with deluxe cooking areas, abundant living space, a host of interior and exterior storage compartments, and fancy bathrooms and showers. Cavernous interior heights, multiple slide-out rooms (some units boast as many as five slide-out rooms), and large bay windows are also trademark features. Sleeping accommodations for as many as eight passengers are possible. Fifth-wheels come in lengths ranging from 20 to 40 feet and must be towed by a large pickup truck or conversion vehicle.

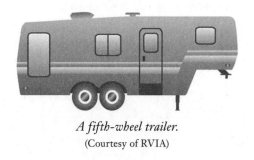

A fifth-wheel trailer.
(Courtesy of RVIA)

Conventional Travel Trailers

Versatile in terms of usage and floorplans, your average travel trailer suits full-time travelers and young families equally well. Sizes range from approximately 20 to 35 feet in length. They can be equipped with bare-bones necessities in smaller models to luxurious accommodations in larger versions. Slide-outs are common on larger models, which might be able to sleep up to eight passengers.

A conventional travel trailer.
(Courtesy of RVIA)

Sport-Utility Trailers

Despite the fact that towable RVs have existed in some manner for more than 70 years, the RV industry managed to incorporate a new style of trailer into the mix. The sport-utility trailer (SUT; commonly called a "toy hauler") is one of the fastest-growing segments in the marketplace. The beauty of these trailers is the pull-down ramp and rear cargo area that allows travelers to transport such goodies as motorcycles, jet skis, sand rails, or, well, whatever. The trailer's front section remains more typical, devoted to human crew, complete with bedroom, kitchen, bathroom, and living quarters. Sport-utility trailers usually range from 20 to 35 feet in length. Now there are also toy hauler motorhomes.

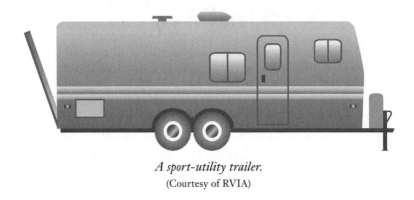

A sport-utility trailer.
(Courtesy of RVIA)

Lightweight/Hybrid Travel Trailers

The towable market was once fairly simple—that is, until the lightweights, super lightweights, and the often-curious-looking hybrid models came into vogue. These RVs are lightweight and overall are smaller versions of larger trailers. Usually weighing in at less than 4,000 pounds (I'll talk about the importance of weight in upcoming chapters), these towables are easily transported by many everyday vehicles, including trucks, SUVs, minivans, and, in some cases, large sedans. This is by far the most active towable category, with units made from everything from aluminum, to fiberglass, to tenting fabrics. Families enjoy reasonably low starting costs and easy towing. Standard living amenities are provided in lengths ranging from 12 to 25 feet. Sleeping capacity usually ranges from two to six people. Hybrid units feature unorthodox but highly versatile expandable book end(s), which extend bedding areas outward from the unit.

A lightweight/hybrid travel trailer.
(Courtesy of RVIA)

Fold-Down Campers

Considered the perfect entry into the world of RVing, fold-down campers resemble hard-sided tents, capable of being towed by even smaller trucks and larger cars. Fold-down units, also known as pop-ups, tuck in during transit for aerodynamic travel and easy transport. When the destination is reached, the unit is often manually deployed, usually via a hand crank or sometimes with the push of a button, raising the roof and readying the trailer for domestic bliss. (That is, assuming your mother-in-law isn't coming along for the ride.) Two bedding areas generally bookend a central living and cooking area. These types of trailers usually can handle up to six people.

A fold-down camper, also known as a folding camper or pop-up.
(Courtesy of RVIA)

PULL OVER

Contact your city officials to find out if you can legally store your RV on your property. Some ordinances prohibit this practice, citing obstructed views and potential eyesores as the reasons. (How dare they?) It's best to know beforehand whether your RV is welcome in your community or whether you must make other provisions for storing your vehicle.

The Least You Need to Know

- A "recreational vehicle" must meet three basic criteria—a place to sleep, cooking facilities, and a living area—but most go well beyond those.
- Motorized RVs include converted buses, Class A motorhomes, Class B motorhomes, Class C motorhomes, and truck campers.
- Towable RVs include fifth-wheel trailers, conventional travel trailers, sport-utility trailers, lightweight/hybrid travel trailers, and fold-down campers.
- Varying floorplans, sizes, weights, methods of propulsion, onboard amenities, sleeping capacities, and costs mean every RV is different.
- RVers enjoy all sorts of advantages in terms of traveling and living onboard their vehicles. The biggest perk is the ability to go where you want, when you want. Spending time with family, rediscovering the great outdoors, taking advantage of low cost, avoiding the hassles of commercial travel, and lowering your carbon footprint are just some of the noteworthy advantages.

The World of Motorized RVs

In This Chapter

- Learning the pros and cons of motorized RVs
- Examining specific types of motorhomes in depth
- Learning about the costs, specifications, and onboard features
- Determining who might benefit from each kind of vehicle
- Learning about new trends in RVing

Life in a motorized RV is like a condensed version of life at home. You can watch TV, listen to music, lounge about on couches and chairs, eat, shower, use the bathroom, sleep in comfort, play cards, write the great American novel (or the next great *Complete Idiot's Guide*), work, or do whatever. If you're a couch potato at home, there's nothing stopping you from assuming that relaxed state in your new converted bus, motorhome, camper van, or truck camper. Family gourmets can knock themselves out in the galley while the kids do their homework (yeah, right) in the living room or dinette area. Even the dog's daily routine needn't be interrupted. It's basically life as usual—except, of course, the fact that, well, your house now has a motor.

Ah, yes, the motor. Depending on whom you ask, it's the very source of the motorhome's undeniable appeal or the reason to take your business into the towable market. Prospective buyers must weigh driving ease and convenience against the added costs and potential longevity issues associated with such a purchase.

In Chapter 1, we explored the two basic vehicle types: motorized and towables. In this chapter, motorized RVs take center stage.

More Than a Motor

The motor. The engine. The mechanical muscle that separates a fully packed, ready-to-hit-the-road motorhome from a trailer that's all dressed up with nowhere to go. This is the very heart of the matter—and the source of all the advantages and disadvantages of motorized RV ownership. Your fondness for life in a motorhome probably boils down to your comfort level with its associated costs, driving ease, and under-the-hood challenges, something we're going to explore in great length. But first, here are some of the unique perks of motorized RVs.

All-in-One Vehicle

No hitching, no connections, no need to learn just what the heck tongue weight is (see Chapter 13 for the answer). The biggest advantage of motorized vehicles is that they're truly self-sufficient vehicles—everything needed is under one roof. Your motorhome is just waiting on you, your gear, and a full tank of gas (or sometimes diesel) to get your leisure time started. Walk triumphantly from driver's seat to refrigerator to bedroom without getting your shoes dirty. When it's raining, say "It's good to be King!" secure in the knowledge that your towable neighbors are scrambling between the raindrops while you're warm and dry.

Easy Street

Driving a solo vehicle (a lone wolf, if you will) is much easier than towing a trailer, especially when it comes to parking, backing up, and tight cornering. For starters, most trailer configurations are longer than most motorhomes; the combined length of the tow vehicle and medium-size trailer can easily exceed 50 feet. That's a whole lotta vehicle to take into the gas station or minimart, or weave in and out of rush-hour traffic. And when you consider the agile maneuverings of camper vans and truck campers, the driving benefits multiply rapidly. Motorized RVs require positioning only one vehicle into a campground space or parking lot during backups, not two. Keep in mind: one vehicle = one direction and two vehicles = many directions.

In-Motion Access

Wouldn't it be nice to watch *CSI* while someone else drove down the road? You might not care where you ended up. The fact is, motorized passengers have access to all their RV's interior bounty while in motion. Although passengers are discouraged from spending too much time moving about the coach—accidents happen—you certainly can reap the advantages of an onboard television, DVD, refrigerator, bathroom, and the like. Buckle up and play a game around the dinette table. Let the kids watch movies, play Xbox, or make a sandwich as you melt the miles up front. Ah, now we know why they're called homes on wheels.

One-Time Costs

The sticker price is the only obstacle to beginning one's motorhome adventures. Granted, this is usually a heavy expense, but motorized units require no extra equipment to start out—there's no pricey tow vehicle, hitches, sway bars, or connections of any kind (stay tuned to Chapter 13 to learn more). Think of your motorhome as an all-inclusive paid vacation, kind of like a Club Med, only without the flirty bartenders.

Hitchin' a Ride

All this, and the ability to tow a boat or secondary vehicle, too? In many cases, yes. The bigger the motorized RV, the more power it has, and the more weight it can support. After hauling around you, your crew, and all your stuff, your motorized RV just might have enough gusto left over to tow a car, truck, or small trailer with a boat, snowmobiles, or a pair of jet skis. A hitch, a series of connections, and a firm knowledge of your RV's weight ratings and towing capabilities are all that's needed to bring such items along for the ride. We'll discuss how to tow a secondary vehicle or trailer with your motorhome in Chapter 13. True, this practice, of course, negates some of the benefits of drivability listed earlier. Ah, well.

Sticker Shock and Motor Awe

In the issue of fairness, motorized RVs in all of their awesomeness also offer their share of possible disadvantages, depending on one's point of view. RV wannabes should be well informed and consider the ramifications of any buying decision. Not surprisingly, the sticker price tops the list when considering the possible negatives.

For a similarly sized, similarly equipped towable, motorized RVs are more expensive. How much more? The starting cost for a 20-foot conventional travel trailer is approximately $15,000 to $25,000; the same size Class C usually starts at $50,000. And as a separate motorized vehicle, insurance costs fall under the requirements of automobiles, and the vehicles must be insured accordingly. For this reason, costs for these RVs always exceed those of any towable, no matter what discounts or tall tales you spin to your insurance company. Routine maintenance, in the form of oil changes, tune-ups, and any (cover your ears) breakdowns are more likely—and, yes, more expensive—than what a motorless trailer will put you through.

Getting Cocky

I've referred to the place where the driver and co-pilot sit as the "cockpit" several times already. Why do we call it this? It's just fun to say, I guess. "Honey, I'll be in the cockpit if you need me." Well, don't kill the messenger, but when not in use, the cockpit is pretty useless, which qualifies it as another disadvantage. In fact, the rest of the interior must compensate for its very presence, jamming amenities and living areas into the remaining space. Sure, you can hang clothes to dry on the steering wheel or showcase your *Star Wars* figures on the dashboard, but it's basically valuable, wasted space when you're not behind the wheel.

Mobility Issues and Floorplans

After the destination is reached, the driving advantage swings back to the towable owner. Why? That nifty car or truck that's been pulling the trailer for the last 400 miles can now be disconnected and ferry the family around nice and easy. Motorhomers who have decided against towing a second vehicle (or "dinghy," as explained in Chapter 1) must make all side trips, errands, and sightseeing jaunts in their RV—and everyone must go together. Whether you're going to the movies or Mom's underwater basket-weaving class, everyone's along for the ride.

Not only that, but motorized floorplans also lack the variety of their towable brethren. The cockpit is always up front; the bedroom, in some form, is most always in the rear. And that's how it's been forever. Sure, kitchens and bathrooms may move from one side of the coach to the other, and onboard standards and options change somewhat. But basically, the room layouts are nearly identical, meaning fewer interior choices for prospective buyers.

You Are Depreciated

We've all heard the cautionary tale about depreciation. Buy a new car, drive a mile, try to sell it, and what do you get? Because it's now a *used* vehicle, it's suddenly worth less. Is that example kinda silly? Sure, but it doesn't make it any less true. Motorized vehicles have a dirty rat onboard in the form of their odometer. It tells new buyers everything they already suspected, dating mileage and creating doubt about the mechanical aspects of the RV.

Not only do motorized RVs cost more, but they also lose their value faster. An engine means more can go wrong. Try selling your two-year-old motorhome after logging a few cross-country trips, and you'll experience this motorized bias firsthand. Trailers, with fewer mechanisms to wear down and break, endure the prying eyes of trade-in time much better.

With an idea of the pros and cons of the motorized world, here is an in-depth look at the five kinds of motorized vehicles: converted buses, Class A motorhomes, Class B motorhomes, Class C motorhomes, and truck campers.

Converted Buses

It almost seems crass to lump a custom-made, converted bus in with the likes of the much more common, mass-produced motorhomes rolling off assembly lines. These one-of-a-kind dream machines usually begin with a 40- to 45-foot Prevost chassis and shell (think Greyhound bus), with the interior usually outfitted according to the wishes of an affluent buyer. Think of your basic converted bus akin to owning a tailor-made suit rather than buying off the rack. Simply put, a converted bus is as good as it gets.

Naturally, this kind of luxury comes with a heavy price tag. Costs usually won't dip much below $600,000, with "average" prices hovering around the million-dollar-plus range—which explains why everyone doesn't have one parked in their driveway. However, for those who can afford them, there are a handful of prominent companies all too happy to design and build the perfect vehicle for you and yours.

It takes big bucks to break into the conversion bus market, but those who can afford it receive a bus of their very own design.
(Courtesy of Liberty Coach)

What Is It?

Perhaps the better question is, what is it not? A converted bus is *not* inexpensive, *not* mass-produced, and certainly *not* for everybody. Those few companies in the bus game usually create fewer than 100 units per year, pouring as much as 1,000 man-hours into each bus to get it just right. Although customers are certainly welcome to select a more standard model from inventory, these folks are more likely ponying up substantial costs for a bona fide original. And just what can a potential buyer expect? Whatever they want, whether it's an onboard Jacuzzi, his-and-her bathrooms, state-of-the-art entertainment systems, ceramic or granite tile, residential-style kitchen appliances, washer/dryers, fish tanks, or technological gadgetry never before seen on the road. And let us not forget the massive diesel engines that power these bad boys, huge holding tanks and storage compartments, and whopping air conditioners, furnaces (even hydronic heat, using hot water to warm the interior), and inverters.

Actors, musicians, and sports stars are prominent members of the bus market. One manufacturer has even come up with a model designed to keep out nuclear radiation and chemical/biological agents. Things can get pretty extravagant inside and out. For instance, one country singer paid dearly for his favorite artist to paint a mural on the coach's exterior. That was after spending a staggering sum for the Mexican tile and special hardwoods for the interior. And we certainly applauded the efforts of the celebrity who couldn't live without eight plasma TVs onboard so he could watch a different game on every channel. As you're seeing, it's anything goes.

Get Some Sleep

Obviously, a million-dollar ride is going to come with some special bedding. In most cases, the master suite is still relegated to the back, but that doesn't have to be the case. We've heard stories of king-size waterbeds and bedding that folds into the wall when not in use. Multiple sets of bunks, for those traveling in larger groups, are quite possible, as are any number of sleeping configurations in the main living area, whether it be a pair of leather sleeper sofas, fully reclining lounge chairs, or other nighttime concoctions.

Just Relax

With vehicle lengths of 40 to 45 feet, space isn't going to be much of an issue onboard. Add a slide-out room or two or three, and expect complaints of close quarters to be at a minimum. Such motor coach designs rarely go timidly into creature comforts, with the biggest benefactor often the coach-wide entertainment offerings. Multiple flat-screen televisions and a DVD are commonplace. Sadly, the universal remote control that runs these systems still gets lost. Obviously, it would be a crime not to install a pricey in-motion satellite system so you don't miss news, weather, or the comedy channel while on the go. Some companies offer link-ups to their vehicles so they can diagnose mechanical problems from back at the manufacturing plant. After all, why shell out this kind of money only to have to limp back for service? However, what goes onboard is generally up to the buyer. Sure, there are limits to what can be done, but as one designer recently confessed, there aren't many.

Typical Specs

Buyers have input in even some of the basic specs. If a cavernous fresh water tank is important to you (doing some camping in the Sahara Desert, are we?), who's to quibble? Again, bus builders aren't in the business of saying no.

Standard Specifications for a Converted Bus

Self-Containment Features	Gallons
Fuel tank	Starting at 100
Fresh water storage system	Starting at 100
Gray water holding tank	Starting at 75
Black water holding tank	Starting at 75
LP gas container(s)	Starting at 80
Water heater	Starting at 20

Price Tag

Are you sitting down? Got some smelling salts handy? Custom buses generally start at $600,000 and, if you're driven like a mad scientist to get everything you could ever want onboard, can even hit $2.5 million. The "lower-end stuff" is usually prebuilt on spec by the manufacturer to have a little something in inventory. The used bus market is quite active as well, with lower costs part of their appeal. However, any way you look at it, it's not cheap. Compounding the dollar purge is the fact that you can't take your dream machine just anywhere for an oil change or service. Such maintenance is beyond the scope of most RV dealerships and service centers, often forcing bus owners to drive well out of their way to find a shop that can handle their needs. A vehicle this size also escalates everything from the costs of fuel to the price of insurance, storage, and the fancy RV resorts that cater to the bus-only crowd.

Final Analysis

Unless your last name is Gates or Trump, a custom bus is probably more fantasy than anything else. But we can dream, can't we? However, if you've got the cash—and lots of it—there's no better way to see the sights and travel on your own terms. Prospective buyers should also note that such custom jobs take time—a couple of months at least for the building stage, assuming there's nobody ahead of you. And who knows how long designing the bus of all buses will take? Otherwise, there's nothing but blue skies for those who wish to climb to the top of the RV heap.

Class A Motorhomes

Pretty much everyone knows one of these when he sees it. In a sea of trendy SUVs, kid-carrying minivans, and monster pickup trucks, Class A motorhomes continue to impress, ranging in size from 21 to 45 feet in length and tipping the scales in excess of 20,000 pounds. Class A RVs are fully self-contained vehicles, complete with a separate master bedroom, kitchen, bathroom with shower and/or tub, living area, and cockpit. You can also expect lots of interior and exterior storage for all your trip essentials. Multiple slide-outs are common.

Class A motorhomes can exceed 40 feet in length and offer the full range of comforts and amenities.
(Courtesy of Winnebago Industries)

Class A motorhome with four slide-out rooms.
(Courtesy of Winnebago Industries)

What Is It?

Class A models are built on a specially designed chassis (an emerging trend) or existing chassis from manufacturers such as Ford, Workhorse, and Spartan. Engines may be either gas or diesel. *Diesel pusher* models feature a diesel engine, usually located in the rear of the coach, to better and more quietly propel you down the road. Engine noise is virtually eliminated in the cockpit area while riding in a diesel pusher model. We'll talk more about the differences between gas and diesel engines and the usefulness of wide-bodies in Chapter 4. *Wide-body* models are fairly common and boast an extra-wide interior space, but come with somewhat of an extra cost. Wide-body vehicles are restricted to designated highways in some states. A trucker's atlas, available in most truck stops, highlights roads on which it is permissible to drive a wide-body vehicle (the Rand McNally GPS for RVers highlights these roads as well). *Basement models* have a sort of basement (hence the name) that allows for much greater storage capacity and accessibility to packed items. If a high-end Class A doesn't have what you need, you may need to reconsider whether RVing is right for you. The range of onboard options should leave travelers with plenty to do and plenty of space to do it in.

RVOCABULARY

Motorhomes powered by a rear-mounted diesel engine, so equipped to propel rather than pull larger vehicles, are known as **diesel pushers.** They are generally found in motorhomes 35 feet in length and larger.

Any recreational vehicle wider than 96 inches is considered a **wide-body.** Most states limit vehicle width to 102 inches, although that number does not include the added dimensions of expanding slide-out rooms. **Basement models** are RVs with a separate storage section located between the chassis and the interior floor.

Get Some Sleep

Mom and Dad are happy in their private master bedroom with queen-size bed. Other couples might share the sleeper/sofa and/or convertible dinette table and bench seats. Reclining chairs sometimes deploy into impromptu sleeping areas, often with mixed results. As always, numerous sleeping options are available, including bunk beds and double beds (instead of a queen-size) and other furnishings that might work in a pinch. Larger coaches are well suited for 6 to 8 passengers, and 10 is not out of the question.

PULL OVER

Examine and verify any claims in terms of sleeping capacity prior to purchasing an RV. Test out all bedding to see if it's fit for an adult or would be better suited for a small child. Sleeping capacity estimates do not follow any legal definitions. Some claims may be wishful thinking on the part of the manufacturer. Untested bedding may leave passengers cranky, come morning.

Just Relax

Lots of living space makes larger motorhomes the most popular motorized RVs in the marketplace. Nearly every model is offered with at least one living room slide-out floorplan. Two and three slide-outs may expand the kitchen, bedroom, and main living area. A model with quadruple slide-outs opens up the space dramatically. The dynamic of the communal space follows that of the quintessential American living room: loads of comfortable furnishings revolving around a large flat-screen TV or two. Of course, your house probably isn't equipped with a slide-out room if you're feeling a bit cramped. Couches turn into beds, recliners, well … recline, and even the chairs in the cockpit most likely swivel to join in on the conversation. A host of side tables, interior lighting, and plenty of storage compartments in all shapes and sizes grace the coach.

Motorhome designers rarely hold back in terms of luxury appointments for their Class A buyers. Carpeting is thick, and interiors come in multiple color schemes. Window blinds, including electric shades, cover the large windows scattered throughout the interior. Home theater systems that include a DVD/CD player and AM/FM or satellite-ready radio and computer workstations are offered as a standard or as an affordable option. A powerful furnace and air conditioner—sometimes two—should come standard.

> **ROAD SCHOLAR**
>
> RV buyers usually have their choice of several color schemes. Different colors for everything from the wallpaper and blinds to carpeting and upholstery are yours to choose. While it's hard to believe you won't like what you see in the brochure, if you don't find what you want, no worries—you can usually customize to your heart's content.

The typical Class A bathroom simply outguns any other motorized vehicle in terms of spaciousness, aesthetics, and features.

Typical Specs

A larger RV allows for larger self-containment options. This means you can stay away from civilization (if you want to) for a greater length of time, boondocking without having to go into town to refill the propane container or empty your various holding tanks. Onboard generators create power where there is none and are almost always listed as standard, fueled by a seemingly bottomless gas tank. Holding tanks and LP containers are cavernous, allowing for greater periods between emptying and fill-ups.

Standard Specifications for a Typical Class A Motorhome

Self-Containment Features	Gallons
Fuel tank	75 to 200
Fresh water storage system	50 to 125
Gray water holding tank	40 to 100
Black water holding tank	40 to 100
LP gas container(s)	20 to 50
Water heater	6 to 10

Price Tag

A Class A may start at $76,000 for a small, "entry-level" gasoline model and evolve into as luxurious and pricey RV as you desire. A million dollars is not out of the question if you go hog wild, choosing the biggest version and loading it to the gills with goodies. And there's absolutely every kind of model in between.

Fuel is the next major cost, as even the more fuel-efficient motorhomes (warning: oxymoron alert) might earn a dozen miles per gallon, at best. A modest diesel engine may better that average by a few miles. A more expensive RV purchase such as this also necessitates a larger insurance premium, storage costs (if necessary), and repairs. Unlike your serviceable everyday vehicle, routine maintenance in the form of oil changes, tire service, and basic troubleshooting can be performed only by an RV service center, with facilities adept at handling the big rigs.

Final Analysis

The question is not so much who Class A motorhomes are good for, but who can afford them. All that space and luxury comes attached with a fairly significant price tag, requiring a more serious commitment from their owners. Folks looking for casual weekends away might find a more suitable RV for their needs for less money, as might anyone just starting out and new to the lifestyle. A large motorhome demands thoughtful consideration to your types of usage. However, if you love RVing, with all its bells and whistles, you really can't do much better.

The major drawbacks usually come down to drivability. Maneuvering a 35- or 40-foot motorhome is just too daunting a challenge for some folks. Buying a Class A does merit some attention in this respect. Finding a parking space large enough to accommodate your rig is also tough. Uncovering a spot in a residential neighborhood, in that charming resort town, or within a metropolitan area is especially trying when you feel like you have the Seventh Cavalry in tow. Storing your motorhome for the winter requires a special facility (and special costs), which may or may not be located nearby.

Class B and Class B Plus Motorhomes

It looks like a van and drives like a van, but when you venture inside, it takes but a moment to realize you're not in Kansas anymore. These vehicles are popular with people who want to incorporate their recreational vehicles into their everyday lives. By day, a Class B serves as a dutiful second vehicle, great for shuttling the kids to school, running errands, and getting you wherever you want to go without the angst of lugging around an enormous RV. A large motorhome or travel trailer just seems strangely out of place at the PTA meeting. There's lots of space for all the kids (the whole soccer team, too), a menagerie of golden retrievers, and all those great buys you found at the antique auction. Class Bs drive like a dream and should easily fit in conventional parking spots. Class Bs are also known as conversion vans, camper vans, and van campers.

When the weekend comes, look out. This is where these motorhomes really shine. Grab the kids, dogs, and gear, and head north to the state park for a day of hiking, swimming, and picnicking. Arrive at the football game early for a little traditional tailgating, with a mobile kitchen to cook the feast, a refrigerator full of tasty beverages, and a TV to watch the pregame show. Arrange a spontaneous getaway for you and your better half, confident in the knowledge that there's always a place to sleep.

A Class B motorhome doubles as a highly functional everyday vehicle when not in use as a vacation machine.

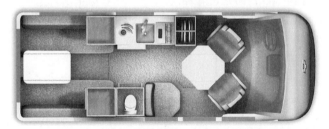

Also known as camper vans, most Class B motorhomes typically feature couch bedding, a modest-sized galley, a communal living space, and a small bathroom.
(Courtesy of Home & Park)

What Is It?

Credit the many Summers of Love of the late 1960s and early 1970s for the advent of these vehicles, when more and more people began customizing their vans with bedding and basic cooking equipment to accommodate their, ahem … lifestyle. (Insert your own Grateful Dead joke here.) This craze led to the growth of conversion companies, willing to do the work in a more professional manner. Thus, the conversion van segment of the RV marketplace was born. These days, conversion vans fall under the category of Class B motorhomes.

Despite their sometimes everyday looks, Class Bs are card-carrying members of the recreational vehicle community. Underneath lies the same chassis as in normal vans, with engines from such familiar names as Dodge, GM, and Ford. The cockpit area is virtually the same, too. But after that, all bets are off.

The conventional seating is removed in favor of a convertible or queen-size bed, small kitchen, bathroom, shower, and storage space. A drop floor might be installed and the rooftop extended to provide adequate standing room. Interior heights vary from 5 feet, 5 inches to nearly 8 feet. One point to note is that many parking garages are unable to accommodate vehicles over 6 feet, 8 or 9 inches. Since some of these bad boys can reach 7, 8, or 9 feet in height, sometimes you've got to bite the bullet and park on the street. Wide-body designs are common. The same holding tanks, electrical functions, and fresh water system that make an RV, well, an RV, are all present.

Class B Plus

Class B Plus motorhomes are an embellished version of a Class B. These rather plush RVs are slightly larger than a Class B for more interior room and storage, and they often have a slide-out. Also a plus are the surprisingly spacious bedroom and bath facilities. The exterior tends to have a lower profile than its Class C cousin, typically utilizing the sloped space over the cab for storage. They are easier to drive than a Class C, too.

Get Some Sleep

Depending on the size of each passenger, most vans can sleep two people reasonably well. Four people is possible, depending on the model and floorplan. As always, the flexibility and willingness of kids to contort into a smaller sleeping area is a big plus. Bedding comes in many forms. The wraparound sofa might pull out to make a double or two twin beds, or a queen-size mattress might fit unaltered in the back of the vehicle. In some cases, chairs lay completely horizontally, creating a usable night's sleep for the junior members of the crew.

Just Relax

You might be lounging about on a sofa, sitting in leather chairs, or chatting around a dinette table in bench seats. Again, floorplans vary, but every camper van has a place for the family to talk, play games, and dine together. With the TV/DVD/CD player, you can happily spend nights watching TV or a movie or listening to your favorite tunes. Windows slide open for breezes and views. A forced-air furnace and air-conditioning keep you comfortable in variant temperatures. An optional generator keeps things going when shoreline power is out of reach. Life onboard is snug, depending on the number of passengers, but it certainly blows the doors off any other family vehicle in terms of functionality.

Typical Specs

Easy driving, modest lengths and widths, and an optional generator make Class Bs as adept at surviving in the backwoods as Rambo. A few companies produce four-wheel-drive models, kicking up such excursions to the next level of terrain and excitement.

Standard Specifications for a Typical Class B Motorhome

Self-Containment Features	Gallons
Fuel tank	25 to 35
Fresh water storage	15 to 35
Gray water holding tank	12 to 30
Black water holding tank	10 to 20
LP gas container(s)	5 to 30
Water heater	6 to 10

Price Tag

Camper vans aren't cheap, especially when you consider that some larger motor-homes offer much more livable space and amenities for less money. Prices range from approximately $41,000 to $100,000, certainly a great deal more than the minivan you're used to. Cost is factored by overall size, onboard amenities, and choice of engines.

Expect gas mileage to drift between 10 and 25 mpg. If you plan on storing your van for the winter, your garage should work, saving you several months' rent at a dealership or storage facility. Otherwise, there are those costs to consider. Insurance is similar to the cost of your everyday vehicles, with adjustments made for type of usage.

Final Analysis

Nimble maneuvering, low profiles, and conventional looks make Class Bs 24/7 recreational vehicles. Their ability to adapt equally well to both life in the city and weekend getaways puts camper vans in unique territory. No other RV functions as well as an everyday vehicle, a consideration that should be factored into a somewhat inflated sticker price. Although three to four passengers could get along okay onboard, Class Bs are better suited for singles, couples, and families with small children.

Gains in drivability and the perks of a usable second vehicle are somewhat tempered by the fact that life onboard can be fairly restrictive. Accessing the interior through the side- or rear-entry doors can necessitate an awkward entry. A few models, usually those boasting sleeker profiles, don't have enough room for taller passengers to stand up straight. A larger motorhome at roughly the same cost is much better suited for extended travel. Enjoying several extended weeks on the road is surely possible, assuming that the lack of moving-around room doesn't bother you. But there's no better RV for tailgating, day trips, and weekends spent touring the countryside.

Class C Motorhomes

Think of a Class A motorhome and a Class B van camper zapped by a morphing laser from a mad scientist—or your local RV manufacturer—and you come close to what a Class C delivers: decent space in a very drivable vehicle. Getting around, not to mention parking and backing up, is just that much easier, making these RVs an all-around good bet. Class C motorhomes, also known as mini-motorhomes, are a nice compromise in the world of motorized RVs. These vehicles feature everything their larger counterparts do—bathrooms, bedrooms, kitchens, living area, storage, slide-outs, cockpit, and loads of standards—but at a reduced size. Although lengths usually range from approximately 20 to 32 feet, sleeping capacity can rival that of the big boys. Up to eight slumbering passengers is possible in some units. A few Class C brands feature a rear ramp and cargo area for storing motorized fare such as motorcycles, ATVs, or snowmobiles.

A Class C motorhome has many of the same features of a larger Class A, only in a smaller, more maneuverable package.

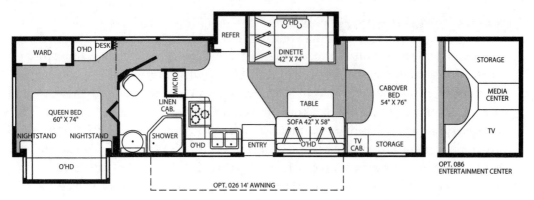

A typical Class C floorplan, complete with rear bedroom and a cab-over sleeping area.
(Courtesy of Fleetwood RV)

What Is It?

Mini-motorhomes start with the same basic van chassis as a Class B, courtesy of Dodge, Ford, General Motors, and others. However, a specially manufactured frame is then added, giving them a unique profile. Class Cs are capped off with the trademark "cab-over" design, which creates a habitable space over the cockpit area and works as a serviceable, albeit tight, sleeping area or spot to store larger items. Slide-outs are common. Diesel engines and four-wheel-drive models also are available.

> **PULL OVER**
>
> The acceptance of the cab-over sleeping area is usually determined by the age of the guest. Youngsters seem to find the tiny area a space ship in the making and usually offer little resistance to sleeping there. Older passengers might struggle with the awkward ascent and find the cryptlike clearance somewhat troubling.

Get Some Sleep

The rear private bedroom paired with a sleeping nook over the cab remains the best way to cram in the most passengers. Throw in a sleeper sofa and/or convertible dinette table and bench seats, and sleeping for six is a breeze. However, in recent years, Class C manufacturers loosened up and started creating more radical layouts. Wander into the back of some models, and you might be greeted by the smell of bacon and eggs cooking from a galley kitchen, complete with a three-burner range, oven, microwave, and refrigerator. Enjoy your meal at the booth dinette. Before bed, take a shower in the private bathroom. The debate over the usefulness of the cab-over sleeping area rages on. Assuming you can find someone to sleep in this smallish space, you'll be rewarded by a higher sleeping capacity and one less body to step over in the morning. Kids really seem to enjoy it, towering high above the rest of the crew in their secluded fortress. A privacy curtain and windows only add to this effect.

Just Relax

All the usual components and furnishings are included, with ingenious methods of incorporating a lot of onboard offerings in a relatively condensed package. The living room, often the benefactor of a slide-out or two, usually delivers a dinette and sofa (J-shape sofas are popular) to create plenty of space to gather. In models under 25 feet, expect one or the other, but not both. A flat-screen TV/DVD/CD and cable TV hook-up are standard or available as relatively painless upgrades. All temperature controls (furnace and air-conditioning) are present to keep you cool in summer and warm when temperatures plummet.

Interior and exterior storage compartments rank somewhere between Class A and Class B motorhomes. Unless you're an insufferable packrat (guilty as charged), finding a spot for all your "must-haves" shouldn't be a problem. Deep cabinets, a variety of drawers, wardrobe closets, and dressers should withstand most families' onslaught of provisions. And assorted exterior compartments—many of which are insulated, carpeted, and well lit for nightly rummaging—are best suited for durable fare such as golf clubs, folding chairs, and that gorilla suit for fun around the campfire.

Typical Specs

A more agile alternative to larger motorhomes, Class Cs can squeeze through most awkward terrain to reach that remote camp-out location. Generators are usually standard or, at the very least, wired for future installation. Depending on the size of the vehicle and one's conservation practices, the various tanks and power sources should keep any hook-up–free adventures running for several days without interruption.

Standard Specifications for a Typical Class C Motorhome

Self-Containment Features	Gallons
Fuel tank	40 to 55
Fresh water storage	30 to 60
Gray water holding tank	20 to 40
Black water holding tank	20 to 50
LP gas container(s)	7 to 40
Water heater	6 to 10

Price Tag

Do I buy that new Lexus or a mini-motorhome? Isn't the choice obvious? With a starting price of around $50,000, you, the kids, and the cat (and her scratching post) can travel, sleep, and eat your way across the nation. Larger and more expansive models might reach $85,000, still a bargain compared to bunking down in a pricey import. Take that, luxury automobiles.

A few smaller, lower-profile models might just tuck away nicely in your garage, thus eliminating the need for offsite storage expense. Insurance is a factor, probably somewhere between a Class A and a Class B motorhome, although routine maintenance should be relatively reasonable. Because your Class C started with a van chassis, larger repair shops should be able to handle many maintenance concerns. However, you might need to take it to a certified RV dealership or service center if your local garage balks at servicing recreational vehicles.

Gas mileage is just okay. Large models feast on fuel like a group of Boy Scouts at the local Dairy Queen; smaller versions may deliver up to 20 miles per gallon with a strong tail wind. But don't count on Smart Car–like fuel economy here.

Final Analysis

Class Cs are useful for most any type of traveling situation. Call it the Goldilocks effect: a Class A is too big, a Class B is too small, but these mini-motorhomes are just right for many. Their relative driving ease, coupled with surprising passenger capacity, arms travelers with a multifaceted leisure machine. Factor in these pluses with reasonable start-up costs, and the case for the mini gets stronger and stronger.

As a full-timing machine, Class Cs work exceptionally well. Everything is onboard to create a truly memorable year-round living experience. Traveling in a 30-foot version with double slide-outs leaves nothing to be desired. A queen-size bed, along with the overall dimensions and appointments of the master bedroom, is sometimes sacrificed in smaller models to complete the rest of the interior. A dwarfed bathroom and cramped shower also sometimes come with the territory. However, that's always the key to any RV—knowing what you can live with and what you can't live without.

Truck Camper

The rugged truck camper, also known as a pickup camper or slide-on camper, provides a steady mix of comforts and nimble transportation to most any destination, in a very inexpensive package. This is simply one of the most economical ways to camp in comfort if you have a pickup.

Truck campers affix to the bed of your pickup truck, providing owners with a go-anywhere camping machine.

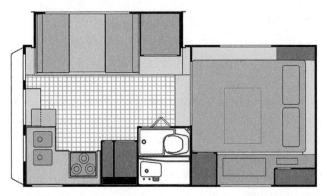

This truck camper floorplan features a slide-out dinette and couch, in addition to a small galley, bathroom, and cab-over bunk.
(Courtesy of Lance Campers)

What Is It?

A truck camper is essentially a pickup truck with a hard-sided camper, or cap, secured to the cargo bed (there is also a pop-up version). Then, presto, your everyday, hard-working vehicle is magically transformed into a genuine recreational vehicle. Who would have thought that the bed of that old pickup, formerly used only to haul around tools, firewood, and your boss's patio furniture, could suddenly transform into a year-round home on wheels. Neat, huh?

The interior plays host to relatively the same basic features of any other RV, only in a much, much smaller package. There's a spot to sleep, various cooking appliances, storage, and places to sit, relax, and plan your next camping escapades. Temperature functions are regulated with a heater and air-conditioning; you can open the screened windows if the weather's nice or employ interior fans found in the ceiling. Nearly all truck campers have hot and cold running water, boast lighting, and are powered by the use of LP gas, or can run off the generator (if so equipped) when you're away from a conventional power source. Bathrooms and showers are fairly common. Truck campers usually sleep between two and four, depending on the size, the floorplan, and your passengers' willingness to cuddle. However, the modest dimensions can make for long days onboard.

ROAD SCHOLAR

One of the nice perks of a truck camper is its flexibility. When the camping adventure is over, truck camper owners have the option of removing the cap, storing it away, and resuming their civilian lives until the call of the wild strikes again.

The Perfect Fit

Trucks and camper sections are rarely sold together in one package. Camper caps come in many sizes, so fitting one to your current truck, whether it's a monstrous or compact version, shouldn't be a problem. The most important criteria is not to exceed the truck's payload capacity, which should be listed in its owner's manual. To gauge this, add the weight of the camper itself (your dealer should know this, or it will be listed in the unit's owner's manual) to the estimated weight of passengers, their gear, and fully loaded holding tanks. If this number is less than your pickup's carrying capacity, your truck can safely do the job.

Another factor is the overall center of gravity. It's not unusual for the camper to hang several feet beyond the end of the cargo area. However, your dealer should help make sure you have the best fit for your truck.

Truck campers are situated fully into the bed of the pickup and secured with turnbuckles and tie-down brackets—two on each side. Manually operated hydraulic camper jacks, permanently bolted to the four corners of the camper, make loading and unloading relatively easy. Extending each jack eventually raises the camper above the level of the truck bed, providing plenty of maneuvering room to back the truck under or to pull the truck out. For safety, always have a buddy—or burly mountain man—help you.

ONE FOR THE ROAD

Electric or hydraulic jacks make the loading and unloading of a truck camper way easier. Having a second person, while not mandatory, is helpful in getting the camper aligned and mounted on the truck bed.

Get Some Sleep

A large bed (sometimes a queen) is situated in the area over the truck cab and should yield a comfortable, albeit somewhat cramped, night's sleep for two passengers. Some floorplans boast additional bedding, in the form of either trans-formable couches, bench seats, dinettes, or double beds. RV manufacturers have a lot of clever ways to create beds out of otherwise functional space. Some campers claim accommodations for six, but so many adults in this small amount of space will undoubtedly lead to calamities that would make even the Three Stooges blush. Bunk bed models are sometimes available for the younger set.

Just Relax

A table with bench-style seats or a wraparound couch (both of which might turn into beds) is common, creating a good spot to chat, plan the next day's events, or feast on the catch of the day (or frozen fish sticks, if the big one got away). TVs and surround sound are sometimes offered. A few interior cabinets and drawers house everything from silverware to clothing. One model might feature a small wardrobe closet; another might be stocked with a storage chest and a row of over-head cabinets. Lights come on and off with a switch, temperatures are controlled via a thermostat, and an exhaust fan helps remove stale odors. You should find adequate lighting and enough room to move around without coming to blows with your fellow passengers. Year-round camping is certainly possible, thanks to adequate insulation practices and optional furnaces and air-conditioning.

Interior height is problematic for your NBA pals but adequate for most folks. An average height is approximately 6 feet, 2 inches, but this number varies from unit to unit. Some *pop-up* (a.k.a. fold-down) models can expand (or pop up) upward when not in transit, giving inhabitants more headroom and space. The emergence of slide-out rooms adds valuable inches onboard.

RVOCABULARY

Pop-up (or fold-down) truck campers lay flat in transit and must be deployed, usually by use of a hand crank or the flip of a switch, after the destination is reached. Advantages of these types of vehicles include less wind resistance dur-ing transit and, in many cases, increased headroom upon arrival. Pop-up models aren't as heavy and drive a little more easily.

Important Add-Ons

With the help of a few accessories, you can guarantee yourself an uneventful trip for both you and your camper. Tie-downs secure and fasten the camper to the bed or frame of the truck. Use these in conjunction with bounce-aways, shock-like devices attached below the cab-over section to the truck, to reduce bouncing down the highway.

It is also necessary to invest in electrical connectors to operate your brake lights and taillights, which are obscured by the camper. Not having these is an easy way for the local sheriff to fill his monthly quota. These cords also charge all the onboard functions while in transit. In some cases, depending on the overall length of the camper, rear bumper extensions may be necessary so the license plate is visible. Remember, the truck is licensed, not the camper, even though some come equipped with a plate bracket. The telescoping type simply extends when the camper is in place and retracts when using the truck as, well … a truck. Finally, make sure your truck camper comes with four mounted jacks, one on each corner. The purpose of these is twofold: to keep the trailer off the ground when not in use and to elevate them so you can back your pickup between them for easy loading.

Typical Specs

Adding a camper to a four-wheel-drive truck gives owners relatively endless possibilities in terms of where to travel. Few recreational vehicles can compete with a truck camper's off-road capabilities. Keep a truck camper's "go anywhere" advantage in mind.

Standard Specifications for a Typical Truck Camper

Self-Containment Features	Gallons
Fuel tank	Same as the pickup truck
Fresh water storage	10 to 50
Gray water holding tank	10 to 25
Black water holding tank	10 to 25
LP gas container(s)	5
Water heater	6

Price Tag

With a start-up cost of between $5,000 and $20,000 for the camper portion, truck campers are among the least expensive recreational vehicles, ideal for "first-timers" with small families or for a couple eager to get away for shorter trips. Of course, if you don't have a pickup, you will need to factor that price into the overall price.

Ancillary costs such as insurance are relatively minuscule compared to those for most recreational vehicles. Besides, in most cases, you were already paying insurance on your pickup, so adding a camper won't do much. Most insurance companies might simply add the camper as a rider policy for a marginal fee. Again, most routine repairs and maintenance (tune-ups and oil changes, for example) are what you would have spent to keep your truck in good working order in the first place. A monthly storage fee probably won't be necessary because campers are small enough to be stored in the garage, in the backyard, or at your lucky in-laws' house. All in all, truck campers are a bona fide travel bargain.

Final Analysis

Outdoor types love truck campers because these vehicles are tough—capable of reaching the most remote places, such as that deep-woods hideaway or off-the-map backwater fishing hole. And depending on your pickup's towing capacity, there's probably still enough power and carrying capacity to hitch up a small trailer to carry a boat, jet skis, motorcycles, or snowmobiles for even more active pursuits upon arrival.

For many, extended trips onboard a truck camper are out of the question. Although these vehicles are surprisingly comfortable and livable, considering their diminutive size, the accommodations do take some getting used to. Just as you wouldn't want to spend entire weeks at a time inside your tent, the same rule applies here. All these factors make truck campers best suited for shorter getaways.

Becoming a Trend Setter

There's nothing faddish about today's trends in motorhomes and RVs. Fads come and go, but broader sweeps of functional luxury, personal space, and environmental partnership have the staying power to become mainstream. Here are a few things to look for if you desire to be considered RV fashion-forward.

Lean and Green

Keep your eyes peeled for a third-party environmental certification sticker. A Certified Green designation means consumer expectations are met without sacrificing the planet. It identifies recreational vehicles that meet net energy-efficient and water-efficient benchmarks and standards for efficiency in use of resources, such as lighter, green building materials; indoor environmental quality, operation, and maintenance procedures; and innovative practices that increase performance.

Solar System

Thanks to factory-equipped solar panels, instead of installing a solar panel kit on Saturday, head out for a weekend in the wilderness. Wherever the sun shines, RVs sporting solar panels can tap into its energy to charge the RV's battery. When the battery is fully charged, campers can turn into fans to catch *Man vs. Wild* or *Mythbusters* on TV.

Off the Grid

Need an attitude adjustment? At the campsite, replace HP with foot and pedal power. Walk to the camp store or unload one of the bicycles to ride over. Circulate air within the RV by opening windows with cross-ventilation in mind. Remember to leave no trace by taking out what you bring into the great outdoors, and honor campground recycling programs. When in doubt, don't take out the trash; take it home.

High-Tech

Bigger boys have bigger toys, even in a motorized or towable RV. With multiple larger flat-screen LED HDTVs secured to walls and, in some cases, the ceiling in the bedroom, it's high time for high-tech RVs. Wi-Fi? Check. Blu-ray players? Check. Integrated surround-sound systems? Why not? Docking stations are built into counters with space reserved for laptops. If hunger strikes, find something cold in a full-size refrigerator or bake a pizza or two in a full-size oven. Slide-outs now create an extra room like an outdoor kitchen, with a second refrigerator, maybe an infrared grill, and definitely a canopy. How about an ice fishing hut, an extra bathroom, or a fireplace?

Good Things Come in Small Packages

RV manufacturers have responded with vigor to the growing demand for fuel-efficient chasses and engines. Watch for motorized RVs and towable RVs to get lighter through the use of more efficient building materials to meet the demands of an energy-conscious populace. And the advancements don't stop there. Enter the EFOY (Energy For You) fuel cell for all of your power needs. The size of a toaster oven, the EFOY fuel cell is sufficient enough to power an ultralight motorhome and eliminates the need for gasoline and diesel-powered generators.

The Least You Need to Know

- Class A motorhomes cost from $76,000 all the way up to over a million dollars. Sizes range from 25 to 45 feet and can sleep up to eight passengers. They're a favorite with full-timers and large families alike.
- Class Bs, also known as conversion vans, van campers, and camper vans, are built on a standard van chassis but are customized with living quarters. Costs range from $40,000 to $100,000. Driving ease and their smallish size allow for everyday use.
- Class C motorhomes, or mini-motorhomes, cost between $50,000 and $125,000. Lengths range from 20 to approximately 34 feet, and due to a special cab-over area, they can sleep up to eight passengers.
- Truck campers combine a standard pickup truck with a hard-sided cap. Costs range from $8,000 to $30,000, not including the price of a truck.
- New trends in RVing include smaller, more fuel-efficient motorhomes, lighter building materials, and solar panels. Functional luxury items include larger flat-screen TVs, full-size appliances, and maybe even an outdoor kitchen.

The World of Towables

In This Chapter

- Defining the pros and cons of towable RVs
- Examining the specific types of trailers
- Looking at the costs, specifications, and onboard features
- Learning who might benefit from each kind

Abbott and Costello. Green eggs and ham. The Chicago Cubs and futility. Like all life's great combinations, towables and the tow vehicles who love them comprise a tag team for the ages. It's a partnership that has paid off in terms of lower costs, longer usage, and big-time creature comforts for owners and guests alike since the first commercially made trailers rolled off assembly lines more than 75 years ago.

The evolution of the towable enthusiast sometimes goes like this …. With young children and faced with the expensive costs of getting out of the house, a couple purchases a small, inexpensive fold-down camper to pull behind the family vehicle. As the children age and everyone demands a little more space, a travel trailer is considered, perhaps even one complete with a slide-out room, just for kicks. It won't be long before the parents, now empty-nesters, enjoy the luxury and easier towing found in a fifth-wheel trailer. However, others jump right to the head of the class with a large first-time trailer purchase. As always, there's no right or wrong way to do it.

Affection for the towable lifestyle usually comes down to your comfort level with the thought of towing another vehicle. To some, the idea is peculiar and scary, especially when there's a perfectly good motorhome or camper van just waiting for a driver. But for others, the thought of RVing in any other manner and paying the higher costs associated with the motorized life is outrageous. I'll take your interest in this chapter as a sign that towables might be for you. Here's a closer look at what's offered and the ins and outs of each.

Tow: The Way to Go

The choice seems so obvious for some. What could be more sensible than one vehicle for driving and another for living? Trailer aficionados favor two distinct driving and livable vehicles, a kind of separation of church and state, if you will. Here are some of the obvious advantages of life with a towable RV.

RVing on the Cheap

Looking for the travel deal of the century? Buy a fold-down (pop-up) camper or lightweight trailer; hook it to your sedan, SUV, or minivan; and vacation on the cheap. (And just for the record, a pop-up camper and a fold-down camper are the same thing). When the kids get a little older—and less tolerant of you—opt for a 25-foot trailer, with room for four and all the goods. The price of two towables combined is less than the cost of nearly any motorized RV. Small towables such as these provide the least expensive way to travel, hands down. Fact is, engines equal money, and big engines—such as those found in medium- to large-size motorhomes—cost big money.

Your trailer never needs an oil change or tune-up, and will never leak radiator fluid or blow a gasket. All things considered, the towable world is pretty uneventful in terms of repairs and maintenance. (Onboard systems and appliances require regular upkeep, just as all RVs do.) Opening up your insurance bill won't send you into a Hulk-like rage, either. Towables are fairly inexpensive to cover, certainly lacking the automotive legalities of their motorized counterparts. In many cases, insuring the new (small) trailer may be as easy as adding it as a rider to your existing automobile policy. We'll chat all about that in Chapter 8.

Double the Fun

Yes, motorized vehicles necessitate only starting the ignition to kick off their adventures, leaving trailer owners in the dust as they hitch up their towables.

However, revenge comes in many forms. For starters, the vehicle doing the actual towing (a.k.a. the tow vehicle) serves double duty as easy transport when the destination is reached. After the trailer is set up, the tow vehicle is free to depart with you and your crew to have some fun while the dutiful trailer stays behind. Enjoy a night at the movies, a gourmet meal at the local bistro, or day trips to scenic locales without a cumbersome motorhome to worry about parking in unfamiliar environments.

Two separate vehicles also deliver peace of mind during times of trouble. If anything ever happened to either your tow vehicle or the trailer behind it, you wouldn't experience the horrors of seeing both home *and* transportation holed up at the mechanic's, a very real threat in the lives of motorhomers. Believe me, there's no worse feeling than witnessing your RV up on blocks while you're scrounging around for cab fare.

Longevity

No, the family pop-up doesn't have super powers. That super lightweight trailer isn't impervious to harm or wear. Fifth-wheel manufacturers don't employ secret space-age technology from NASA to add years to their products. But it may seem like it, because many towables outlast those members of the motorized world. Mechanical parts—engines, drive trains, and transmissions—break down over time. All moving parts do, which is exactly why your towable may surprise you, because the "box-on-wheels" design incorporates little in the way of breakable mechanisms. As previously mentioned, this is the reason motorhomes are more expensive to buy and maintain. Don't be surprised if the same pop-up purchased for you and the kids has grandkids in it someday.

ONE FOR THE ROAD

Park models aren't technically RVs. These residential-style structures are designed for setup in one location for greater lengths of time. They resemble conventional travel trailers, but some have peaked, shingled roofs. Two of the best features of the Park model are the large sliding patio doors and lots of windows. Inside you'll find at least 400 square feet of space, with larger appliances and furnishings straight out of a home. A second floor is common. Park models are more home than vehicle. They're just towable enough to lobby for true RV status, but they're really in a class by themselves.

Spatial Orientation

Did you know that a 30-foot fifth-wheel delivers more space than a 30-foot motorhome? How can this be? Illusions? Smoke and mirrors? A government cover-up? None of the above. The motorhome's cockpit area is to blame, taking up vital interior real estate, rendered virtually useless upon arrival to the campground. As with all towable RVs, the absence of a driving compartment results in more bang for your buck and more usable space for you and your crew.

In addition, motorhome floorplans follow the same basic model—cockpits up front, bedroom in back. The good old travel trailer, on the other hand, has no such obvious limitations, allowing designers to put things wherever they want. Bedrooms can go anywhere, front or back. The kitchen may be enormous (perfect for those who love to cook) and dwarf the rest of the coach. Or go with a rear living area with large bay windows and a slide-out, the center of all things inside. It's not unusual for a regular trailer to be available in double-digit floorplans. That's a lot of options for those looking for the perfect RV. And it gets better: with towable manufacturers outnumbering motorized manufacturers, there are more models to choose from.

Vacation Home

Not everyone wants to roam the country, living life on the go. A job and a family may require more realistic vacationing, a sad fact that may limit travelers to weekends up at the lake or quick jaunts to a favorite campground. With this in mind, many owners prefer to simply unhook the trailer and leave it full time at a seasonal campsite or other purchased property a reasonable drive from home. Instead of worrying about towing, these folks treat the trailer like that cabin in the woods or timeshare, using their everyday vehicle to shuttle them and the kids up to their new "second home."

Towing Woes

Yes, there may be a few disadvantages. Or perhaps none at all, if you are comfortable with the costs and traveling differences associated with this awesome, exciting, every-day-is-new-and-different lifestyle. Again, these are disadvantages to the towable persuasion only if you allow them to be. Here's a closer look at some of the potential pitfalls in the life of a towable owner.

The Big Tow

The pattern is simple: big towables need big vehicles to tow them; small towables need smaller ones. Sure, it's a little more complicated than that rudimentary explanation, but in either case, *something* is required to pull that pop-up, travel trailer, or fifth-wheel from place to place. Fitting a trailer to an existing truck or car (in a few cases) is great—it saves from writing a second check. Otherwise, that new fifth-wheel you've got your eye on may necessitate buying a much larger pickup truck to handle the load. And these big rigs ain't cheap. Prepare to easily drop another $30,000 to $50,000 for a tow vehicle large enough to do the job.

A medium-duty truck, sometimes referred to as a "baby-semi," is usually required for towing the largest fifth-wheels and their Herculean weights of 18,000 to 22,000 pounds. Armed with massive diesel engines, such trucks also often feature surprisingly nice sleeping and living quarters of their own. True, this much muscle comes with a steep price tag: $60,000 to $90,000 if you go all out. However, this higher price tag is offset by its much longer life span. One of these trucks can sometimes outlast several pickups, so in the long run, they may actually be cheaper.

> **ROAD SCHOLAR**
>
> What good is a trailer that sleeps six when your tow vehicle can accommodate only your spouse, one child, and maybe his or her hamster? If future towing plans (fifth-wheel wannabes, take note) call for a pickup, entertain the idea of one with an extended cab with additional seating for everyone. Transporting six is not impossible, and customized vehicles may allow for even more passengers.

Separation Anxiety

Plenty of interested RVers are simply fearful of towing a trailer. Certainly, it's an unfamiliar situation for some, one that I compare to owning a Beagle. As much as you'd like that towable to behave, sometimes Daisy, er … I mean, the trailer, wants to do its own thing. Here you are turning down the sidewalk, and she's licking dirt off the mailbox. Of course, I've never seen a trailer that can catch a Frisbee.

This, of course, is an exaggeration to make a point. Towing is different, not difficult. Turns must be taken a little wider. Back-ins mandate patience and a Zen-like oneness with your surroundings. Winds and speed may cause your RV to sway some, which can be disconcerting (and remedied in Chapter 13). And you may get wet from time to time hooking up the towing connection in the rain. Some RVers are willing to explore this challenge, while others say, "No way, not for me." Hopefully, I can make this a less intimidating prospect in the chapters to come.

Meeting Your Match

Prospective buyers become giddy walking into an RV show. The choices are mind-boggling. All those shiny trailers dazzle the mind. For some, finding a husband was easier than choosing the perfect RV. And it gets harder. The towable you buy and the tow vehicle—be it a car, truck, or van—needs to be properly matched, based on their weights, hitch/receiver, and towing capacity. In this case, opposites definitely do not attract.

I break this down in detail in Chapter 13, but here's the CliffsNotes version: Your tow vehicle must have the ability (tow rating) to pull the towable in its loaded state (gross vehicle weight rating). Your hitch must also be rated to do the job. A tow vehicle's and trailer's fortunes and fates are intertwined, and a suitable match is the only way toward a safe RV experience. So whether you're buying a trailer to match your vehicle or a tow vehicle to match a would-be trailer, your choices are not as limitless as they might seem.

Accessorizing

A shiny new pickup sits ready in the driveway. Across the way is your beautiful new trailer or fifth-wheel. They're like kids at a dance: interested, but not sure how to make that connection. The third-party matchmaker comes in the form of a hitch, which makes the introductions, and a series of connections (brakes, lights, safety chains) to seal the deal. After that, it's a good idea to purchase such *aftermarket* devices as an additional *antisway device* and other products to create a safer environment. All this, by the way, costs money, and should be factored into the bottom line. I take a closer look at towing accessories in, you guessed it, Chapter 13.

RVOCABULARY

RVers may choose to add options and accessories to their vehicle during the buying stage or later from separate companies and retail outlets, generally referred to as the **aftermarket.** Most products offered by the manufacturers themselves can be found throughout the aftermarket, allowing buyers to be patient with such decisions concerning add-ons and accessories.

An **antisway device** is an accessory that helps stabilize the connection between the tow vehicle and the travel trailer and restrict motion while in transit. This is an especially useful item for negating the effects of high winds and turbulent conditions caused by traveling at higher speeds.

Towable Types

There are two schools of thought regarding the purchase of a towable RV. Either match up an existing vehicle (sedan, minivan, SUV, pickup truck, or medium-duty truck) to a suitable towable, or vice versa. Of course, which route you take depends on a lot of things, but it starts with pondering your needs and how much you want to pay. As we've discussed, this vehicle tandem must be properly matched, based on your tow vehicle's tow rating and the towable's overall weight. You'll need to pour research and thought into this decision; I assist you with this in Chapter 13.

There are five types of towable RVs: fifth-wheel trailers, travel trailers, sport-utility trailers, lightweight/hybrid trailers, and fold-down campers (or pop-ups). An in-depth look at each is given in the pages ahead.

Fifth-Wheel Trailers

Fifth-wheels are the granddaddies of the towable world. Walking inside, you may feel that you've crossed the threshold into a rolling condo—there's even a small set of stairs in the front portion of the unit, usually leading up to the master bedroom. There's no cockpit taking up valuable space. Fifth-wheels, with their noticeable "goosenecks" (mentioned in Chapter 1), which hitch snuggly to within the bed of large pickups, deliver the most usable space of any type of recreational vehicle. Sizes go up to 40 feet (in which case, a powerful 1-ton or even larger hauler is needed).

Interior heights are enormous, and slide-outs—now as many as five—are now the norm, not the exception. But that's not to say entry-level models aren't offered, with smaller weights and lengths for easier towing—and prices to match. These days, there's a fifth-wheel trailer aimed at every type of buyer and any kind of tow vehicle, as long as it's a truck.

The upfront gooseneck section is the distinguishing feature of a fifth-wheel trailer.
(Courtesy of Newmar)

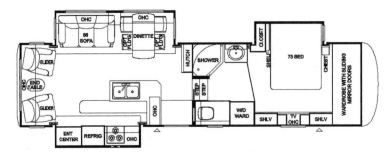

Fifth-wheels usually come equipped with slide-out rooms, such as the three found on this floorplan.
(Courtesy of Newmar)

What Is It?

So how does a fifth-wheel differ from your average travel trailer? And what about that goofy name? Both of these questions can be answered by examining the manner in which fifth-wheels are towed. Instead of a conventional hitch and connection made at the bumper or frame of the tow vehicle, a specially designed fifth-wheel hitch, also the genesis for its name, rests in the cargo area in the back of the truck. Because this area must be open to store the hitch, pickup trucks, medium-duty diesels, and a few custom-made conversion vehicles are the only types of vehicles capable of towing a fifth-wheel trailer. Sorry, SUVs need not apply. The trailer's trademark gooseneck front-end hangs over the truck's payload area, creating a much greater fit between the two vehicles, and a unique, bi-level recreational vehicle.

Fifth-wheel sizes range from 20 to approximately 40 feet, with weights sometimes tipping the scales at more than 22,000 pounds, fully loaded. Heavyweight models mandate a big-time truck or specially made conversion vehicle. Smaller models may or may not be compatible with your existing small- or medium-size pickup. Again, we get to that in Chapter 13.

Life Onboard

In addition to easier towing, the ramifications of the gooseneck overhang are felt throughout the interior of the trailer. Much in the same way that Class C motorhomes use their cab-over area as a supplemental sleeping or storage area, fifth-wheels make great use of this specially designed space. Of course, this area is a whole lot bigger, with dimensions large enough to accommodate a master bedroom, bathroom, tub/shower, closets, and nightstands, with decent headroom to boot. A few steps (creating a true second floor) separate the front end from the rest of the interior, making for a nice oasis from the noise of the television or conversations in the living room. Interior heights are staggering when compared to other recreational vehicles.

Although not nearly as diverse as travel trailers (the undisputed kings of floor-plans), varied fifth-wheel room layouts reward buyers with a wide range of interiors. As always, color schemes and choice of fabrics are offered, as is the obligatory long list of options, as found in most other RVs. Storage is usually immense, aided by multiple slide-out configurations and basement model floor-plans, which are becoming more common in higher-end products.

Sleeping Beauty

Sleeping four is easy and up to eight is possible, depending on the model and the size and contortion abilities of your passengers. The master bedroom, almost always outfitted with a queen-size bed, and a sleeper sofa perform the yeoman's work, come nighttime. Some floorplans might even offer two bedrooms, or bunk beds, to really pack 'em in. A convertible dinette and bench seats and/or reclining loungers also transform into sleeping arrangements. Double beds can occasionally be substituted for the master queen-size, but don't count on it.

Inside Out

An illusion is at work in many fifth-wheels. No, Criss Angel isn't in the RV business—yet. Rather, awesome interior heights work on the collective psyches of trailer owners, making rooms appear larger than they really are. True, the area between your head and the ceiling isn't exactly usable space, but it creates a more spacious, open feel. As a result, taller closets, cabinets, and pantries can be added, holding everything from clothes, to televisions, to family heirlooms.

Furnishings come in the traditional forms of various couches, recliners, and a communal dinner spot, either a dinette table with bench seats or a free-standing table and chairs. Multiple slide-outs are extremely popular, changing the dynamic (and size!) of the interior in mere seconds. Many fifth-wheels now dazzle with opposing slide-outs in the main living area, which can expand that total living area to 15 feet across. Amazing!

Towability

Thanks to a more snug fit in the payload in the back of a pickup truck—and therefore less sway and overall length—fifth-wheels help take some of the stigma out of towing. With the trailer's hitch mounted to the pickup truck's bed instead of the bumper or frame, fifth-wheels generally ride smoother and are more maneuverable than conventional travel trailers. The symmetry between the two vehicles makes for easier backups, cornering, and parking, while reducing choppy movement and sway during transit.

The secret's in the geometry. The pivot point of a conventional trailer/tow vehicle combo is behind the rear bumper. The pivot point of the fifth-wheel hitch is directly over or slightly ahead of the tow vehicle's rear axle. The shorter the distance from the turning wheels of the tow vehicle to the pivot point, the easier it is to maneuver. Plus, with a fifth-wheel trailer, the hitch weight is carried by the rear axle of the tow vehicle rather than having to be distributed mechanically and therefore less efficiently. It may sound like coursework from MIT, but the bottom line is an easier towing experience for all.

Because the truck and fifth-wheel combination "bends" in the middle, it can be more maneuverable than the larger motorhomes, and having the overlap of trailer and truck shortens the length and makes turning easier than with a travel trailer of the same length. Fifth-wheels tend to be better built than travel trailers and are the choice of many full-timers. In fact, quite a few companies focus on building units for full-timers exclusively.

Typical Specs

With exterior heights exceeding 12 feet, added to a fairly lengthy towing package, fifth-wheels may struggle to reach the more elusive, exotic locales not listed (thankfully) in travel books. Places with low clearances, rough roads, and tight corners are problematic for larger models. Assuming that you can make it there, a series of large holding tanks allows for longer getaways than usual. An onboard generator may or may not come standard, so make sure your dream machine is equipped with one if you plan to camp away from shoreline power and covet the use of larger appliances, such as the microwave and air conditioner.

Standard Specifications for a Typical Fifth-Wheel Trailer

Self-Containment Features	Gallons
Fresh water storage	25 to 100
Gray water holding tank	40 to 85
Black water holding tank	30 to 50
LP gas container(s)	20 to 60
Water heater	6 to 12

Costly Matters

Sure, you can spend a not-so-small fortune on a roving palace, leaving you longing for nothing. But more realistically, fifth-wheels start at around $25,000 and can reach $122,000 if you get really fancy. Smaller, lighter-weight models start at as little as $15,000 and may be towed by a smaller pickup truck, saving you another costly trip to the local truck dealership. Unfortunately, the most difficult part may be deciding what to tow it with. As explained, the flexibility of choices afforded most trailer owners is narrowed to what type of pickup truck is up for the job. As mentioned earlier, for those who haven't priced a medium-duty truck lately, they're not cheap. Expect to pay at least $62,000 for one to safely haul the largest fifth-wheels. Otherwise, a $\frac{3}{4}$- or 1-ton truck can be had for $29,000 to $48,000. Towable owners won't need to waste another Saturday changing belts or plugs, driving down to the RV dealership for a costly tune-up, or searching for the origin of that brown puddle collecting underneath the engine. Insurance premiums are relatively low—contingent on the sale price—so pat yourself on the back for your frugal purchase.

Final Analysis

Ample space and storage make fifth-wheels popular with full-timers, as well as families with more than a couple of kids. Your canary will love the high ceilings, and the edginess that sometimes accompanies life in a confined space should be blissfully absent from days onboard. As previously mentioned, the resemblance to a rolling condominium is uncanny in higher-end models. Manufacturers do their best to woo buyers with loads of luxury appointments. Large windows, plush fabrics and carpeting, and quality hardwoods continually position fifth-wheels among the most livable RVs in the industry. You'll also discover some of the finest and most thorough examples of kitchens and bathrooms in the marketplace. The rest of the interior ain't too shabby, either.

Unfortunately, relatively modest start-up costs must be tempered with the possible purchase of an expensive tow vehicle. If you've already got that truck in your driveway, you're in luck. The fifth-wheel lifestyle is closer than you think. However, it's best to price both the trailer and tow vehicles to make your accountant happy—the combination can cost more than a suitably sized motorhome. This cannot be overstated. After scanning prices for medium-duty trucks at a recent RV show, I nearly fell into a coma.

Travel Trailers

The backbone of the towable marketplace, travel trailers come in all shapes and sizes, from basic to luxurious, super lightweight to those requiring a larger tow vehicle. For this reason, I've created a subgroup—lightweight/hybrid travel trailers—in the pages ahead.

Free of a cockpit and lacking the gooseneck area of fifth-wheels, designers are free to create a full gamut of varying interiors. Like a crazed Dr. Frankenstein bent on showing his unbridled genius (a slight exaggeration, perhaps), travel trailer manufacturers mix and match layouts in ways that might surprise you. Bedrooms may be front or back—or both. Kitchens can take up the entire rear of the unit, share space on either side, or be scattered about, refrigerator here, pantry there. Bathrooms range from lean and functional to spacious and opulent. You also may find up to three or four slide-out rooms onboard.

A conventional travel trailer plus a tow vehicle.
(Courtesy of Fleetwood RV)

This travel trailer features a pair of rear bunk beds, living room slide-out, and upfront master bedroom.

(Courtesy of Fleetwood RV)

What Is It?

A box on wheels is as good a description as any I've heard. Traditional travel trailers often lack the slopes and quirks found on most other RVs, although many have been rounded somewhat over the years in an effort to maximize aerodynamics. Unlike fifth-wheels, these trailers attach to a frame-mounted hitch, with the load distributed over anywhere from one to three axles of your dutiful tow vehicle. Conventional travel trailers vary from 24 to 40 feet. A good-size truck or SUV with a V-8 engine or better is often capable of handling the towing duties, assuming that it's equipped with a compatible hitch and the vehicle used has the appropriate tow rating.

For inclusion in the category, travel trailers should exceed 5,000 pounds, unloaded. Anything less places them in the category of lightweight travel trailer, as described in the following section. That weight does not include your portly cat, your collection of shot glasses from all 50 states, or that supplemental canned ham in case the fish aren't biting—just the trailer and nothing else. More on calculating these numbers and their importance in Chapter 14.

ROAD SCHOLAR

When comparing various RVs by size, it's important to know how vehicle lengths are calculated. Fifth-wheel measurements are taken from the tip of the front extension (gooseneck) to the back bumper. Travel trailers start at the end of the trailer tongue (where the connection to the hitch is made) to the back bumper. In both cases, this adds several feet of superfluous space to the number. Motorized RVs are measured bumper to bumper.

Life Onboard

Don't be alarmed—designers remembered to include a couch and a television. Your hours watching highlights on SportsCenter aren't in jeopardy. In fact, everything you've come to expect of the RV lifestyle should be present, no matter what size travel trailer you favor (but as always, in varying degrees, based on the size and weight of your chosen model). Cooks continue to work their magic in the kitchen, bathrooms and showers are standard, and everyone remains free to fight over who gets the master bedroom.

Sleeping Beauty

Sleeping capacity can hit as high as eight in larger models. Of course, this mark is easiest reached if passengers aren't overly finicky in terms of where they lay their head at night. Four to six sleepers is a much safer number. A master bedroom with a queen-size bed is common, although double beds and bunk beds (even triple bunk beds) are routinely offered. The usual cast of convertible furnishings transforms the living space into a nightly snoozefest.

Inside Out

Buyers worried about interior space—not to mention a trailer full of bored teenagers—should feel at ease after kicking a few tires at the local RV show. Large flat-screen TVs, DVD/CD players with surround sound, plus satellite, cable TV, and iPod connections are common. Various-sized sofas, loveseats, and recliners also help champion the cause of true leisure and contented passengers.

Bench seats around a dinette table continue to be the perfect place for eating dinner, playing games, or writing angry letters to the mayor for your town's lame-brained RV storage laws. And because there's no cockpit, every inch of the interior is utilized, whether it takes the form of larger rooms, expanded furnishings, or greater storage. Interior heights average a respectable $6\frac{1}{2}$ feet.

Towability

There's no way to sugarcoat it. Many would say that a lengthy travel trailer is the hardest of all recreational vehicles to command. That doesn't keep millions of people from towing these babies every day, and travel trailers continue to rank among the most popular RVs in the marketplace.

Unlike fifth-wheels, which attach snuggly to their tow vehicles like teenagers during a slow dance, travel trailers rely on a lone undercarriage hitch receiver or frame-mounted hitch. As a result, a 40-foot trailer and a 15-foot tow vehicle combine to form a whooping 55 feet of vehicle cruising down the highways, parking lots, and campgrounds of America. Backups might take longer, as the trailer might want to veer to one side. Because the tandem is less than aerodynamic, headwinds affect fuel economy worse than any maniacal oil baron ever could, while heavy crosswinds can unleash more trailer rock 'n' roll than Elvis on the *Ed Sullivan Show*. Worried? Having second thoughts? Want to jump ahead to the lovable fold-down camper and forget all about it? Don't be silly. These potential problems can be lessened with the aid of a couple products and some advice dispensed in Chapter 13.

Remember, tow vehicles and trailers must be matched to the job. I can't think of any regular automobile capable of hauling a trailer of these proportions. This is a job better left for your muscle-bound pickup truck, especially if you fall head over heels in love with a 40-foot model with enough slide-outs for a roving block party.

Typical Specs

Travel trailers, regardless of size, boast fairly lofty self-contained specifications. Holding tanks are comparable to those in motorized RVs and fifth-wheels of similar size. LP tanks, a standard 20 to 40 gallons in most cases, may be removable or permanently installed to the front end, so keep that in mind, come buying time. A generator might be a no-show, due to the fact that space for it as well as the separate fuel supply (such as that found in a motorized vehicle's gas tank) might be lacking. As a result, boondocking gets a little more complicated. However, I give you potential solutions in Chapter 18 for roughing it.

Standard Specifications for a Typical Travel Trailer

Self-Containment Features	Gallons
Fresh water storage	30 to 60
Gray water holding tank	30 to 50
Black water holding tank	25 to 50
LP gas container(s)	20 to 40
Water heater	6 or 10

Costly Matters

Compared to a similarly sized motorhome, travel trailers—all towables, for that matter—always win in terms of initial sticker price. Remember the mantra: motors equal money. Inch for inch, trailers are the blue-light specials of the industry, provided that there's a nice shiny truck in your driveway eager to meet the towing challenge. Expect to pay somewhere from $25,000 to $80,000 for a trailer in the 25- to 40-foot neighborhood. Extra costs rear their ugly heads for such importances as a tow vehicle (assuming you don't have one), $500 to $1,000 for a hitch, and a few bucks to equip it with the extra gear recommended in Chapter 13.

As mentioned during our chat about fifth-wheels, less expensive, motorless vehicles skirt the heavy insurance premiums and required automotive coverages of motorhomes. You can expect fewer trips to the mechanics, too. Routine maintenance is mostly limited to the refrigerator, air conditioner, and similar appliances, saving owners more than a few bucks over the lifetime of the trailer.

Final Analysis

A 30-foot trailer is a one-size-fits-most situation. The right floorplan dares most families to try to outgrow it, and it works as well for year-round living as it does for the Boy Scouts' trips into the mountains, merit badges included. The variety of types and sizes gives buyers unparalleled options and buying power. Don't like one? Move on to the next. There are literally thousands of floorplans to choose from within the trailer marketplace. Be choosy. Be picky. Be happy with your purchase.

Trailers do equally well towed or settled down as a vacation home. Tour the nation with your apartment on wheels behind you, or plop down stakes at a nearby seasonal campsite, commuting back and forth to your new second home via the family vehicle. Ever wanted a spot in the mountains, among the tall pines, or adjacent to a wonderful lake? Their ability to serve as permanent housing without fear of mechanical failure from idle engines is a great plus. Travel trailers go where the family cabin or high-priced motels never could.

The knee-jerk reaction of some is to dismiss the idea of towing a separate vehicle altogether. "It's too hard," they say. "I've never done it before. My trailer will get mad and run away." Don't fall prey to such rash judgments. Towing is just like any new skill—strange at first, made easier over time. Travel trailers can provide you and your family years of inexpensive and fulfilling travel. A frugal purchase saves you tens of thousands of dollars over an equally stocked motorhome, so don't be too quick to dismiss it. Just find the right vehicle to tow it and let the adventures begin.

Sport-Utility Trailers

A continued RV phenomena are called sport-utility trailers (SUTs), toy haulers, garage units, and probably a half-dozen other names. Whatever you call them, they're arguably the most versatile recreational vehicles in existence, combining a unique mix of residential living amenities, a separate cargo area, and a loading ramp. Perfect for toting motorized toys such as motorcycles, jet skis, and snow-mobiles, SUTs are the ideal way to add a little adventure to your travel itinerary. There simply is no better way to haul and unload (via deployable ramp) a pair of Harleys for the local rally while maintaining suitable sleeping quarters, all in one. Those sportsters who enjoy camping off the grid with their jet skis or ATVs ccommodations for both them and their machines. And although the aveler still makes up a large majority of this market segment, studies Vers are switching to these units with large storage space to use for a , a place for dog kennels, and a plethora of storage they just can't get among other uses.

A deployable ramp and separate rear garage area allow sport-utility trailer owners to easily transport such items as ATVs, motorcycles, and jet skis.

(Courtesy of Coachmen)

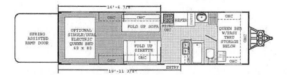

There's enough space aboard sport-utility trailers for both human and motorized cargo.

(Courtesy of Coachmen)

What Is It?

Sport-utility trailers come in fifth-wheel, travel trailer, and motorized designs. The front section is reserved for humans, complete with a kitchen, bathroom/shower, living spaces, and bedding configurations. The rear of the unit contains a large (depending on the model) garage section, with metal flooring and tie-downs to secure items such as motorcycles, snowmobiles, mountain bikes, or anything else you can squeeze in. A drop-down bed and/or fold-down or removable furniture is sometimes equipped within the space for times when the motorized faire doesn't make the trip. In most cases, a wall, often called a vapor wall, separates the living space from the garage area. Loading and unloading gear is easy, thanks to a drop-down rear door that forms a heavy-duty ramp. Ramps are usually in the 7-foot length category and most often can handle up to 2,500 pounds. Some travelers with disabilities have reported that the ramp and layout are a great aid in dealing with their mobility issues.

In an effort to support the off-the-grid lifestyle that usually accompanies these kinds of buyers, SUTs usually deliver a host of amenities designed for such boon-docking adventures. Units usually offer heavy-duty shock absorbers for the extra poundage, as well as larger water and wastewater tanks to facilitate longer stays away from civilization. Exterior fuel stations, beefed-up generators, outside show-ers, spotlights, screened-in patios, and a host of creature comforts for both people and machines are becoming more common. The SUT is the perfect RV for the adventurous owner.

Life Onboard

Interior refinements used to be rather ho-hum. Sure, all the living functions were present (AC and heat, bedding, kitchen, and bathrooms, and so on), but all in all, it didn't exactly dazzle. Life onboard was usually pretty sedate. And until recently, no one really cared. After all, the fun was sitting in the back of the trailer, in the form of motorcycles or what-not. Who wanted to sit inside and watch *CSI* reruns? Of course, before long, the inevitable happened. Customers wanted their cake and their dirt bikes, too, to mix metaphors. All of a sudden, things onboard got, well, nice. The living space became rather plush and fancy. The bathroom became less of an afterthought and became more accommodating. More thought and time went into where people would congregate, how and where they would sleep, and what they might do on a rainy day. In short, floorplans and amenities became more amenable. During the surge in SUT popularity, the market began to split, as all towable products inevitably do. A somewhat lightweight SUT segment developed. And then there were the super-upscale, elegant fifth-wheel designs, something worthy of a pair of Fat Boys in the back (we're talking about Harleys here, not your plump teenagers).

Sleeping Beauty

We've talked at length about the versatility of towables, and the SUT is no exception. This fact is evident in the bedding. Depending on the model, owners might enjoy a private master suite up front; a drop-down, queen-size bed in the garage area; bunk beds; sleeper sofas; and what have you. It's really up to the whim of that specific company. However, the one thing you can count on is that the garage area is always in the rear. It's just a matter of whether humans are asked to share that space come nighttime.

Inside Out

Interior furnishings vary but most likely follow the typical RV assortment of a dinette table, a sleeper sofa(s), and a chair or two thrown in for good measure. Again, any number of variations are possible, as is the case with nearly every towable.

Towability

SUTs that favor a typical travel trailer design remain the toughest units to tow. Their long lengths (usually the same as typical travel trailers) and heavy weights (bumped up by what's in the garage area) usually make for necessary upgrades in the tow vehicle. Count on SUT weights starting at 6,000 pounds (GVWR) and going up to 18,000 pounds, give or take, for the largest fifth-wheel versions. Fifth-wheel versions make for fairly uneventful towing due to their snug fit in the back of the pickup truck. Whether you have the right truck parked in your driveway warrants investigation, which we'll conduct in Chapter 13.

Typical Specs

As previously mentioned, holding tank limits are often enlarged for the typical SUT. And this makes sense, considering that most users prefer to camp in desert climes (for sand rails), along watery banks (for jet skis), or in frozen backwoods (for snowmobiles)—settings usually void of fresh water hook-ups, sewer hook-ups, and dump stations. For the same reason, an onboard generator and fuel tank are often included.

Standard Specifications for a Typical Sport-Utility Trailer

Self-Containment Features	Gallons
Fresh water storage	40 to 150
Gray water holding tank	25 to 125
Black water holding tank	25 to 125
LP gas container(s)	10 to 60
Water heater	6 or 10

Costly Matters

The move toward smaller SUTs has lowered costs significantly. After all, not everyone needs a massive storage area. As such, costs can start at $15,000 but more typically are twice that to get started. High-end fifth-wheel models can easily reach $50,000 to $60,000, perhaps more if you want to equip it with a wide assortment of gadgetry and comforts. Larger weights certainly affect the bottom line in terms of fuel costs. Expect a heavily loaded unit to earn you the worst fuel economy of any towable. Insurance costs won't differ much, considering that your Harleys and motorized goodies are probably already insured, right?

Final Analysis

In the old days, those longing to bring motorcycles or dirt bikes with them on their RV adventures had to tow them. This, of course, was an impossible feat for towable owners, because towing the travel trailer and a secondary utility trailer is both impossible and illegal. The advent of the sport-utility market changed all that—and, with it, changed the face of the RV industry as well. Now RVers across the country can see their advantages. Simply put, there's no better RV for the person looking to transport and store wheeled gear while maintaining a suitable residence for the human crew after reaching the destination.

Lightweight/Hybrid Trailers

In an attempt to woo (don't you just love that word?) young families, the RV industry has spent a great deal of time building an entire new segment of light-weight travel trailers. Weighing in at less than 5,000 pounds, the majority of them can be towed by the many minivans, small- and medium-size trucks, and scores of SUVs on the road today. And America simply loves its big vehicles, which routinely surpass the forgotten automobile in terms of annual sales. A suitably powered sedan can also handle towing jobs, in some cases.

The classic "teardrop" design is the hallmark of this super-lightweight trailer.
(Courtesy of Dutchmen RV)

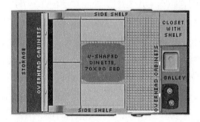

With modest dimensions onboard, this trailer converts a wraparound couch into a bed.
(Courtesy of Dutchmen RV)

What Is It?

Lightweight travel trailers fall somewhere between a fold-down camper and a conventional travel trailer in terms of size, weight, cost, and amenities. Sizes generally don't exceed 25 feet because the extra materials would tip the scales into the next weight division, the conventional travel trailer. The hybrid trailer, as it is usually called, is a lightweight version that, well, just looks different. The biggest difference is usually the bedding, which utilizes fold-out bunk ends on one or more sides to expand the room and sleep count. When deployed, the trailer can take on a kind of UFO appearance. Some models sprout "wings" upon arrival, extending the bedding outward in a tentlike material; others must be manually deployed, or popped up, via a hand crank to access the interior. It might sound bizarre, but owners don't seem to be complaining, as this is currently one of the fastest-growing segments of the RV market.

Life Onboard

Perhaps only a supermodel understands the plight of the poor lightweight trailer. Just how does it stay desirable to consumers without exceeding its waifish physique? Want to bet this problem has kept many an RV engineer up at night? In the world of 30,000-pound motorhomes, you can imagine the limitations imposed on a 4,000- or 5,000-pound trailer. In fact, some units may be only a piece of chocolate cake away from losing their good standing in the lightweight community. But kudos to manufacturers who continually make it work—a durable trailer with just enough functionality for the average family to enjoy for years to come.

Larger models reflect all the comforts associated with conventional travel trailers. Heat and air-conditioning, full kitchens, adequate bedding, bathrooms, and living space are usually all included. Interior heights average 6 feet, 5 inches, which is about the norm for any RV. Even slide-outs are sometimes offered. On the smaller side are "teardrop" trailers so named for their unique shape. Teardrops are miniaturized versions of RVs but deliver all the basic requirements of cooking, sleeping, and congregating. They can usually be towed by the midsize family car.

Sleeping Beauty

The master bedroom often achieves martyr status, sacrificed for the greater good of the interior. In these cases, expect substitutions to take the form of convertible sofas, unfolding mattresses (also known as bunk ends) that extend beyond the perimeter of the unit, or more ingenious designs. Sleeping capacity reaches six in larger models, but that's a lot of people and belongings sharing a 20- to 25-foot space. Finding a traditional floorplan, with the bedroom in the rear, shouldn't prove difficult for those desiring a private room, a respite from the television and Uncle Lou's version of *Swan Lake*. A double bed might take the place of the preferred queen-size version, however.

Inside Out

Like Forrest Gump says, "Life is like a box of chocolates. You never know what you're gonna get." The same can be said about any "typical" interior. Many times the entire unit acts as the living area. Other floorplans appear as if they were puréed in a blender, creating a wonderfully unorthodox collage of rooms rolled into one. The main living area sometimes moonlights as the bedroom. Several additional feet may be granted, thanks to a small slide-out room. Couches can encase the entire front end, work in conjunction with a dinette table, or be absent altogether. The only thing we know for sure is that numerous floorplans are available, so keep looking until you find the best one for you.

Towability

We saved the best part for last. Smaller and lighter towables require only the services of—you guessed it—smaller and lighter tow vehicles. For many models, vehicles with a six-cylinder engine should do, provided it possesses the necessary hitch setup. That means even the family sedan may get a crack at the RV life. And in a world of trucks, SUVs, and vans (maxi and mini alike), most families already own a tow vehicle to do the job. Congratulations, you're halfway there.

Typical Specs

Passengers lack for none of the usual onboard offerings. Standard electrical systems prevail, as does a fresh water system, holding tanks, and propane gas containers for fueling the furnace and stove. However, space and fuel limitations leave a generator off the list of standard—and even optional—equipment in most cases. Owners can power 120-volt appliances through the aid of a portable generator in the event of camping in remote locations, void of shore power.

Standard Specifications for a Typical Lightweight Travel Trailer

Self-Containment Features	Gallons
Fresh water storage	15 to 40
Gray water holding tank	20 to 40
Black water holding tank	10 to 40
LP gas container(s)	5 to 14
Water heater	6 or 10

Costly Matters

A few hundred pounds may be all that separates a lightweight trailer from a trip to a higher weight class. In these cases, costs are similar to those of travel trailers. Otherwise, expect these reductions in size and weight to pay off when making out the check to the local RV dealership. Fully loaded and pushing the 5,000-pound weight limit, a handful of models might flirt with a $25,000 sticker price. However, $8,000 to $20,000 is more likely.

Again, engineless living benefits owners with a virtual blackout on any major exterior repairs. The biggest concern is probably the tires, which are susceptible to wear and tear just like any others. As with all RVs, some preventative maintenance will need to be performed inside. Routine tinkering with the unit's air conditioner (if so equipped), furnace, and refrigerator rounds out the list of likely interior projects, some of which most backyard mechanics can undertake.

The amount and degree of insurance are up to you, but as with all towables, costs are relatively cheap and coverage can often be attached to an existing automobile policy. Save additional cash by storing trailers in the garage or on the premises when not in use. Fuel costs will rise for the tow vehicle, now asked to pull a heavier load. However, costs should be among the most reasonable in the towable class.

Final Analysis

The lightweight/hybrid trailer market continues to be hot, hot, hot. Nearly every RV manufacturer has scurried over the past several years to gain entry into this competitive arena. Buyers are blitzed with choices ranging from stripped-down versions of larger and therefore heavier models, to brand-new creations to fit the family station wagon.

Pick the right trailer, and it should deliver many years of faithful service. Low starter prices and upkeep expenses compensate for just about any budget. Furthermore, the availability of many likely tow vehicles grants easier entry into the lightweight trailer fraternity than ever before. Add a suitable hitch, and you're in business. In fact, there's probably a vehicle in your very driveway that's more than up to the job.

Couples and small families can't do much better. Multiple floorplans with emphasis on cooking, sleeping, and living space means there's something out there for everyone. True, lightweights pale when compared to the onboard offerings of most fifth-wheels and motorhomes. However, RVing isn't about one-upmanship—it's about providing a comfortable and functional way to complement your leisure. The lightweight RV signals an easy and satisfying entry into the world of RVing.

Fold-Down Campers

Maybe you know them better as pop-ups, camping trailers, or tent trailers. Regardless of the name, fold-downs serve as the best and most cost-effective way for young families to camp and travel. For starters, they are easily towed, ranging in weight from 1,500 to 4,000 pounds, and form a terrific pairing to most SUVs, trucks, minivans, and some larger automobiles. After that, you're free to roam the country, confident that a dry bed, storage for your gear, and a hot meal (or cold one, if you prefer) await you.

What Is It?

Pop-ups deliver a major upgrade from a tent and sleeping bag, not to mention a much more reliable and durable barrier against the elements. Resembling boxes in transit, you wonder just how anyone could possibly get, let alone live, inside. However, that question is quickly answered upon arrival at the family's favorite campsite or for a true getaway in the back country. The once modest 12- to 18-foot box unfolds (pops up!) via a manual crank or (hopefully) a push-button deployment system, now assuming the appearance of a tent on wheels. Unfolded lengths can exceed 25 feet. Not a bad little trick, is it?

Fold-down trailers remain one of the most inexpensive ways to enter the world of recreational vehicles.
(Courtesy of Starcraft RV)

Your standard pop-up features a mix of hard walls and durable fabrics, resembling a tent with wings when it's completely set up. Nearly all models feature two identical sleeping areas that bookend the middle living and cooking space. More expensive units boast a shower, a toilet, a manual slide-out room (which greatly expands the roominess inside), and more deluxe cooking features. Travelers are protected from the elements by a combination of heavy canvas and hard-sided roof.

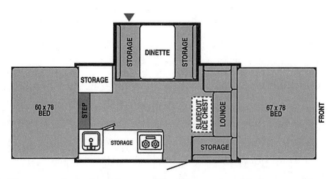

With bedding on either side of the towable and a convertible dinette and couch, some fold-down trailers can sleep up to seven passengers.
(Courtesy of Starcraft RV)

Life Onboard

Space is at a premium, with most units totaling less than 20 feet in length. Be prepared for communal living, with all passengers sharing one small living space for cooking, eating, and hanging out. Labels such as "kitchen," "bathroom," and "living room" are misleading here, because they are all simply offshoots, not separate entities. In fact, they're not "rooms" at all. Say adios to the walls and doors that divvy up larger trailers and motorhomes, serving to create a private oasis. Instead, think of a pop-up as similar to life in that first studio apartment you rented after college, minus the beer keg in the corner.

Many pop-up owners are transplanted tent campers, so dealing with small space isn't really an issue. After all, they're used to much less room, with only a zipper and light fabric separating them from the rest of the world—not to mention angry grizzlies. A night in a pop-up feels like the penthouse at the Four Seasons after a few seasons of soggy tenting. Interior height is often surprising, averaging 6 feet, 6 inches for most units. Some manufacturers achieve a whopping 8 feet, although this cathedralesque height is not always present throughout the entire interior.

Sleeping Beauty

Remember the old Wrigley chewing gum jingle, "Double your pleasure, double your fun"? What that had to do with gum, I have no idea. But it's extremely appropriate to most fold-down floorplans, because matching sleeping areas are found on either end of the unit. It's more accurate to say "areas" instead of "bedrooms" because of the lack of true, closed-door privacy and the fact that a mattress is usually all that's involved. His-and-her nightstands, fancy vanities, and hulking wardrobe closets are rarely present. Typical bed dimensions average 70 by 80 inches, which is doable for most couples.

Further bedding may come in the form of a convertible dinette and/or a sofa bed. A few select models can sleep eight, assuming there are some youngsters in the mix. Otherwise, four is a safe bet and six is possible.

PULL OVER

Although sinks are almost always present, holding tanks to collect the gray water aren't always installed on smaller towables. In these cases, water from the sink empties out the side of the trailer into a bucket or other receptacle for later emptying. Travelers are required to collect and empty gray water in a safe and responsible manner. Be sure to follow all campground rules and city ordinances regarding proper disposal.

Inside Out

Don't expect too many variations from the traditional floorplan: beds on either end, living area in the middle. However, dimensions are getting larger thanks to slide-out areas that add crucial feet of living space.

A dinette table with bench seats serves as the chief locale to eat, work, and rally the troops for another day of fly fishing or another trip up the mountain. A couch is offered in larger models, so Dad and dog can assume their most natural state—napping, and dreaming of playing centerfield for the Yankees or chasing rabbits (whatever the case may be). Storage is often catch-as-catch-can, with smaller compartments dotting the interior. Relief usually comes in the form of one larger interior cabinet or storage compartment. Enlist the tow vehicle to store extra items such as firewood, patio chairs, and that set of *World Book* encyclopedias. A small furnace and air conditioner (sometimes optional) help control temperature fluctuations.

Unfortunately, the chances of finding a unit with the big three—TV, DVD, and stereo system—are somewhat remote. However, true campers won't be too put out by this fact, because the outdoors isn't just another setting to watch the 6 o'clock news and get the latest stock tips. Besides, David Letterman and the great outdoors is an unsettling combination. For those who must get their TV fix, a quick trip to the local electronics store for a few necessities can remedy all that. Just bring a credit card or two.

Towability

Look around the highways, and what do you see? Pop-ups towed behind smaller trucks, vans, and sedans. There are even smaller automobiles up to the job, bolstered by the trailers' low weights. Rarely will a pop-up exceed 3,500 pounds, and 1,500 to 2,000 is about average. This is good news for folks eager to get started and hoping the everyday vehicle is up to the job. The right hitch, either bumper or frame mounted, is usually all that separates many decent-size vehicles from doubling as tow vehicles.

Fold-downs are the easiest vehicles to tow in the RV world. The biggest challenge owners face is probably backing into their campsite. Just take it slow and have your co-pilot hop out and give you directions. Or better yet, opt for a pull-through campsite and skip the process altogether. Cornering, turning, and parking are much more easily accomplished than with any other towable, with common sense and patience the most vital ingredients. But more about that in Chapter 13.

Typical Specs

As previously mentioned, the presence of a toilet and/or shower dictates what—if any—type of holding systems are found onboard. Even the water heater is a possible no-show, so conduct a thoughtful search if these attributes are important to you. An onboard generator is extremely rare, as is LP gas and fresh water capacities capable of lasting more than several days away from civilization. However, fold-downs commute reasonably well to off-the-beaten-path locations. Agile maneuvering is complemented by small traveling lengths and virtually nonexistent traveling heights.

Standard Specifications for a Typical Fold-Down Camper

Self-Containment Features	Gallons
Fresh water storage	5 to 20
Gray water holding tank	Up to 20
Black water holding tank	Up to 15
LP gas container(s)	5 to 15
Water heater	Up to 6

Costly Matters

You can buy most new pop-ups for between $5,000 and $15,000, a bona fide bargain, considering its livability. A family of four (particularly if the kids are still young enough to consider sharing a bed fun) should have little problem eating, sleeping, and dressing onboard, provided you don't plan to spend countless hours in a space that is still relatively tiny. Aside from the cost of the hitch, a pop-up adds little in the way of extra expenses. Your tow vehicle's gas mileage will suffer somewhat, but only marginally, and insurance and maintenance costs are a fraction of those of higher-end towables.

A recent study declared camping by fold-down camper the least expensive way to vacation. When compared to other forms of travel, including planes, cruises, rental cars, and even motorized and other towable RVs, each fails to deliver as much bang for the buck as the pop-up camper.

Final Analysis

A sign hung above the office window of a car service center read, "Cheap, fast, and good. Pick two." Had someone else's vehicle been on the blocks, the slogan would have been hilarious. But pop-ups meet all three criteria. Low sticker prices and virtually maintenance-free living establish them as the cheapest way to RV, by far. Because most folks already have a usable tow vehicle, you and the family are just an RV show away from finding the right vehicle for you. Standard floorplans and uncomplicated offerings hasten search time. Finally, is it good? Absolutely. What's not onboard, you won't miss. And the money saved can help put the kids through school.

As a full-timing choice, well, it's not so good. We're talking about a 365-day home, so it's best to get the biggest RV possible. Pop-ups are also easily outgrown. When those adorable kiddies start to "mature," preferring a set of headphones and a video game to conversation with Mom and Dad, it might be time to upgrade to a travel trailer or fifth-wheel. Furthermore, winter and fold-downs really don't mix. Most lack proper insulation, and the heavy canvas and tentlike fabrics aren't much consolation in December. Finally, it takes only a few adult bodies to cramp everyone's style onboard. Factor in who's coming and for how long prior to any such purchase.

Families who spent one too many camping trips suffering through cold nights and gear mishaps often soon find themselves on an RV dealer's lot scouting out these "entry-level" units. And for many, buying a pop-up represents a couple's first foray into the world of RVing, with the purchase of a larger trailer or motorhome not far behind. RV manufacturers know this and hope travelers use a pop-up as a springboard to a larger, more expensive RV later. Until that time, however, enjoy these small camping wonders, the best value in the industry.

The Least You Need to Know

- Fifth-wheel trailers are the largest, most luxurious, and most expensive towables on the market. Costs vary from $15,000 to $122,000, with sizes ranging from 25 to 40 feet. Their gooseneck design and special hitch require a pickup truck to serve as the tow vehicle.

- Travel trailers offer the greatest flexibility in terms of manufacturers, models, and floorplans. Sizes range from 24 to 40 feet, and double and triple slide-outs are common. The price range is $15,000 to $80,000. Travel trailers can usually be towed by vehicles with a V-8 engine or greater.

- Sport-utility trailers are travel trailers and fifth-wheels with one major difference: a garage area, complete with heavy-duty ramp for toting items such as motorcycles, jet skis, and snowmobiles. Costs range from $15,000 to $60,000.

- Lightweight travel trailers weigh less than 4,000 pounds, allowing for most trucks, SUVs, and minivans to perform the towing duties. They are extremely popular with buyers, thanks to low costs ($8,000 to $20,000), large sleeping capacities (up to eight in some cases), and sizable amenities.

- Fold-down campers are the quintessential family-friendly RVs, with low start-up costs, easy towing, and a major step up over tents. Most units cost less than $10,000.

Narrowing Your Choices

Chapter

4

In This Chapter

- Choosing the right RV for you
- Sorting out differences among manufacturers, standard equipment, building materials, and other key factors
- Deciding between a new or used RV

So far, we've talked about recreational vehicles in the abstract. You learned that RVing provides a comfortable, reliable, and affordable way to live and travel and is loved by all different types of people. I've asserted that RVing is all about choices, with plenty of options regarding where to stay and a variety of vehicles to launch your family getaways. You understand the uniqueness of a motorized as opposed to a towable RV and the various selections within these two categories.

The goal of this chapter is to provoke a discussion about which RV is right for you. We're not after the brand, the exact size, or who makes it—just what kind is right for you. Is it a small motorhome or a whopping fifth-wheel? Do you want to put the family SUV to use with a lightweight trailer, or is a camper van or truck camper more your speed? Could it be that a 40-foot diesel pusher is in your future? New RV or used RV? Let's find out.

Talking the Talk

In the RV equivalent of *Fantasy Island*, such decisions would be easy. In the absence of such reality, we'd probably all just take the biggest and the best. Money would be no object. Other "little" annoyances, such as weight, towing ability, and where to park, wouldn't factor into the decision in the slightest. But sadly, we awake to the real world, with a Beagle licking our face, hungry for breakfast, and maybe a quick walk around the block while we're at it. Alas, narrowing the RV choices requires a little work. Pondering the questions in the following sections should help in the search.

> **PULL OVER**
>
> Good common sense regarding any big purchase applies here. Be realistic with your bottom line. Know what you can spend, and don't deviate. Looking out of your price range only leaves you frustrated and complicates the matter further. Remember, there's an RV made for every budget. Put that motto to the test, and you won't be disappointed.

The Bottom Line

Every other part of the decision-making process comes second to determining how much money you can spend. Believe it or not, the local RV lot wants more than a smile and a handshake to close the deal. It takes money, and sometimes a great deal of it. Buying an RV is just like buying a car. Assuming your proverbial ship didn't come in, financing is the way to go. How much money can you afford to part with every month? How much can you scrape together for a down payment? Be sure to leave a little leftover cash for some actual trips, factoring in fuel, tolls, insurance, and campground costs. We'll discuss such matters in the chapters ahead.

Jumping into the high-end world of an ultra-extravagant motorhome or towable just might not make financial sense at this point. Besides, it's never a bad idea to start small and work your way up to a nicer vehicle over time. As is the case with any major purchase, overbuying creates a sense of dread and remorse. Would you rather spend your free time rationalizing an expensive RV or enjoying it? A $5,000 fold-down camper can provide the same bonding and fellowship any larger towable can—and at a fraction of the price.

Motorized or Towable?

Chances are, you made this decision 50 pages ago. Most people fall into one of the two camps (pun intended) explained early on. Like the idea of operating just one vehicle (a.k.a. a motorhome) with easier driving and trips free of hitching up? Already have that tow vehicle in place and are just an inexpensive towable away from launching your next big camping adventure? We discussed the pros and cons of each type of RV in Chapters 2 and 3. Deciding on the motorized or towable route will make all other decisions a little easier, and thus help narrow your search.

Who's Coming Along?

The probable headcount should make all kinds of decisions for you. Generally, the two-adult, two-child dynamic lends itself to most kinds of RVs. Truck campers and smaller Class Bs may or may not oblige, but most others should. Add another adult or two to that mix—or a brood of growing teenagers—and choices point to larger trailers and Class A and C motorhomes. Think at least 30 feet of vehicle for five or more people and their gear.

ROAD SCHOLAR

Because passengers are *strongly* discouraged from riding onboard a trailer while in transit, your tow vehicle is really what determines how many people can come along. Sleeping for six aboard your new trailer is useful only if the tow vehicle can get them all there. Have I harped on this point enough? I think so.

Where Are We Going?

Although it's mostly true that RVs do well in all kinds of environments, some versions are better suited for specific activities than others. For the family who plans to stick to the highways, opting for local campgrounds and major attractions, any RV should suit. However, those wanting to off-road and basically go where none have gone before require a highly maneuverable, rugged, well-equipped, fully insulated machine. That lengthy fifth-wheel or monstrous motorhome may struggle compared to hunting and fishing trips utilizing camper vans, truck campers, and smaller towables. More active types dreaming of side trips aboard motorcycles, snowmobiles, and the like might consider a sport-utility trailer or Class C equipped with a special cargo area to store motorized goodies.

How Much Room Do We Need?

I've met full-timers who were happy as clams touring the country in their camper van, as well as those who felt claustrophobic aboard a 40-foot motorhome with multiple slide-outs. Towables are cheaper per foot than motorized vehicles and are further aided by the absence of a cockpit. As you inspect any new RV, ask yourself one question: Can I live here? Large amounts of time spent indoors are probably worth the investment of a bigger vehicle. A few rainy days in tight quarters raises everyone's annoyance level a few degrees. Conversely, making do with less requires a less costly investment.

PULL OVER

Is your spouse afraid to operate the new fifth-wheel or motorhome? Situations in which one member of the family does all the driving invite trouble down the road. What if the perpetual driver gets hurt, gets sick, or needs a rest? What then? A true driving partnership is always the goal of any new purchase, so buy only what both of you feel comfortable with.

What's My Driving M.O.?

It's an irrefutable rule: the smaller the overall length of your RV, the easier it is to move around. And because many hours are spent in transport, give careful thought to this most underrated consideration. Is the extra space of a Class A worth the extra diligence required for finding a parking space, backing up, or changing lanes? Is the lesser expense of a travel trailer worth the added sway and towing considerations over most fifth-wheels? Opting for a camper van amortizes its initial expense with use as a second vehicle. If so, is this what you envisioned as your everyday, 24/7 vehicle?

What Do I Need Onboard?

Deluxe showers and fold-down campers are mutually exclusive. Triple slide-outs and truck campers simply don't coexist. Camper vans cannot accommodate a washer and dryer, a gigantic kitchen, and bunk beds for the kids, as the big rigs can. Thinking about what, if anything, you can live without should break through a decision deadlock. Again, roomier—and more expensive—RVs reward buyers with added options and accessories.

Even More to Think About

Making any progress? Is the soul-searching paying off? Before I und...
the local dealership for the buying stage (soon, in Chapter 6), reach a consen...
about the type of vehicle you covet. Is it a towable or motorized? Fifth-wheel or
trailer? Class A, B, or C? Lightweight travel trailer or fold-down camper? Ideally,
you should also know what you want to spend, how many people the RV must
transport, and what kinds of things you'd like to see onboard (besides a dozen
donuts). Get closure on these issues before proceeding. Go ahead, I'll wait.

Great, glad that's decided. But there are a few more things to consider before
busting open the piggy bank. Again, we want to avoid impulsive decisions on
the dealer's lot. A little forethought can go a long way to making a good buying
decision. Here are a few other wrinkles in the decision-making exercise.

ONE FOR THE ROAD

The first slide-out room appeared in motorhomes built by Newmar Corporation
in 1990. The advent of the slide-out turned the RV industry on its collective ear.
Vehicle lengths had plateaued for many years, so the chance to expand outward
threw buyers and dealers into a collective frenzy. Slide-out rooms are now so
common that it's unusual to see a model without at least one onboard.

Gas or Diesel?

You've decided on the motorhome or tow vehicle of your dreams, and just one
question remains: gas or diesel? Most Class A, B, and C manufacturers offer at
least one model with a diesel engine. These extra choices (with larger price tags)
beg the question, which type of engine is indeed better?

A good rule of thumb is to seriously consider a diesel engine for an RV greater
than 35 feet in length. This is doubly true if your driving adventures take you
through much hilly terrain, where a rear-mounted diesel engine's extra power
comes in handy. Of course, the 37-foot gas-powered motorhome I just test-drove
did fine, but generally, the rule is still a good one.

Today's Diesel

Today's diesel engines are quieter, harder working, and more efficient than ever, as best exemplified by the latest offerings from Cummins and Caterpillar. With today's diesel pushers (rear-mounted diesel engines), noise is almost a nonfactor. Noise may be a different story when sitting in the cab of a diesel pickup, where passengers are much closer to the engine. If that's a concern, a gas-powered pickup such as a Ford 350 with a Triton engine might be a better choice—it purrs like a kitten in comparison.

The diesel smell is also not the greatest, and cold-weather start-up problems can still hamper engines when the temperature dips below 30°F. However, when properly maintained, electronically controlled engines shouldn't really be hard-pressed until temperatures plummet below 0°F. Again, this isn't a problem with a gas-powered pickup.

Diesel Dilemmas

Consider the cost factor. Diesels are more expensive, whether it's for your RV or tow vehicle. Still, fuel costs are competitive while usually delivering better overall fuel economy than their gasoline counterpart—a very big perk for a motorhome struggling to earn double-digit miles per gallon.

With cold weather comes a set of fuel considerations for diesel owners. Icing and gelling in the fuel tank, associated with the changing of temperatures, often necessitates special care. A number of additives are available to remedy these problems if they occur. Travelers also have to be sure their diesel fuel is fresh, because it doesn't share the popularity of unleaded fuels and thus runs the risk of being old. It's probably best to fill up along the interstate, where the hordes of 18-wheelers keep the diesel supply fresh and the turnover rate higher than at other locales.

Your diesel engine will probably need less routine maintenance over time (no tune-ups or spark plug changes necessary), but when work is required, it will definitely cost more—and not every shop can do the job. A $100 oil change is very possible. However, diesel engines are extremely durable and should last a long time. Stories about pickups besting 500,000 miles are not uncommon. This workhorse reputation should serve you well come trade-in time.

ONE FOR THE ROAD

Diesel engines surely have gasoline versions beat in terms of overall lore. Ever heard the one about the owner who got 500,000 miles out of his medium-duty pickup? I personally have seen countless examples of diesels exceeding 200,000 miles and look primed for more. How about the motorhome that rolled out 300,000 miles and is still going strong? True or false, such tales are certainly a part of the diesel mythology.

What's Their Rep?

Unlike the automobile industry, limited to a few giants and their subsidiaries, there are loads of RV manufacturers. A few can boast 75-plus years in the business; others started last Thursday. Company XYZ might build every type of RV under the sun, while another focuses on one or two kinds. Every manufacturer brings something new and different to the table in terms of design or engineering, presenting the dilemma of who to trust to build yours.

At some point, the choice might boil down to an RV from company X and company Y. The prices are competitive. Each passes all your tests as far as livability goes (as you'll see in Chapter 5). Even your goldfish seems impressed. I recommend letting the manufacturers' reputations break the tie. Listening to the opinions of customers, the media, and even wacky Cousin Al will reveal certain patterns about a company's products, accountability, and commitment to customers. Talk to that RV owner at the rest stop or gas station about his thoughts on his particular unit. Ask your local RV dealer why he carries the products he does. Read as many publications as you can, particularly ones conducting RV road tests. Go online for reviews and solicit opinions from members of various RV-related forums and message boards. Useful sources for your search are listed in Appendix A.

Walking the Walk

It's time to leave the nest. Hitch up the horses. Polish up the shoe leather. In short, this part of your quest cannot be accomplished in your favorite easy chair. Okay, you can bring the remote control if it makes you feel better. It's time to hit the streets in search of answers. The best way to truly narrow your choices is to tour the RVs themselves—lots of them. If a picture is worth a thousand words, what, then, is an afternoon spent looking at vehicles worth? The answer could put me out of the book-writing business.

Examine the floorplans, see how a slide-out really works, get behind the wheel, and make loud driving noises. Compare the living quarters of one type of RV to another. Ask questions. Listen. Repeat. Eliminate the vehicles you can't afford, can't drive or tow, or feel are too big or too small. You're not here to buy—that comes later. Leave the checkbook at home—or leave that wad of cash safely tucked away in the mattress. No transactions today—only fact-gathering and lively discussions with you, your spouse, and the family about what type of RV is best for the group. The following is an itinerary of sorts, a list of places and ways to refine your opinions in an effort to, say it with me, narrow your choices.

It's Showtime

There's an RV show happening somewhere nearly every week of the year. The local convention center or football stadium is awash in a sea of recreational vehicles, a sight so profound for those who love the lifestyle that traveling hundreds of miles to attend is not unheard of. I know couples who struggle to name the date of their anniversary but are quick to drop the date and time of the next big show. Events such as these are created with three goals in mind: sell, sell, and sell some more. Area dealerships showcase their wares, with salespeople in a frenzy to make a deal.

In addition to a bunch of shiny new RVs, exhibitors may offer entertainment, food, and events to lure potential buyers. Representatives from nearby campgrounds and resorts, the latest accessory products, food, and probably a juggler or two are also common RV show sights. But remember your mission: to tour every RV you can and make a decision about which is best for you. There's simply no greater opportunity than this to survey the RV landscape. Okay, you can have some cotton candy, too.

The local newspaper usually has show dates and times. The travel or auto section is the best bet. Otherwise, the Recreation Vehicle Industry Association (RVIA) features a comprehensive listing of RV shows nationwide. Visit www.rvia.org/?ESID=rvshows for a comprehensive listing.

Kicking the Tires

The next best way to sample RVs is to visit area dealerships. Of course, you may be spoiled rotten after the head-spinning selection at the RV show. Instead of hundreds of units on display, most medium-size dealerships might have fewer than 50 available to tour. The price and space requirements of inventory minimize the amount of overhead most can handle.

RV dealerships vary from their automotive counterparts in several ways. Unlike the massive Honda, Ford, or Mercedes dealerships you're used to seeing, most RV lots feature a scattering of different manufacturers and a mix of vehicle types. For example, dealer X might sell fifth-wheels by one manufacturer, travel trailers from another, and a few lines of motorhomes thrown in just for fun. Meanwhile, dealer Y offers three kinds of fold-down campers, a number of lightweight trailers, and truck campers from several different makers. Be sure to call ahead to eliminate unnecessary visits. For example, if you've ruled out motorized vehicles all together, coordinate visits to only those selling towables.

PULL OVER

Rental companies are notorious for some rather oddball—and pricey—provisions found within the fine print. Beware of extra charges for cleaning the unit, refilling water and LP tanks, and emptying the holding tanks. Also hammer down any possible extra mileage costs or per-diem insurance before you leave the premises.

Overdue Rent

Because the driving/towing segment of RV life is crucial to your level of comfort and enjoyment, it's prudent (if at all possible) to take your preferred type of RV out for a spin. Renting a vehicle for a few days takes this one step further, offering consumers the chance to actually live onboard and experience the lifestyle firsthand. The benefits of such a trip are twofold: first, to determine how much you like traveling by RV; and second, to see if this is the right kind of vehicle to do it in. Sure, the differences between a 35-foot motorhome and a small camper van are fairly obvious upon first review, but an extended trip reveals key insights into the strengths and weaknesses of each. Buyers often discover a great appreciation for what they're looking for after a weekend sleeping, cooking, showering, using the bathroom, and lounging about in an RV. Fortunately, rentals are available for such introspection.

The good news is that rental companies exist. The bad news is that towables are rarely on the menu. The deliberations required to match up a tow vehicle correctly to the trailer *du jour* is more fuss than most customers and renters want to endure for a spontaneous getaway. Opportunities for fifth-wheel and travel-trailer owners are few; smaller fold-down campers and lightweights are more common but still represent a minority of the nation's rental fleet. Life on the motorized side is much better because nearly everyone rents Class Cs. Larger Class As, camper vans, and truck campers are also available, although to a lesser degree.

The drawback is that renting isn't cheap. Expect to pay $100 to $200 a night for the vehicle itself—possibly more, depending on when and where you rent. Campground costs, fuel, tolls, per-diem insurance, dumping fees, and miscellaneous costs might appear in the contract. A mileage fee may or may not be included.

The nation's largest RV rental chain, Cruise America (1-800-327-7799; www. cruiseamerica.com), is a sure bet. At this time, the company rents various sizes and kinds of motorhomes, including a Fun Mover model with a ramp and cargo area for dirt bikes, snowmobiles, and other motorized goodies. A handicap-accessible unit is also available at select locations. Someone I know recently recommended a smaller RV rental company named El Monte RV (1-888-337-2214). Otherwise, an online search is warranted. For a complete catalog of rental companies, contact GoRVing (1-888-467-8464; www.GoRVing.com).

ROAD SCHOLAR

GoRVing is a great resource designed with the consumer in mind. It can aid in your decision-making process by giving you a list of local RV dealerships, rental facilities, and info on the RV lifestyle. Coupled with this book, you will go from idiot to expert in no time. The Recreational Vehicle Industry Association (RVIA) is another great resource tailored more to manufacturers, investors, and the media. They offer RV news, technical information, market data, and a lot more. Here's the info: (703-620-6003), www.rvia.org.

Take a Sunday Drive

Test-driving a little beauty off the dealer's lot is another option. This is useful only for getting a feeling for how she handles, not for gauging the living quotient onboard. Walking around in your PJs and drinking milk straight out of the container is usually frowned upon. However, a decision between a 35-foot Class A and a 30-foot Class C motorhome might just come down to the driving ease of each. Maneuverability, parking ease, and your anxiety level behind the wheel will help make your decision—you might just set your sights on a mini-motorhome or something even smaller.

Towable enthusiasts fare only slightly better here than in the rental sector. If matching up an existing vehicle is a potential influence on a buying decision, some dealers might allow you to hitch up the trailer to your existing tow vehicle and take it out for a spin. Otherwise, don't expect a loaner vehicle on the premises to transport the fifth-wheel or travel trailer you've been eyeing.

A Friend in Need ...

With more than 10 million RVs on the road, somebody you know has to own one. Perhaps that person will even let you take it out for a spin. An in-law, a cousin, the neighbor with the black socks and the Bermuda shorts, the boss's nephew whom you helped move last summer …. When you locate that person, bend his ear and see if you can arrange a visit. Two words: ask nicely.

Read All About It

There's also no shortage of up-to-date information about the RV lifestyle, whether it be online, on magazine shelves, or through scores of publications devoted to specific RV travel clubs. Check out an internet discussion group, post a barrage of questions on bulletin boards (the cyber kind, not the one at work), and question fellow RVers about their RVs and preferences. Be prepared for forthright and eager responses, as my experience is that we RVers love to talk. Sure, some folks have an axe to grind or may be ill informed, but such candid discussions are still usually beneficial.

Buyer's Guides

You can find more comprehensive information in an RV buyer's guide, available on an annual basis from *Trailer Life* and *Woodall's.* These guides feature detailed information on a wide range of RV offerings for the upcoming year. Sizes, weights, floorplan choices, standards and options, prices, and a shiny photograph are the least they offer. RVs are broken down into classes, allowing for an easy glimpse of many of the hottest new designs in one specific category.

Do Your Homework

After a lengthy investigation, everything might start to blur into a never-ending collage of fiberglass, rubber, and wheels. Taking in this much new information should leave your brain more fried than a chicken leg from KFC. Grab brochures of favorite models and scribble down notes and costs. At some point, you'll begin to recognize the makers of a specific RV by their unique features. Eventually, the pendulum might swing in favor of a couple specific manufacturers, perhaps due to their aesthetics, user-friendly floorplans, or obvious quality. You may not know what RV you want, but perhaps company XYZ is the answer.

Pinpoint your search by going directly to the manufacturers themselves. Visit their websites and tour their product galleries. Send away for brochures and read everything printed about that company, their reputation, and their customer service.

Campfire Chats

The mood is serene. A parade of campfires flicker away in the summer night. Kids are passive, watching the burning embers and readying marshmallows for a thorough torching. The smell of hickory dances in the air. And then someone starts talking about his RV. It never fails. RVers love to talk about their vehicles. During my various road tests, it's common for curious strangers to approach me about what I'm driving. "Come on in," I'll say. "Have a look around." This kind of RV showcasing isn't braggery—rather, it's an inquisitive look at what the other folks have. Surely they'll return the favor and walk you through their motorhome or talk about what they love about their 10-year-old trailer. Ask your neighbor for opinions. Next thing you know, you'll be sharing beef stew talking about why she prefers a certain brand of Class C. Bring over dessert, and school is in session.

New or Used?

The new or used debate is a classic one. Many owners treat their recreational vehicles as luxury items, subjecting them to relatively low mileage, wear and tear, and light periods of use. As a result, it's not unusual to see 20-year-old rigs out on the road (avocado interior included). Factor this in with the expense of the latest models, and the appeal of a previously owned unit becomes obvious. However, a secondhand product comes with a fair share of risks. Why are they selling? How did they treat it? What if it breaks a mile down the road? Determining whether to cut a larger check for a new RV or roll the dice on an older model is a major decision. Let's look at some of the key factors.

Secondhand Views

That sinister little foe, depreciation, makes buying a used RV very attractive. Purchase a new vehicle, drive it around for a while, resell it, and what have you got? About 10 to 20 percent less money than you started with. This is especially true for motorized units, with an engine and more mechanisms to wear down from use. Of course, you probably don't need me to tell you that the lower price is the single biggest advantage to buying used.

Depreciation affects all those neat doodads onboard, too. Those pricey upgrades—the leather sofas, dishwasher, and undercarriage rust-proofing the dealer sold you on—are also used and therefore should be less expensive, too. That one-year-old GPS and the awning you just installed also fall under this category.

ROAD SCHOLAR

It's worth the money to have an RV service technician look over any used RVs you're serious about buying. Undetected trouble doesn't stay that way long, which is why it's best to have the pros take a look-see. And speaking of trouble, keep in mind that the older the vehicle is, the harder it is to find parts for it. In an age when mechanics need computer degrees just to pop the hood, servicing an older RV can be problematic.

Used and Abused

The dream is that you'll find that little old lady who drove her RV only to church. The reality is that, like you, a used RV has a past, one that may reflect a history of abuse and little respect for itself, kind of like you back in college. Did the owner take care of it, or was he too busy chasing squirrels off his lawn? Was routine maintenance performed on the appliances, electrical and LP systems, and plumbing? Was the vehicle properly stored when not in use and eased back into service in the spring? Did the owner drive it like a government mule—or, worse, like a rental car? As we'll discuss in Chapter 7, there's a lot we can do to verify the overall condition of a vehicle. Unfortunately, Jerry Springer won't be there to uncover all its secrets for us. There are some things about a used RV that you may never know.

Inspector General

Buying used is always risky, but it can be rewarding, too. Here's where it's worth the investment to have an RV specialist or even a home inspector appraise the RV. Tell the seller that the purchase is subject to the RV passing an inspection by a professional. This will give you peace of mind. One of the best things about buying a preowned RV is the bargain price. It allows you to start RVing sooner than if you had to save for a new one, and that's always a good thing. Get warranties in writing and leave no stone unturned, new or used.

The Benefits of New

Price. Plain and simple. That's the one solid argument against buying new. A higher sticker price and higher insurance premiums await all new buyers. If cash is short and you're feeling frisky, a terrific case can be made for a preowned unit. I would rather have you out there RVing, living life on your terms, reaping the rewards of spending time with your family, than sitting at home pondering all the what-ifs. Now, here's what's good about buying new.

Choice

Face it, new RVs come with more choices. Size, color, engine, and so on, it's a smorgasbord of opportunity. Just visit an RV show to see what I mean, which is much more tempting in terms of driving out in a new 40-foot diesel than the slim pickings found on the waiver wire of the weekend classified section. While frugal buyers comb the used dealer lots and websites for deals, you've got the pick of the litter. Hundreds of choices await, and dealers are more than happy to show you all around. Play eenee, meenee, minee, moe to determine a favorite. This is doubly true for floorplans, with multiple variations in every unit, from every manufacturer.

Rest Assured

The RV is brand new. Plastic is draped over the furnishings; the floor is unspoiled, pristine, and beautiful. The odometer is fresh as a daisy. The driver's seat lacks the butt groove of any previous owners. A sparkling clean engine radiates under the hood. Appliances sit clean and shiny. Everything is untouched, unspoiled. Inhale deeply. Notice the smell of honest clean. That is what you're paying for.

Not only that, but newer is usually better in terms of quality. Newer materials such as Corian, gel coat fiberglass, and Thermopane windows (to name a few) are superior to their predecessors. With every production year, RVs get better made, safer, more aerodynamic, and probably more durable than a unit made 5 or 10 years ago. You won't find air bags or top-of-the-line innovations on some older vehicles. Nor will your investment be protected by a warranty as comprehensive, giving new buyers a level of confidence.

The Least You Need to Know

- Determining a budget and then such factors as driving or towing abilities, number of passengers, and types of usage is paramount to picking the best type of RV for you.
- Reading and researching online for information about RVs and manufacturers is an important step in selecting the dream RV.
- Visiting RV shows, touring dealer lots, renting, and taking test-drives help many buyers discover their needs and further narrow their list of must-haves for their future RV.
- Using the services of an inspector to check a used RV gives the buyer peace of mind. New RV buyers pay more for the confidence of the latest product design, warranties, floorplan choices, and a clean driving history.

Buying or Renting an RV

Call the accountant, notify the bank, wake the dog—it's time to buy or rent an RV. A close financial inspection revealed that you do indeed have enough money in the reserves to jump into the recreational vehicle fold. Congratulations! Your hard work has paid off, and now you, the family, and relatives you've never heard of can soon hit the road in search of ... well, whatever. So what's it gonna be? A snazzy 35-foot motorhome for you and your better half? A modest fold-down or pop-up camper for use behind the family SUV? A medium-size travel trailer that sleeps six? Hey, what about a sport-utility trailer for those shiny new Harleys? Or maybe you've just been lured into the fun of renting an RV (by your best friend) for your dream trip to Graceland. Hopefully you've reached some sort of a decision about what you're looking for, since this part of the book is dedicated to pulling the proverbial trigger on a new RV or renting an RV. Get out your checkbook—buying or renting time is here.

What to Buy?

In This Chapter

- Testing the livability index of any RV
- Performing a thorough RV inspection
- Knowing what to look for during a test-drive

By now, you should have a working model of what you're looking for—or, at least, what you definitely *don't* want. A financial summit has produced an acceptable budget, and a headcount has determined just how many people your future RV needs to transport and sleep. If you're not at this stage, go back to Chapter 4 and get a handle on these most important factors. Believe me, it's a lot easier to find the perfect travel trailer under $25,000 capable of sleeping six than it is to find, say, "whatever towable will work." Otherwise, you may wilt under the pressure of a charismatic salesperson. A sort of RV-show paralysis is all too common for those unfocused in their buying decisions.

Now hop aboard—the perfect RV awaits.

Livability Tests

Your eyes meet from across the lot. Could it be love at first sight? A thoughtful glance at the sticker price only steels your resolve—you can afford it! You walk inside, trying to imagine the whole family in a peaceful coexistence. After a slow walk-through, you're still smiling. You like it. Now it's time to get serious. Every vehicle claim will be tested, every nook and cranny thoroughly examined. The purpose of such a "livability test" is to determine how user-friendly this new motorized or towable truly is. Can it really sleep eight passengers? Is the shower of adequate size? Can you see the TV from the couch? Is there enough storage for all your bowling trophies? Remember, this is your hard-earned money. Make sure your new RV is worthy of this investment.

Let's start inside, because this is the make-or-break spot for most of us.

ROAD SCHOLAR

You might look at dozens of RVs before settling on one you like best. As such, keeping the details straight from one unit to the next can be difficult. Most dealers carry brochures on each RV, so make sure you grab one. Take deliberate notes. Circle the floorplans you've toured, including prices and noteworthy points. Some buyers find it useful to record video of their findings for later review.

It Sleeps How Many?

For the most part, RV manufacturers do a reasonably good job with their sleeping claims. Of course, a few are a wee bit too optimistic. If a unit says it sleeps up to six, make them prove it. Is that six adults or six children? Can your sister who played center for three seasons in the WNBA fit anywhere? Start in the master bedroom (if applicable), home to the most important bed in the place. Why? Because it will most likely be your bed, that's why. Lie down. Ask your spouse to come along, too. Is there room for the two of you, or would this tight fit create a nightmarish situation for the both of you? Is there a spot nearby for the alarm clock, journal, and eyeglasses?

Don't stop there. Test every sleeping configuration the RV has to offer. Deploy the sofa bed, convert the dinette table sleeper, crawl up in the cab-over area (Class Cs only), and lie down. Are these spaces comfortable, easy to deploy, and accessible? Do you fit? Will cousin Benny? After all these tests, determine just how many the RV can sleep—and sleep comfortably.

ONE FOR THE ROAD

Most, if not all, convertible dinettes are too short for adults. Sofa beds vary a lot in terms of overall mattress size and comfort. Be sure to watch that metal bar underneath (you know the one) that can make for long nights for your guests.

Food Fight

Assuming that cooking—and eating—is important to you, the kitchen area should definitely be somewhat chef-friendly. Consider space issues. Is there enough storage for pots, pans, and place settings for everyone onboard? How about the sink? Can it hold more than two dirty plates at a time? Do you have enough counter space to chop vegetables, set bowls for mixing, or prepare sandwiches for the gang? Where will the garbage go (remarkably, not all RVs come with a garbage can)? Where might any recycled items go? Is the underneath-the-sink storage a usable space or is it dominated by plumbing fixtures? Are the drawers decorative or functional? How about outlets, lighting, and a place for larger or awkward cooking items?

Check out the appliances. What comes standard and which are options? Will a two-burner stove be enough, or can you find three or more in your price range and vehicle type? Can the oven accommodate anything larger than a tray of cupcakes? A small refrigerator and a large family equals trouble. Visualize all the usual staples—an endless assortment of soft drinks, cumbersome leftover dishes, and the catch of the day—and see if they will fit. Do you have a freezer or icemaker? Do you really need one? Is the microwave standard or an option? Do you care? Would a convection oven be the best of both worlds? Where will paper towels, silverware, and spices go? Give adequate attention to these small but ultimately significant issues.

PULL OVER

The bigger the vehicle, the larger the kitchen. In this case, you usually get what you pay for. If the budget calls for a fold-down camper, don't expect the island kitchens, double-door refrigerators, and dishwashers found in some high-end fifth-wheels. The question, rather, should be whether there's a *reasonable* mix of storage, space, and functionality present. If not, perhaps the next model will work better. Unrealistic expectations can plague the buying experience.

What About My Ukulele?

Keep tabs on all interior drawers, cabinetry, and storage compartments. Open each one. Are they there for show or are they ready to serve? Are they skinny or deep, tall or tiny? Is there a wardrobe closet onboard? Does that matter to you?

Does each room possess enough storage to prevent the endless searching for your gear? I once saw an interesting trailer in which the largest concentration of storage was in the bathroom. Would such a situation work for you?

Are there larger compartments for blankets, cleaning supplies, and bulkier items? A great development is the advent of underneath-the-bed storage, where the bed easily lifts to provide a sizable, out-of-the-way compartment. Plenty of overhead storage onboard is also great, but it's useful only for lighter items. Heavier stowage belongs closer to the floor, to prevent a top-heavy condition. I'll cover proper packing and what to bring along in Chapter 14.

Going Through the Motions

I guarantee that you're going to feel goofy standing in the shower fully clothed with that perplexed salesperson looking on, but do it anyway. Step inside and go through the showering motions (no water required here). Otherwise, this watery tomb may prove to be a constant source of annoyance after the purchase. A roomy shower is a joy; conversely, a tight squeeze should be reserved only for orange juice. In the case of smaller RVs that often lack their own paneled showering room, it's doubly important to try it out. How does it work? Does a curtain wrap around the middle of the camper van, with water going down an in-floor drain? Just because a shower is offered doesn't mean it's a satisfactory experience. Walk the walk so you know what you're in for.

You know what's coming next, don't you? If a bathtub is present, go ahead and test it out. Ask the salesperson to scrub your back if you like. Can you spread out? Is it worth the extra cost? Showers with tubs can be more difficult to access than flat-floor showers. Keep this in mind for passengers struggling with mobility issues. Garden tub/shower combinations are becoming more common. They don't take up as much room as a full-size bathtub, yet they feel quite roomy.

Is there a spot for soap, shampoo, conditioner, and rubber ducky? How about towel racks and outlets for the hair dryer? How do the sink and vanity rate? Generally, bathrooms don't possess too much storage, so a medicine cabinet is a nice touch. Actually sit on the toilet (yes, I know how this looks). Do your knees knock against the walls? Are you constricted like a Houdini stunt? One of the nicest fifth-wheels I ever saw didn't have a roll for toilet paper. Certainly not a deal-breaker, but it's important to think about the little things.

Live and Let Live (Inside)

No matter how sporty you are or how active the itinerary, spending some time lounging about the interior is inevitable. During these times, the comforts of the couch and size of the TV matter a whole lot more than whether the fish are biting. High-line RVs come with all sorts of entertaining options; that list is whittled away somewhat as you move down to the more entry-level offerings. But a few key questions remain. Are the chairs and couches comfortable? Does the swivel chair swivel, the recliner recline, and the expandable table, well, you get the picture. Can everyone see the TV? Do you require a second one in the bedroom? In many motorhomes, the cockpit chairs swivel around to join the conversation, for additional seating. Is this important to you? Would a slide-out living area (or two) provide the finishing touch?

Where will drinks go? How's the lighting for reading? Got enough headroom? Interior heights and widths vary, so don't settle for dwarfish dimensions onboard. Keep looking—you're bound to find a manufacturer capable of getting the most out of every inch. Would a freestanding table, capable of being moved, be better than a stationary dinette with bench seats? I was just in a travel trailer where all the furnishings were movable, in stark contrast to the nailed-down furnishings of most coaches. Would a J-shaped couch be better than a loveseat? Does the motor-home have enough seat belts? Where will the laptop go? Deploy all slide-outs to gauge their impact in terms of space.

Other Keys to Victory

Honor your first impressions. Does the interior feel homey and welcoming? Can you picture the family running around within, husband snoozing away peace-fully on the couch, the dog licking her chops in front of the refrigerator? Is there enough light? Are there enough windows and skylights to allow the sunlight to radiate throughout? Are overhead lights, outlets, and heating ducts abundant? What about cable TV hook-ups, an HD TV antenna for better reception, or a place for newspapers and magazines? Does the décor reflect your taste?

Take It Outside

Because you won't be living outside, poking around the exterior isn't technically a livability test. That doesn't mean you won't be spending some quality time out there, however. Expect plenty of moments rummaging through the various exterior compartments, hooking up to campsite utilities, deploying the awning, and the like outside your new RV.

Storage

Go outside and open the storage compartments. In nicer models, expect to see carpeting, insulation, lighting, and locks for safekeeping. Is this the case? Is there enough room for bulkier items such as fishing poles, life vests, and lawn chairs? Believe me, bags of charcoal and firewood don't make for great chaperones inside. Pass-through storage means gear can be accessed from either side of the unit. Basement storage models, as discussed in Chapter 2, are cavernous and great for those traveling with larger numbers.

You cannot have too much storage space in an RV. Ask any seasoned RVer what his biggest gripe is, and the majority will side squarely with the "place to put stuff" issue. Some of the fancier coaches feature nice, sturdy, slide-out trays that extend from outside storage compartments (think of them as industrial-grade spice racks). Of course, slide trays are also available in the aftermarket as an upgrade for your existing storage space. And don't overlook the possibility of adding a roof-mounted storage pod when the area below the floor or in the basement isn't quite voluminous enough.

ROAD SCHOLAR

Slide-outs are truly amazing—that is, until you need to get at something located in a compartment stuck underneath the extended room. Your choices are but few—go inside and retract the room, or crawl on your belly to get that meatball recipe. Thankfully, a few manufacturers have patented systems in which exterior storage compartments expand right along with the room. This may be worth a look if a slide-out is in your future—and you love meatballs.

Awnings, Steps, and Little Extras

Plan to spend any quality time on the roof (not a good idea with a pop-up or small RV)? A rear ladder is your gateway to impromptu roof inspections or meteor showers, not to mention a great seat at the races. Otherwise, consider yourself grounded. What about the entry step? Is it strong and resilient, or spongy, propelling you in and out of the coach like an Olympic diving competition? Electric and manual models are available. Handrails in the entryway are a must for older passengers and generally a good idea anyway.

Awnings—sometimes gigantic, electronic versions—are included as standard on many RVs to create shade and shelter from the rain. Is yours easy to deploy or a bear to operate? Some older models require the patience of Job to deploy, negotiating a never-ending series of latches, clasps, and a supplemental pole for extracting. These days, more manufacturers are going the motorized route, which removes most of the ill will from the process. Does your RV have an awning? Do you care? Window awnings might also be offered, which keeps the sun off the interior and prevents furnishings from fading. Is this important to you? Aftermarket awnings aren't cheap, so try to get one in the buying process, if you can.

PULL OVER

Just because there's a ladder doesn't mean going topside is entirely safe. More than a few unwilling participants have tap-danced their way off their rubber roof after a morning rain. Please be careful. Wear rubber-soled shoes, as if you were boarding a slippery sailboat. Watch the air conditioner, antennae, and seams. Don't let children transform the top of the motorhome into a treehouse.

The Inspection

Any RV that passes these livability tests is probably in the running for your hard-earned dollar. You liked what you saw and went through the appropriate examinations, and this RV should be considered a finalist in the single-elimination tournament that is buying an RV. But a final hurdle still awaits: the inspection. Get out the magnifying glass and overcoat, Sherlock—it's time to see what makes this baby tick. What we're looking for now is quality—quality craftsmanship, quality materials, and a quality product built to last.

I don't believe in assumptions, especially when it requires signing over a great big chunk of money. The quality of a new RV isn't necessarily a given. Just because the motorhome has less than 100 miles on the odometer and has a pretty pink ribbon on top doesn't mean we should let it off easy. Was it built right? How long has it been sitting on the lot? Was it professionally crafted or does it resemble work done by a monkey with a caulking gun? Is that bluish puddle underneath a sign of a leak or just the remains of your kid's snow cone?

Make doubly sure all previously owned RVs receive a close inspection, both inside and out. With that said, I agree that today's RVs are built better than anytime in their history. Computer technology, refined building practices, and decades of learning what works and what doesn't have helped manufacturers construct the finest RVs ever. However, I still favor leaving no stone unturned come buying time. Repeat after me: every RV purchase demands a close inspection.

Take It Inside

Ascertain the maker of a prospective RV's dedication to quality building and craftsmanship. This is a nice place to begin when searching for a new RV. If either quality is lacking, don't even bother with the rest. Move on and find another. Depending on what you're looking for, this can rule out a lot of units and really save time. Start your inspection inside out. Poor engineering of the roof, sidewalls, or windows and doors will undoubtedly result in future leaks, electrical and plumbing problems, and other sneaky damage.

Floor It

Look down. What do you see? Is the carpeting plush and springy or beaten down by life? How is the coloring? New patches or cut-outs indicate work done to that area. Was it a leak, a hole, or what? Walk the coach, taking careful note of any spongy or tilted areas beneath you, all possible indications of rotten floorboards or other looming problems. Examine around baseboards, underneath doors and windows, and near appliances where leaks are most likely to develop.

Though some squeaks may be inevitable, listen for excessive noises as you walk the floor area. Improperly secured flooring may manifest as squeaks or groans. If the galley or bathroom area is tiled, look for cracked or loosened tiles that may indicate a subflooring problem. For me, problems with the subfloor are a deal-breaker.

Woodworking

Don't shortchange the importance of durable woods and craftsmanship, affecting drawers, cabinets, closets, doors, tables, and chairs. Nothing dooms resale faster than shoddy work and flimsy materials. As a rule, solid woods are better than particleboard; screws and glue are superior to staples. Open and close the drawers and tug on the cabinets. Is the woodworking rugged or set to come apart 5 miles outside Albany? Do the side tables, bookshelves, coffee table, and magazine racks feel like they can go the long haul?

ROAD SCHOLAR

Follow your nose—it always knows. Involve your sense of smell in the search, with a whiff of mold or mildew being a prime giveaway of leaks. In such events, determine what, if any, maintenance has been performed to correct the problem—or whether it's the responsibility of a new owner. In any event, you've got damaged goods on your hands. It's now just a matter of gauging the damage and deciding whether you want such an undertaking.

Don't let the price fool you. One of the most beautiful (and expensive) RVs I ever tested had marble (yes, marble) countertops on top of cheap and amateurish woodworking. The same brand-new RV concluded my three-day road test with several broken drawers, an end table with a bum leg, and a pair of wobbly side mirrors. I didn't do it, I swear! Moral of the story—you don't *always* get what you pay for.

Furnishings

Most folks know quality when they see it, and cheap fabrics are about as obvious as a $4 necktie. Are the fabrics strong and durable or already showing signs of wear just from a few walk-throughs and sit-downs? Is this the couch that will take you through countless Sundays watching NFL football? Can the chairs hold up against your 2-year-old with the penchant for biting? Do the cushions spring or sag?

As you manipulate the sofa hardware, listen for any squeaks, rattles, or rumblings that may be a precursor to spring or support problems to come. Will that fold-down table really fold down? As for convertible dinettes, as mentioned earlier, be sure the cushions configure as they should in any and all positions.

Seals of Approval

Improper sealing around doors, windows, roofing, and slide-outs is the most likely suspect for future leaks and other problems. Inspect doorways and windows for a tight fit. Wetness or incoming air suggests a less-than-snug situation. Double-check rubber seals for fading and cracking. Inspect the seams in the walls, where pieces are joined. Any spots, buckles, or fading? Any mismatched wallpaper or paint jobs, clear signs of past repairs? Watch the slide-out as it expands and retracts. Does it keep out the debris, air, and moisture?

> **ROAD SCHOLAR**
>
> If possible, tour prospective units during inclement weather, namely rain. This is the surest way to determine an unforeseen leak problem. It's not a bad idea to take your test-drive under less than favorable situations as well. Wind, snow, and rain are a part of life, and how this RV handles at its worst can be very telling. Now if only I had listened to this advice when I bought my house ….

Appliances

You must be convinced that all appliances and onboard systems are in proper working order. Don't take anyone's word for it—see it for yourself. This goes double for used units. RVs with faltering heating or cooling, batteries that won't hold their charges, or drains that won't send gray water promptly away are about as fun as ants at the family picnic. At the very least, you should ask for a full rundown of all appliances, how they work, and troubleshooting information prior to taking possession. More on this in Chapter 8.

Let the seller know ahead of time that you intend to check everything onboard. Yes, everything. This should give him the opportunity to fill the tanks (water and propane), fuel the generator, and precool the refrigerator.

Out and About

Leave the white pants at home: it's time to get dirty. A careful examination of the exterior—roof, chassis, sidewalls, and so on—should reveal whether this vehicle can keep up with all your heavy-duty plans. True, you won't always know what you're looking for, but it's worth the effort anyway. Surely you can spot obvious trouble when you see it. Crawl around underneath, go on top, look at the RV from every angle. What you detect now might save you trouble down the road.

Chassis

Just what, exactly, is going on underneath that thing, anyway? Leaks, puddles, critters' nests, dangling wires, rust, and more obvious signs of damage should cool off the trip to the ATM for your down payment. Follow the exhaust system for cracks and rust. Take your time and maneuver underneath as much of the rig as possible. Shiny new parts on an older unit indicate a new repair. What was the work for? Is it a sign of things to come?

Inspect tenaciously for cracks or openings into the living portion. Critters, especially mice, can enter and exit through the tiniest of holes or gaps between the floor and sidewalls. Check closely around the drain pipes that extend below the floor line also.

Tired Out

Check the tires for wear, cracking, and fading. Even relatively new, undriven tires fall victim to oxidation from that pesky ozone and from UV radiation. Uneven tread may mean an alignment problem. Use a flashlight and a mirror, if necessary, to inspect the sidewalls between the rear dual tires on a motorhome. The sidewalls are the most vulnerable, and any cracking mandates replacement, regardless of the age of the tire. Better to find this out now, as a trip to the tire store is an expensive outing.

Sidewalls and Roofing

Unsightly seams and excessive caulking are red flags of a rushed job or poor work. Be skeptical if your new RV looks hastily put together, which just might be the sad truth. Various viewing from aft and stern discloses any problematic tilts, leanings, or bulges in the sidewalls. Such findings are significant enough to cause you to rethink this purchase. Follow the line of all seams, looking closely for a tight fit. Rust, new paint or panels, and stucco are calling cards for Trouble, Inc.

PULL OVER

No matter how hard we look, most of us possess the skills to detect only the more obvious problems (for example, loose wires, colorful puddles, gaping holes). That's why it's probably worth the investment to have a professional RV specialist appraise a prospective purchase. Upon narrowing the field, make an appointment with an RV technician (someone not affiliated with the dealership) to shake down the vehicle for any signs of trouble. This is a must for all preowned vehicles.

In the case of larger vehicles, get on the roof and have a careful look around. Again, question excessive caulking and sealant. Re-examine seals, particularly around roof-mounted air conditioners and antennas. Tears, rips, and cracks can usually be easily repaired, but the extent of the external damage caused could be worrisome.

Popping the Hood

Pop the hood on motorized RVs and take a peek inside. As always, you're searching for the usual suspects—leaks, rust, and worn seals and rubber. A new motorhome's engine should be clean and fresher than a new shirt taken out of the dryer. Evidence of corrosion or excessive wear here should send you scurrying off the lot. On the contrary, a new-looking engine doesn't necessarily guarantee prime working condition because engine washes are easy and inexpensive. Check belts, hoses, and plugs. Are the fluids sagging dangerously below levels, suggesting the owner has been less than faithful in upkeep?

On some older motorhomes, it is nearly impossible to check the brake fluid reservoir without the aid of a trained monkey wearing a miner's hat with a light. Some had access plates under the carpeting near the driver's feet. On motorhomes with engine access covers inside the coach, closely inspect the seals around the cover.

Revving Your Engine

The purpose of the test-drive is twofold: first, to assess your comfort level piloting this particular RV; second, to gauge the likelihood of any mechanical problems that could snafu your adventures. Both goals will be accomplished with one or two reasonable-length outings behind the wheel. Sellers who lobby hard to limit the trip to a spin around the block and five minutes of road time might have something to hide. It's best to bring a co-pilot as another set of eyes and ears and to get input from another vantage point.

The Towable Exception

As you'll see in Chapter 13, trailer operation requires a well-matched tow vehicle with a suitable hitch. Assuming you already have these things in place on the lot and ready to go, a "test tow" can probably be arranged. However, for whatever reason, such tests aren't very common, and most dealers won't have a tow vehicle to loan you if your existing vehicle isn't up to snuff. It's a moot point, anyway, because all tow vehicle configurations are different. What is paramount, however, is learning (1) what, if any, nifty new pop-up, travel trailer, or fifth-wheel your existing vehicle is able to tow or (2) what size tow vehicle you need to haul away the towable you've got your eyes on. The answer to both questions lies in Chapter 13.

Prior to Take-Off

Start the engine and have a listen. Does the rush of power sound triumphant, followed by a steady purr, or rather like the sound the neighbor's cat makes when someone steps on his tail? Soak in all the sounds for a moment before taking off. In the meantime, adjust the seats and side mirrors, and buckle up. You don't want any distractions, so turn off the radio. Turn on the dashboard heat and air-conditioning. How fast does it warm up/cool off? Send the co-pilot out back to test the brake and backup lights. Make sure all doors are closed, see that the slide-out is retracted (you couldn't operate the vehicle if it weren't), and do a quick walk-through to make sure everything is battened down. Now it's time to hit the road.

The Course

Your motorhome is only as good as the terrain it can cover. Mountain grades, crowded city traffic, Autobahn-like highways, and trips to the market are all part of the RV experience. Make it clear to the seller that you want to sample a mix of road situations, and plot a course accordingly. If they hem and haw, restate the fact that this is an expensive proposition and you want to be very sure of your decision. And then remind them that the dealer down the street had no problems with the idea of an extended test-drive.

Keep a careful account of the following:

- **Stopping.** Are you comfortable with the stopping power?

- **Acceleration.** Does it have enough power? An underpowered RV can leave you lacking during inclines.

- **Cornering.** Do you feel like you're at the wheel of an aircraft carrier?

- **Turning.** Is it easy to turn? A vacant parking lot is a good place to test the turning radius. Backups, too.

- **Clearance.** Does the high clearance make you wary?

- **Handling.** Is the steering responsive?

- **Gadgets.** Are the controls user-friendly?

Warning Signs

Inexperienced buyers can't be expected to stroll onto a dealer's lot with an advanced mechanical degree. At some point, most of us must trust that our new vehicles will act as such and that the careful preparation and examinations will pay off in the form of a well-built unit. A nice set of warranties should help erase some fears, too. There are, however, a few telltale, don't-walk-but-run-away signs to avoid in any particular unit. Follow these, and your odds of buying a clunker reduce dramatically.

Rentals

You know that expression, "It's been driven like a rental"? It evolved from the fact that most of us drive such vehicles, shall I say, a little differently than we drive our everyday autos. Okay, most of us drive rentals fast, hard, and with little regard for their well-being. Rental RVs are no different, with scores of novice drivers jumping curbs, backing up into mailboxes, and navigating the learning curve behind the wheel. When rental RVs outlast their effectiveness, they go to dealerships, sporting a "for sale" sign and a nice discount. Many come with an ugly history of overuse coupled with long periods of sitting around. It may just be a personal bias, but I say leave rental resales alone.

Barely Driven Vehicles

It turns out that dormancy is one of the worst things that can occur to any vehicle, especially when improperly stored, as I'll reveal in Chapter 12 on basic care. And this doesn't apply just to the street machine you commute in during the work week. Imagine if it contained the complex plumbing, electrical, heating, and cooling systems that your RV does, along with an array of appliances and sensitive components. Rarely used RVs are often neglected, meaning more maintenance duties for the new owner: you.

Lean and Mean

As previously stated, an RV shouldn't lean like a high school kid working at McDonald's. Rather, it should stand up straight and tall like a fresh graduate from boot camp. Awkward tilts reveal some not-so-subtle foundation woes, problems best left for the next sucker—I mean, buyer.

Water, Water Everywhere

Wayward leaks are the single greatest threat to an RVer's sanity, as well as to the vehicle's foundation. As your soggy basement at home consistently proves, water can be a slippery foe, with the origins of leaks difficult to track and even harder to remedy. When faced with the scent of mildew, squashy floorboards, and buckling paint, repeat after me: "Thanks, but no thanks."

Wish List

There's nothing scientific about this list, just a collection of the "I-wish-I-hads" from the many travelers I've heard from over the years. Learn from their mistakes, and find the best RV you can.

- Garbage can
- Dirty clothes hamper
- Larger refrigerator
- Towel racks
- Place for recyclables
- More interior storage
- Bedside stand
- Deeper sink
- Larger windows
- Full-length mirror

- Separate room for toilet
- Washer/dryer
- Computer desk/workstation
- File storage
- Places for shoes and coats
- Icemaker
- More outlets
- End tables
- Storage, storage, storage

The Least You Need to Know

- A comprehensive series of livability tests is the fastest way to determine whether an RV is for you. Lie down in the beds, pretend to shower, move about the coach as if you owned the place.
- Carefully inspect the RV inside and out. Check the interior for quality materials, evidence of leaks, and signs of previous repairs. Inspect the sidewalls and roof for rust, leaks, and evidence of trouble.
- Test all appliances to make sure they're in working condition. Notify the seller ahead of time to fill up all tanks, start the generator, and prepare for a close examination.
- An elaborate road test is the final factor in gauging whether an RV is right for you. Listen for signs of engine trouble. Take note of the stopping, starting, and turning abilities.

The Art of the Deal

In This Chapter

- Choosing the right seller
- Avoiding typical pitfalls
- Getting the best deal
- Financing, trade-ins, warranties, and taking delivery

You're getting dangerously close to the "big C." That's right, commitment. By now, you hopefully have a sense of the RV you're looking for or have at least shortened your dance card to just a couple possibilities. It's now just a matter of making it all official, finding the right seller, and reaching a deal you can live with.

Some folks regard the buying stage as an epic battle, them versus the dealer. Like Gary Cooper in *High Noon*, they feel it's time to put on their white hat and prepare to shoot it out against a most unsavory foe. Others succumb to a more passive outlook, shrinking away from a situation they find uncomfortable and confrontational. They prefer to go meekly through the process; just wake them when it's all over. My advice is to approach the sale with realistic expectations and a reasonable point of view. Both buyer and seller want the same thing: to get you RVing. When you think about it like that, negotiations take on a different light. Of course, it comes down to who wants it more and what each party is willing to do to get there. That's where this chapter comes in.

Of course, there's more to it than finding a trustworthy seller and an affordable product. Other questions arise. Where and how do I finance? What extras must

I have? How do I redeem a warranty? What about my trade-in? You sure do ask a lot of questions. Good thing, because the answers are coming.

The Hard Sell

Choosing the right seller is important for a number of reasons. Unlike your prom date, this may turn out to be a fairly lengthy relationship, especially if your RV ever needs service or repairs. Financing through the dealer might also ensure some future dealings, so give some thoughtful consideration to the kind of people you're doing business with. Remember, a check with a whole lotta zeroes is the prize for the seller meeting all your criteria. However, to earn it, all questions must be answered, all expectations met. A deliberate investigation rewards buyers with peace of mind—and a fruitful business relationship in good times and bad.

Basically, there are two types of sellers: private sellers and RV dealers.

Private Sellers

As stated in Chapter 4, private sellers offer a somewhat tantalizing proposition. You might find the deal of a lifetime, the perfect used vehicle at an unbelievably low price. Much like that vase bought at the garage sale that turns out to be a lost treasure from the Ming Dynasty, these situations are somewhat rare. More frequently, buying from a private seller requires a small act of faith on your part that their RV isn't a clunker. No warranties or returns will be honored, and there may be some lingering doubt about the possibility of breaking down outside Anchorage. The inspections discussed in Chapter 5 should help assuage some of that concern, and good deals can certainly be had. Your comfort level of gambling on a less-than-sure thing, as well as your troubleshooting abilities in the event of problems, probably determines the appeal of a private seller.

Even in the internet age, your local newspaper remains a good source to find regular folk ready to sell, with the auto section being the best bet. Otherwise, regional buyer's guides such as the *Trader Times,* found at mini-markets, grocery stores, and the like, might feature an RV section. A quick search online should also uncover a host of sellers in your area. Try www.rvsearch.com or www.craigslist.org for starters.

RV Dealers

If a new RV is on the docket, then shopping through an established dealership is a must. The upside is that, unlike private sellers, these people are running a business, with a reputation at stake with every transaction. Consequently, they're less likely to take advantage of their customers—at least, we would hope so. In addition, dealerships offer a greater selection and a deeper inventory, and most likely a service center, financing, a parts department, warranties, and possibly a trial money-back period. You might be able to score a hot dog and some cotton candy, too, but let's not get distracted.

ONE FOR THE ROAD

Much like the rest of the RV industry, most dealerships are still small, independent businesses. Many of these operations are family run, with a loyal customer base and handshake-type approach to doing business. The recent wave of consolidation has resulted in the emergence of the RV superstore, offering incredible inventory, volume discounts, and massive staffs who probably won't remember your name. It's worth a look at each type to determine which situation you favor.

Unlike their automotive counterparts, RV dealerships are not found in every town. In fact, buyers might have to travel a significant distance to find one that carries their specific RV, particularly if it's produced from a smaller manufacturer with a tiny network of sellers. But according to a survey sponsored by Woodall's Publishing, readers said they were willing to travel up to 200 miles to find the best deal. Now that's dedication.

For a list of RV dealerships in your region and a look at their inventory and prices, you go online. Grab a cup of coffee and loosen up those typing fingers. Prospective buyers can search for a specific RV brand, dealership name, or any number of criteria to find who's got what. The Yellow Pages is still a great place to find local dealers. A call to a specific RV manufacturer should put you on the path to the dealer that carries its products nearby. Otherwise, keep your eyes open for one of Woodall's regional publications (see Appendix A for a complete listing), a long-time home to regional dealer advertising, as well as your newspaper's auto section.

Dealer's Choice

A nearby dealer is the best kind of dealer. If you need service or a breakdown occurs, taking a short trip down Main Street for warranty-related repairs or routine service is preferable to heading back across the state. Service and repairs can be performed at most any service center, but nearby is always better. For this reason, start any search locally and spread out accordingly, branching out only as far as you feel comfortable commuting. Determine the important factors in your search. Price is the first and last word for most, so start there. If customer service, knowledgeable staff, repair facilities, and financing are important, then audition sellers based on these concerns.

Incorporate proven techniques here as you would for any big purchase. Be patient. Ask questions. Keep looking. Be assertive—we're talking about a lot of money here. If you're unsatisfied, go elsewhere. An uncooperative or shady salesperson might be indicative of the way this company does business. Take careful notes. And remember, these people are working on your behalf, not the other way around.

Dollars and Sense

If your decision simply comes down to who has the lowest price, you've heard it all before. The mantra is comparison-shop, comparison-shop, comparison-shop. Searching online or making a few calls for quotes is still the fastest route to saving thousands of dollars. It saves dealers time, too, because they don't need to show you around and dust off their standard pitches. Ask each dealership for its rock-bottom price on vehicle XYZ, ask exactly how long this dollar amount is good for, get the name of the person who quoted you this figure, and repeat this process at as many places as you can. Better yet, have them email their best offer so you have something in writing when you show up later.

Conventional views suggest that late in the year ranks among the very best times to buy new RVs. Fall through the first of the year is a transition period, when new models bump last year's versions to the back of the lot. Many sellers historically drop prices on year-old units and good deals are likely. Otherwise, buying out of RV season works well, or when the weather is relentlessly crummy and foot traffic at the dealership is low. Timing and comparison shopping are the keys to great deals.

Money for Nothing

Congratulations—you found the RV you wanted, and you didn't break the bank in the process. So why are you still worried? If it were a can of soup or a clock radio, I would say great. However, RVs cost considerably more, and there are other important issues to consider along with the sale price. What about repairs and service? Is there follow-up after the sale, or are buyers on their own? Will the dealership be around in two years to honor any warranties or contractual obligations? Certainly, price is of the utmost importance, no argument there. There's no sense paying more than you have to. But the savings reaped can quickly disintegrate if problems arise later. Here are some other criteria to include on your next shopping trip.

Again, What's Their Rep?

I talked about knowing the manufacturer's reputation in Chapter 4, but it's important to check out the dealer as well. Know whom you're buying from. Question friends, members of the local camping club, or online RV forums for their preferred dealerships. Why do they recommend them? Did their sweetheart service change after the deal was reached? What salesperson did they like? Did the staff descend on them like a pack of vultures at a carrion convention? Was it like pulling teeth to schedule service?

Finalize your list and start visiting some lots. Does the inventory look scattered, battered, or haggard, suggesting money problems and a possible red flag on the SS *Chapter 11*? Remember, a bankrupt dealership complicates matters after the sale. Buy from the healthiest company you can, to avoid getting stuck with promises unkept and services unfulfilled.

ROAD SCHOLAR

Let the findings from the Better Business Bureau help you decide. A long list of complaints and charges probably means an unwillingness to work with the customer. Although a "clean record" doesn't necessarily guarantee a perfect buying experience, it does serve as further evidence that you might have found yourself a winner.

Save a few questions for the salesperson, too. How long has this dealership been in business? Is it a member of the Recreation Vehicle Dealer's Association

(RVDA)? Why not? Ask for the names of several recent customers to get their important feedback. Be skeptical if the dealership refuses. There's no truer portrayal than from those who have undergone the process before you.

Service with a Smile

At some point, even the finest vehicles need some service. It could be a routine repair, preventative maintenance, or a sizable undertaking, but it's gonna happen. Many buyers prefer to return their RV to their original dealer to have any work performed—and dealers may oblige with perks such as free washings, inspections, and so on for their existing customers. What services and repairs can and can't they do? Can they handle the big jobs, such as engine repair, transmissions, and chassis trouble? What if the refrigerator breaks, pipes burst, or leaks develop? Can they fix most problems there, or is everything just sent back to the factory?

Do customers get special treatment, or are they thrown into the mix with everyone else when it comes to repairs? How many service bays and technicians are on the premises? What are their qualifications, certifications, and areas of expertise? Are their hourly rates outrageous or reasonable? Is a towing service provided? A large parts inventory means fewer delays, come fix-it time. Find out now, before there's trouble.

Worth the Trip

How far are you willing to travel for this transaction? As we've discussed, closer is always better, but it may be worth loading the family into a minivan to scout out nicer deals. Big savings on the RV of your dreams might be enough reason to make a weekend of it a few hundred miles away from home. Factor in any cost breaks with distance required to make the sale. Conversely, are you favoring a local dealership too much, unwilling to journey for the lowest price?

Good Help Is Hard to Find

Good salespeople can work at bad dealerships, and vice versa. However, a lack of understanding or shady practices can reflect the culture of the company, so be careful. Does your salesperson know what he's talking about? Does he RV? How long has he worked there? Is this his career, or was he selling lawn mowers yesterday? Is he demonstrating a strong knowledge of the products or using the brochures like a crutch? Get the sales rep talking. Some professionals don't know a hitch from hot chocolate, so it pays to be a little skeptical at first. Ask questions. Listen. Then decide whether this person is for you.

What is the rep's attitude? Friendly? Confrontational? Interested? Your salesperson is your main liaison before, during, and after the sale. Do you feel comfortable with this person and what he's telling you? If not, leaving the dealership isn't necessary. Politely ask to work with a more experienced employee. Don't mess around with bad service or a mule cart full of BS. Remember, the typical motorhome costs as much as four years of college, the average towable as much as a luxury automobile.

Deliverance

Get a sense of the delivery process *before* signing on the dotted line and pocketing the keys. Will the salesperson walk you through every inch of your coach, explain all warranties, run through each and every appliance, and demonstrate the inner workings of the new unit? Or are customers just a check to cash? Some dealerships have a goodwill period of 30 days to work out the kinks of a new RV. Does yours? What about a follow-up meeting to discuss any problems associated with the new vehicle? A hands-off attitude after the sale is a symptom of poor customer service down the road.

Although still rare, some dealerships pride themselves on after-the-sale instruction in the form of seminars and customer clinics. Classes might range from driving and towing, troubleshooting onboard systems, boondocking, and various how-to's for their customers—usually at no charge. These sellers are demonstrating a commitment to their customers, and such opportunities shouldn't go to waste.

Another growing practice is the emergence of the dealership/campground, giving new and prospective customers a safe haven to acclimate themselves to their new RVs. Smart dealers and buyers know that there's simply no substitute for the experience of spending a few nights in a new purchase. Provisions such as these show a seller's willingness to work with you after the sale, instead of the hurry-to-buy, hurry-to-leave approach taken at some places. I'll explain what steps to take before taking delivery in Chapter 8.

Trade Ya

I like someone who will bend over backward to make the sale. For instance, consider the Florida dealer who prides himself on accepting all sorts of unusual items as trade. Lore has it that he's taken classic cars, boats, even a pair of tigers to help grease the wheels of a transaction. True, most businesses won't accept your llama and pair of dancing chimps, but an existing RV might do the trick. Trade-ins are usually accepted as a means to secure your business. Those uncomfortable with selling their RVs themselves should gravitate toward dealers with a kind and loving attitude toward previously owned models.

PULL OVER

Skip the folks selling RVs in an abandoned lot or along the side of the road. These sellers promote unbelievable deals, hoping for an impulse buy. Avoid these situations, as this is no way to make such an important investment. If a seller looks like a fly-by-night company, it probably is. Where did these vehicles come from? Resist the knee-jerk reaction to get a "once-in-a-lifetime" deal.

Common Buying Pitfalls

Many folks want to get the buying process over as soon as possible. They know what RV they want and dislike the adversarial process of negotiating. Besides, the sooner you buy it, the sooner you can hit the road and start enjoying it, right? Resist the urge to make a quick sale. If the first dealership was great, the second one may be better. And the fifth one might blow the first two away, saving you thousands of dollars in the process. To avoid a nasty case of buyer's remorse, visit as many lots as you can. Listen. Gain insights from salespeople. Take notes. Record prices. Ask questions. Be patient. Repeat as necessary. Most of all, prepare yourself for a lengthy process. A purchase this size demands it. And most importantly, resist each of the following.

Avoiding Hysteria

Avoid quick decisions. "Today-only sales" and "limited-time offers" may or may not be for real. But in either case, don't allow the seller to dictate the pace. Buy only when you're ready, even if it means missing out on a special offer. Sales promotions are like boomerangs—they have a tendency to come back around.

And speaking of promotions, big sales events with balloons, hot dogs, and all the soda you can drink certainly breed goodwill and make the process more enjoyable. However, this generosity fails to address your primary concerns of "Is this the seller for me?" A festival-like atmosphere might be all sizzle and very little steak, designed to get you in the door only. Stick to the mission of buying from the best, most thoughtful, and most service-oriented place you can. You can get a hot dog at the ballgame.

Love Story

The lyrical question was once asked, "Why do fools fall in love?" My only answer is that they like paying full price. Love makes you do funny things, and reveling in an RV that sets your heart all a-flutter is dangerous, come bargaining time. The easiest way to louse up a deal is fretting that the RV might suddenly vanish if you don't scoop it up today. Forget it. These are RVs, not Judy Garland's ruby red slippers. There are a thousand more where that came from. Leave your emotions back at the car. This is business.

Bossy Britches

In the presence of an aggressive salesperson, some people fold like a three-card Monty game in Times Square. Who's in charge here, anyway? You are, so stay the course. If a seller comes on too strong, tell him so. Be candid about your pace, stating that you're in the looking stage and dislike the in-your-face style. If he continues, ask for another person. If you wanted the hard sell, you would have stayed home and chatted with all those lovely telemarketers.

Paralysis by Analysis

Feeling paralyzed with all these options? Then it's time to regroup. Remember, it's a daunting process. Get your bearings and revisit Chapters 4 and 5 to determine exactly what you're looking for. Perhaps in the search for a modest camper van, you begin to fancy a mini-motorhome. Then you find yourself poking around the 40-foot diesel motorhomes. Next thing you know, you've overbought and are forced to work a night job to pay for fuel.

Wheelin' and Dealin'

Now it's time to save yourself some money—perhaps lots of it, if you're patient and persistent. At this point, you've found an RV you like and can afford, as well as a seller you're comfortable with. But unlike the game show, the price *isn't* right. Maybe we can do better. Peeling away the extra costs associated with the sticker price isn't an exact science; there's no magic formula or secret password to make the seller cave to your demands. Short of hypnotism, the next best thing is using a little psychology, knowing the facts about the RV in question, and hoping for good timing.

Remember, transactions are a two-way street, so be reasonable. Dealerships cost money to run and must show something from each sale. Demanding the invoice prices on a unit is unreasonable.

You Scratch My Back ...

Although haggling isn't encouraged when buying shoes or knocking long-distance calls off the phone bill, it's a well-established practice in the field of RV buying. The best deal won't fall into your lap; rather, it is an act of erosion. If you want to save some money, you're going to have to play the game. Of course, you can always skip these negotiations altogether by favoring a seller who lists the lowest price.

There are two starting points for negotiations. The first is to take the sticker price and work your way down. This number should be fully disclosed, usually pasted on the vehicle itself. The second is to learn the *real* cost of the RV, the invoice price, or the sum the seller actually paid for the RV and work your way up. Finding the true cost is more difficult. A few companies, such as the RV Consumer Group (1-360-765-3846; www.rv.org), sell such information. In this case, the goal is to stick as closely to the invoice price as possible.

Paying the Price

With invoice price in hand, examine the sticker price. Subtracting the two amounts will determine the range of negotiations. For example, an invoice price of $50,000 and a sticker price of $60,000 means there's $10,000 to work with.

Obviously, the closer the final sale is to the invoice cost, the more successful your transaction. The difference could be tens of thousands of dollars for an expensive RV or much less for an entry-level unit. However, every dollar counts, and this range is where you should concentrate your efforts.

Patience Is a Virtue

What's your hurry? Take it slow. I have found a little persistence mixed with a relaxed approach can whittle a significant percentage off any new purchase, whether it's a dream house, an RV, or a prized Superman comic book. The key, however, is to remove the sense of urgency and slow down the pace. Operating at breakneck speed only aids the seller, propelling you into a rash decision. Here's the magic formula to remember:

Time + Persistence = The Best Deal

Chances are excellent that you may hit an impasse over price. You and the seller are dug in; neither party is willing to budge. Given the lofty prices of some higher-end vehicles, the two of you might be several thousands of dollars away from common ground. At some point, the seller will say no way, can't do it, no chance, have a nice day. Be patient. Tell the salesperson to sleep on it—meanwhile, you visit the nice dealer down the street. The sight of you walking out the door might be enough to make the sales rep reconsider. Otherwise, call back in a week, when the rep's attitude might have changed. Perhaps your offer will look better after a few slow weeks and a mountain of new inventory sitting idle. Because most salespeople work on commission, they'll consider most reasonable offers.

ROAD SCHOLAR

As the old saying goes, "Always dance with the one who brung ya." If you've found a salesperson you like and you intend to buy her product, work directly with her until the sale is reached. Don't show up on her day off to close the deal with someone else, leaving her commissionless for all her efforts. Reward a professional by taking her card and asking for her for all future dealings.

Creative Bargaining

When the going gets tough, the tough ask for leather upholstery, cruise control, or a rear-mounted camera with cockpit monitor. Extras cost money, too, and can play a role when the money talks deadlock. If they won't come down another $500, how about adding an awning, convection oven, or towing package? What about adding to the extended warranty or granting free oil changes or washings?

Extras, Extras

Most every new recreational vehicle comes with pretty much the same stuff. Sure, floorplans vary, as do size, price, and sleeping capacities, but as features go, well … they're more alike than different: a galley with a stove and fridge, a living space with a TV and a few comfy places to sit, sleeping areas for you and your crew. Power doors and windows and nice adjustable seats are typical cockpit fare. Some RVs and their manufacturers are stingier about what's included than others, but the line between *standard* and *optional* is usually pretty well defined. But that shouldn't stop you from wanting as much stuff onboard as you can get.

Separating yourself and your new RV from the Joneses isn't very hard. All it takes is an open mind—and a checkbook to match—to crack the vault to a world of alluring add-ons, ranging from the latest technological gadgets to the "must-have" accessory *du jour*. There are no shortages of things to buy. However, where and when to buy such things—and the ramifications of such purchases—requires a little forethought.

Who's Got the Goods?

Choosing the RV was the hard part. Deciding what little extra goodies to install is fun—it's the gravy on top of the mashed potatoes. However, a few irresistible, albeit expensive, options can easily transform a once frugal investment into a bank-draining albatross faster than you can say "heated mirrors and electric awning." Deciding who to buy these goodies from can make all the difference. Should you have it installed at the factory or wait and secure it in the aftermarket world?

Don't think all final decisions must be made on your dealer's lot. If you're unsure whether you need—or can justify the cost of—an expensive option, then wait. The marketplace is ripe, full of companies that will gladly fill your vehicle with any and all must-have items after the point of purchase. If you decide six months later that a GPS or high-end generator is a must, don't worry—a quick trip to Camping World (1-888-626-7576; www.campingworld.com) or any number of RV parts and accessories suppliers should remedy that. RV publications are jam-packed with advertisements and editorials showcasing all sorts of exciting gadgets and gear, so keep your eyes open.

Viva Variety

An RV manufacturer might equip its vehicles with only one brand of CD player, leveling system, or backup monitor, accounting for only a small portion of the total suppliers in that given field. If your heart is set on a specific brand-name product, chances are, you'll have to buy it from someone else later.

However, the flip side of that coin is that compatibility isn't usually an issue with a factory-installed item. Installations made at the assembly stage virtually guarantee a correct fit, serviced by professionals used to working on recreational vehicles. This is especially true when debating such electric upgrades as inverters, generators, and big-time electronics. The local superstore may quiver at the challenge of equipping that pricey stereo system inside the confusing world of an RV's cockpit. In these cases, it's probably wise to let the manufacturer do the work.

Price vs. Service

Is the lowest price always the top consideration? Maybe, maybe not. Although the purchase price for small options is usually cheaper in the aftermarket sector, the dealer's price most likely includes installation. (If you're not sure whether there's a separate installation fee, be sure to ask.) Remember, labor is often the most expensive part of any job, so factor these cost differences into the final equation, along with the time and hassle of finding another company to do the work. Factory-installed prices are usually competitive for big-ticket items such as generators, air conditioners, and high-end appliances.

Tradin' Time

Like the two cranky kids in the backseat, keep the trade-in and the new RV transaction separate. Such dual negotiations only swing the pendulum of control back to the seller while complicating the issue of price. Forge a sale price for your new rig or towable before any talk of an existing vehicle arises. In my mind, these are two separate transactions and should be treated as such. If the dealer balks, you can always sell the used RV on your own.

Go Figure

Determining the value of a used RV is as easy as a phone call. Did you know there's a way to value new and older RVs? If you're in the market for a preowned rig or towable, pick up a copy of NADA's *Recreation Vehicle Appraisal Guide* (1997–present), updated three times per year, or its similar guide for more venerable products, the *Older Recreation Vehicle Appraisal Guide*, providing values for RVs from 1977 to 1988. You can order both guides by calling 1-800-966-6232 or visiting www.nadaappraisalguides.com.

Role Reversal

You have more options than you think regarding a used vehicle. Assuming that you can't reach a satisfactory trade-in arrangement, it's up to you to put on your salesperson hat and sell it yourself. A well-placed ad on CraigsList and in the transportation section of a large newspaper should generate interest. Sunny days and warm temperatures are better times to sell than when the doors are frozen shut and the vehicle is trapped underneath a foot of snow. Local vehicle trading guides are another useful spot for a classified ad, and some dealers sell on consignment.

Warranties

A drawer full of warranties is one of the main advantages to buying a new RV. A one- or two-year bumper-to-bumper warranty is common. After that, expect a structural or roof warranty and perhaps coverage on some of the larger items. The refrigerator is governed by a different set of terms and conditions than the drivetrain or water heater. As such, expect different lengths of coverage and repair procedures for just about every moving part onboard your RV.

ONE FOR THE ROAD

Warranties vary, but three years/36,000 miles is typical for the chassis. Onboard appliances are usually governed by a policy limited to 12 to 24 months. The roof may be covered for periods ranging from 5 to 10 years—or longer.

You Break It, You Buy It

Expect to void a warranty if the product breaks and you were the one doing the breaking. Manufacturers are testy about laypersons tinkering with their products and, as such, may not honor a warranty if you're the reason behind its sudden nonworking condition. Read the terms carefully before trying to perform repairs yourself or jamming that screwdriver in with reckless abandon. If the heater went south for the winter without any help from you, you probably have a reasonable claim.

Stake Your Claim

Just what are the procedures for making a claim? Although most service centers can probably handle the work, who will pay to fix it, ship it, and reinstall it when it's well? In the event of a possible challenge to your claim, who has the final say? If the manufacturer refuses a reasonable claim, your original dealer can act as a strong advocate. After all, an unhappy customer is bad for repeat business. Be sure to follow the claim procedures to the letter and get the salesperson involved in case of problems. Because warranties are offered from the manufacturers directly, don't expect terms to vary from seller to seller.

Check, Please

It's time to settle up. Pay the piper. Break out the checkbook and start writing until somebody tells you to stop. But where's the money coming from? Ah, good question. Whether it's time to break into the piggy bank, sell off the IBM stocks, or head down to the bank for a loan, don't expect the keys to the RV kingdom until everyone has been properly paid. Which begs the question, where are you gonna get the money?

Unless your last name is Trump or Gates, chances are good that financing is in your future. Fortunately, all sorts of folks want to help you pay for your RV. A good thing, too, because without the deep pockets of such lenders, most of us would still be confined to getting around on our bikes with baseball cards tucked in the spokes. But just because some people are willing to lend us a few bucks doesn't mean all the deals are the same.

You didn't get this far in life without realizing that borrowing money costs money. At the heart of the matter lies the interest rate, which varies due to the stinginess of the various lenders. I'm sure you've played the interest rate game before during such purchases as a house or a car. In addition to banks, savings and loans, credit unions, and typical lending institutions, a number of RV-specific finance companies are jumping up and down to get your attention. Larger RV dealers might sway you toward their in-house loan departments to help close the deal.

How Do They Rate?

Complement your careful search for the perfect RV by finagling the best financing deal possible. Again, the rules are simple: shop around. RV shows and publications reveal a host of industry lenders experienced at navigating such purchases. Because RVers boast a famously low level of default (approximately 1 percent), coupled with the fact that RVs are longer lasting and depreciate more slowly than automobiles, expect a better deal than what you scored for your little red sports car. A 10- or 15-year agreement is fairly standard, with 10 to 20 percent required for a down payment.

ROAD SCHOLAR

Consider arranging for a loan *before* buying that new RV. For starters, this "voucher" lets you know exactly what you can and—aw, shucks—can't afford. As important, finding a lender early eliminates the rush-rush of financing after a deal is reached. This unnecessary practice might send you scurrying into a bad deal and give you 10 or more years to stew over a bad decision.

To Serve and Protect

Low rates are important, but so is service. Like any contract, know what you're getting into. Make sure all the terms are carefully explained and easy to understand before you comply with a signature. Consider the significance of a prepayment penalty, which prohibits paying off the loan early. What are the fees to refinance? Does the company offer an automatic payment service? How long has it been in business? What is its reputation? Does the company service the loans itself? Rates should be competitive enough among lenders to let a company's range of services break the tie.

Borrow Sorrow

Bad loan arrangements come in many forms but usually stem from not devoting time to a quality search. Taking the first deal is a surefire way to overspend. Remember, even a $1/4$ percent rate difference may end up costing several thousands of dollars more over the life of a loan. Avoid the impulse to just go through your local bank. Chances are, there's a better deal out there. An online search should yield a host of possible suitors, in addition to current rates and range of services.

Interest-ed

This is one time when you won't mind calling the IRS. One of the great perks of RV ownership is that interest on most any type of RV loan is tax-deductible. Sound the cannons. Ring the bells. You're getting a tax break! This savings is based on a recreational vehicle's role as a second home (whether or not it actually is). Some special provisions apply, so it's best to contact your accountant or local IRS office (visit www.irs.gov for a complete listing). Ask for a copy of "Home Interest Deduction" and "Selling Your Home," and you might actually be smiling for a change on April 15.

The Least You Need to Know

- A private seller might offer a lower price but no warranties or returns. Audition RV dealerships based on price, knowledge of staff, service facilities, and reputation.

- Learn the invoice price to reap the best deal. Adapt a slow pace for negotiations and be persistent with price. Throw in optional accessories when talks stall. Discuss any trade-in vehicles only after the deal is done.

- New RVs come with myriad warranties, covering everything from the mechanical parts to appliances. Extended warranties are available through many companies and are worth the extra costs only if they provide peace of mind.

- Shop around to get the best loan rate. Avoid easy routes of working through dealers and your local banks until after you've scoured the marketplace. Clean up your financial records and reevaluate the purchase if you're turned down.

Renting an RV

In This Chapter

- How to rent and return an RV
- Researching rentals
- What you can expect to pay
- Who can drive
- What to do in case of an accident

Let's just call it the "big easy." No, not New Orleans, but rather the experience of renting an RV. That's not to say there aren't a lot of things to consider—that's what this chapter covers. But RV rental companies are all about ease when it comes to offering you an RV travel experience. For many, the rental is a long-awaited first-time opportunity to get behind the wheel of an RV for a family vacation. For many others, the rental is a test-drive to determine whether purchasing an RV is in their future. Some will use an RV on an on-site job as short-term housing; others will use an RV to cast off on a dream fishing trip.

To put your mind at ease, log on to the lessor's website, pop some popcorn, and settle in with your co-pilot to watch the orientation video. Also, plan to arrive early to pick up the RV; taking a walk around an RV is a bit more complicated than looking for dings on a two-door coupe at a rental car company. Allow at least 30 minutes to become acquainted with the RV before you take it off the lot. Don't be embarrassed to ask lots of questions. Better to spend some extra time up front, or your family may end up a little too close for comfort when you can't figure out how to deploy the slide-outs. Go over the inside and out with a fine-tooth comb.

When everything is made easy, the RV experience only gets better—from renting the correct size of vehicle and finding the first night's campground, to settling in by a campfire to reminisce about the day's adventure and how easy and fun life can be in an RV.

Got Reservations?

Unlike with renting automobiles, there's no RV rental counter in most airports or hotel lobbies. They're mainly found in major cities and major touring destinations. Rental companies such as Cruise America have nationwide locations, so check online to locate a rental office near you. As when renting other motorized vehicles, you can make and confirm a reservation online or with an agent using a toll-free number. An online site is helpful because you can view different models of recreational vehicles, available floorplans, and a comparison chart that shows features and models available. Speaking with an agent helps with special requests. For instance, if a member of your party has special needs, ask to speak to a rental agent who specializes in these services. Most RV rental companies offer vehicles equipped with hand controls for driving and/or lifts for access. Use either or both; the point is, you have plenty of options to think about. So while it's true that renting an RV is easy, making some advance decisions is the real key. The following sections help get you rolling.

Cruise America is the nation's largest RV rental chain.

ROAD SCHOLAR

Cruise America (1-800-671-8042; www.cruiseamerica.com) is the largest rental chain, but El Monte RV is another great resource (1-888-337-2214; wwwelmonte. com). The Recreational Vehicle Rental Association (RVRA) also has a complete list of rental companies (1-888-467-8464; www.rvra.org).

Counting the Costs

The base rate (in 2012) for a seven-day rental on a five- to seven-passenger RV is $600-plus, or close to $100 per day. And that doesn't include taxes and mileage fees. Mileage fees vary but currently list at approximately 32¢ per mile. Don't forget that the cash for the fuel that makes those miles possible is out-of-pocket. Then there's an hourly fee for using the generator, too—usually about $3. There's some good news, though: most generators are built into the vehicle.

As you can see, the costs add up quickly, so it's a good idea to check rental websites for specials. You may find half-price miles specials, geographic travel specials to certain areas of the country or continent (if you have Canada in mind), and even specials for one-way travel. Armed with that information, remember that renting an RV is much like renting other modes of transportation. There's high season, shoulder season, and winter. Although it's possible to rent an RV during the winter months, it can be costly. Travel during some holidays, cyclical events like spring break, or within the time frame of major sporting events can also raise the rates. Depending on where they're being held, anything from your favorite team's spring training, to the Super Bowl, to a Bassmaster tournament can be considered prime or high rental season. To ensure the best value, book well in advance and discuss options with a reservation agent.

Note that most rental companies require a deposit at rental confirmation, a security deposit, plus the estimated rental fee when the RV is picked up. When you return the RV, the final charge will be adjusted. Check the individual lessor for which debit or credit cards are accepted and details on the company's policy for accepting cash.

Getting Too Close for Comfort

If there's a theme to this chapter, it's that I *strongly* recommend reservations. Advance planning is essential to get the vehicle with the room you need. If an RV sleeps four, don't try to squeeze in six. Even if pretty Aunt Kay and Uncle Phil are family, it's no fun being uncomfortable while traveling great distances. Just one night of being snored or elbowed out of a good night's sleep can be enough to disrupt an otherwise joyous trip. Count heads and then, if necessary, size up instead of sizing down. You won't regret it.

Adding the Extras

The guy behind the Avis counter won't ask if you want to rent a blanket or breakfast dishes to go along with your Corolla, but RV companies do. Blankets are part of an optional add-on kit that includes bedding and towels. There's another kit for the kitchen, too. A kitchen/provision kit costs about $100, and items must be returned clean. Not so for rented linens: simply tuck them into the furnished laundry bag and leave the bag inside the rental vehicle. To save money, bring your own favorite sheets, blankie, feather pillow, coffee cup, and frying pan.

An RV rental agent won't suggest purchasing additional or special RV insurance, either; coverage is rolled into the total price of the rental. After you sign the contract, supplemental liability insurance kicks in. For other inclusive coverage, see the lessor's web page.

PULL OVER

While researching the internet for rental information, read or download a copy of the leasing company's renter's guide. It should outline step-by-step solutions to common challenges that renters face on the road. These guidelines cover topics from following common-sense campground etiquette and solving mechanical situations with the kitchen sink, to recognizing a roadside scam. No printer? No problem. Renters get a copy of the guide at the time of pick-up. Keep it handy.

Bringing Man's Best Friend

The big question "Are pets permitted?" is easily answered with a resounding "Woof"—or "Yes," for us human folk—with the understanding that you will clean up after your pet. If you don't clean up after your pet, expect a hefty cleaning fee when you return the vehicle—perhaps $200 or more. In general, the policy regarding cleaning up after your pet is to return the RV in the same condition as it was received.

Be sure to mention the species and weight of Fido to the rental agent, as some rental RV companies require an additional deposit.

License to Drive

In general, drivers must be more than 25 years of age and have a valid driver's license. Any driver who plans to spend time behind the wheel must be present and have proper identification when the contract is signed. (For foreign visitors, identification papers also include a valid and current passport.) Some exceptions can be made for drivers between the ages of 21 and 24, but an underage surcharge of about $25 per day will be levied. Ask the rental agent or visit your lessor's website for more information.

Rental Ready

Now you've considered all the options, selected a specific type of RV, and booked a reservation with a rental company. If you are like most RV enthusiasts, your first time will be with a Class C, the most popular rental RV type. Woo hoo, let the fun begin! Before you and yours get behind the wheel, let's look at a few other factors that you should know, like consolidating rental agreements and materials in one easy-to-access place in the cockpit. Or maybe making sure you have your own crib sheet of information that you'll need in a hurry—like the roadside assistance telephone number and your rental contract number.

Steering the Ship

Driving the C-class, or chassis-based, design feels much like driving a regular van. Simply put, if you can drive a car, you can drive a rental recreational vehicle. Most are five-speed automatic drive and come with terrific driving features, like automatic transmission downshifting when descending hills. That said, they don't respond like your Lamborghini, and you'll need more room for stopping and a bigger turn radius. Some models have a built-in GPS. If not, bring your own.

When Accidents Happen

Be prepared. Read the renter's guide that's available on the leaser's website before you pick up the RV. Most sites have a video orientation for renters, too. Check out both. You'll get a copy of the renter's guide at the time you pick up the RV. Keep a copy of it and the insurance certification with the rental agreement that includes the contract number someplace you can easily access it. If an accident occurs, call the police and the lessor's toll-free assistance number. Be prepared to tell the operator the rental contract number, and follow the instructions as given.

Breaking Down

Get off the road first, and then call the toll-free roadside assistance number listed on the rental contract. Again, be prepared to tell the operator the rental contract number, and then be prepared to follow the instructions given. The rental company's 24-hour assistance is designed to help you get back on the road as quickly and easily as possible. Be wary of roadside scams that prey on breakdown situations.

Remember not to abandon the vehicle. One way to avoid problems is to check the tires, fluid levels, coolants, and engine oil each time you add fuel.

Turning In

Before you leave the rental facilities for your planned trip, take time to review what you need to do before returning the vehicle. The renter's guide should have some sort of checklist. In general, return the vehicle on time and in the same clean condition as when you picked it up; waste tanks should be empty and the fuel tank filled to the level it was at checkout. If you neglect any of the required return responsibilities, you'll be charged extra—and you can bet the extras will be costly, compared to simply handling the items yourself. Be sure to check for personal belongings before you drop off the keys.

The Least You Need to Know

- Become familiar with your rental before you leave the lot. Asking plenty of questions up front can save you from headaches on the road.
- Drivers have to be 25 years of age with a valid driver's license to pull out of the parking lot. As with rental procedures for other vehicles, if more than one driver will be at the wheel, all drivers must be at the rental counter and show proper identification when the papers are signed.
- Size matters when renting an RV. Even if you're family, overcrowding spoils everyone's fun. We all need personal space. When in doubt, size up.
- Safety first. Treat the rental like you would your own vehicle—maybe better. Buckle up and clean up.

Life After the Sale

In This Chapter

- Learning the important steps when taking delivery
- Insuring your RV
- Hearing the case for roadside assistance
- Protecting yourself from a "lemon"

Strike up the band. Uncork the champagne. Wake the neighbors. You've just purchased a recreational vehicle. Congratulations, you're almost ready to reap the benefits as a card-carrying member of the RV community. However, amid the euphoria, there's still some work to be done. Stay focused now, for this is a time when many folks miss some essential steps about the ins and outs of their vehicle and ways to safeguard their new purchase.

The sole purpose of this chapter is to protect you and your investment. Before driving off the lot in a hail of confetti and dancing bears, you want to make certain of a few things. For starters, the act of taking delivery should be more involved than the seller saying, "Here's your keys." Making the most of this process can make a lot of difference (for the better) in the early stages of your RVing life.

Then there's the matter of insurance. Surely, it's nobody's favorite subject, but it's imperative to spend some time on the topic. Regardless of whether you're pulling a towable or snuggled in the cockpit of a new camper van or motorhome, a costly purchase mandates adequate coverage. Spending precious time poring over policies might not appeal to you now, but you will appreciate the legwork in the event of trouble down the line. Speaking of trouble, a comprehensive road-side assistance plan is a must, and we'll tell you why. And not to put a damper on things, but a brief examination of your rights under existing "lemon laws" is merited, as are ways to resolve everything from a bum rig to a nasty case of buyer's remorse.

Special Delivery

Like proud new parents, expect to feel a combination of excitement, relief, and maybe an ounce of panic concerning the family's new addition. The long buying process is over, and you'll probably be eager to get home and start living it up. Don't be in too much of a hurry, though, because after you're off that dealer's lot, an ugly sort of transformation occurs: you're now a customer instead of a *potential* customer. Big difference. A quality dealership takes the time to walk buyers through their new purchase, demonstrating how everything works, explaining the warranties, and answering any and all questions before shaking hands and bidding adieu. Buying from a seller with a strong after-the-sale commitment reduces the anxiety many new buyers feel with a new RV and creates a favorable relationship for any return visits for service, maintenance, or whatever might happen down the road.

Walking the Walk

A final walk-through is a must. No exceptions. No, the seller didn't paint the interior lime green while you were off signing the ownership papers. Nor did he or she replace the tires with pothole covers or short-sheet the bed when no one was looking. The primary reason for a final vehicle walk-through is to make sure you know how everything works. And I do mean everything. Plan to spend a minimum of one hour with the salesperson or service technician for this tutorial on the inner workings of your new vehicle. A larger motorhome or fifth-wheel may take considerably longer, but it's time well spent. This is simply the best time and place to learn the particulars of your purchase.

Have this person show you how everything operates (refrigerator, water heater, awning, and so on), and then repeat it yourself. Remember, if it doesn't work at the dealership, it probably won't work in the wild. Get involved. Don't just observe, but go through the motions yourself. Take notes. Ask questions. Ask more questions. Film it with a smart phone, if that makes you feel better. Yes, we'll cover how everything operates in upcoming chapters, but doing it yourself—in your specific RV—is the best way to learn.

The following checklists were created to make sure you don't forget anything on your final walk-through:

How Do I ...

❑ Take a shower?

❑ Get running water?

❑ Get hot water?

❑ Activate slide-outs?

❑ Transform all sleeping areas?

❑ Deploy the awning(s)?

❑ Work the satellite TV, backup monitor, GPS, or TV antennae?

ROAD SCHOLAR

No new purchase would be complete without parting gifts in the form of a mountain of warranties and service manuals. Treat them like family heirlooms and hold on to these. Study manuals for operating tips and preventative maintenance procedures to get the most out of systems and appliances. Keeping these materials together and onboard the RV will pay off when you really need them.

Test Appliances

❑ Stove burners

❑ Oven

❑ Microwave or convection oven

❑ Refrigerator (on all settings)

❑ Furnace

❑ Air conditioner

❑ Fans and roof vents

❑ Water heater

Learn the Systems

- ❏ Filling and draining the fresh water tank
- ❏ Learning the ins and outs of propane container(s)
- ❏ Emptying the gray and black water tanks
- ❏ Hooking up to shoreline power
- ❏ Working the generator
- ❏ Examining all batteries and their fuse locations
- ❏ Locating the 120-volt AC breaker box/identifying all circuits

RV-Specific Checklists:

Towable RVs

- ❏ A full run-through of hitching and unhitching

Fold-Down Campers

- ❏ Deploying and retracting the unit

Truck Campers

- ❏ Installing and removing the camper

Motorized RVs

- ❏ Steps for towing a car or trailer

If a postsale inspection uncovers a problem, have it fixed immediately. Don't take possession of a faulty RV. Expect to go to the head of the line to get this problem righted immediately.

Follow-Up Meeting

Only when you're completely satisfied that everything's in working order—and that you won't be scratching your head when it's time to deploy the sleeper sofa—should you hit the highway. But before heading off into the sunset, schedule a follow-up meeting with the salesperson for a few weeks later. This second meeting is devoted to answering questions and addressing concerns that you no doubt will have after your first "shakedown trip" (see the following section). A quality seller may offer a goodwill period to return the RV if there's a problem or if it requires service. Schedule the meeting within 30 days.

Shakedown Street

Plan a weekend away from home within a week (sooner is better) of taking delivery. As the old saying goes, "This is where the rubber meets the road." There's simply no better way to see what your new RV can and can't do than by, well, doing it. Choose a campground far enough away to get the feel for life behind the wheel or your towing aptitude. Because you want to test all the onboard features, a full–hook-up campsite is necessary. This allows you to evaluate the water, electric, and sewer systems, as well as practice hooking up and dumping the tanks. Consider cable TV service a bonus, if you can get it. Meanwhile, ask the folks in the next campsite for assistance if you forget how something works. You'll be surprised at how willing fellow RVers are to help a traveler in need.

As a secondary measure, we recommend a day spent using the RV's self-contained features to see how they perform on their own. This is especially critical if you're likely to camp off the grid. Test the RV's generator (if so equipped) to power up the appliances. Rely on the fresh water holding tank and water pump for all your water needs rather than a water connection. Get a feel for which appliances work off your coach batteries and which tap into the automotive battery. Power the fridge off the LP gas and coach power to see how it handles on each setting. Again, the goal here is to determine the RV's (and your) ability to rely on itself. Any questions should be addressed at the prescheduled follow-up meeting at the dealership.

ONE FOR THE ROAD

In an effort to ease buyers into their new RVs, some dealerships feature overnight camping facilities on the premises for customers to get acquainted with their vehicles. This is an ideal way to learn the ins and outs of your new RV, backed by knowledgeable personnel nearby if you have questions or problems.

Load up your rig with what you'll need for a weekend away from home. Prepare to do all the cooking onboard, so a trip to the grocery store is in order. Yes, you can have a candy bar. If you didn't already do so at the dealership, fill up on propane and fresh water (see Chapters 10 and 11, respectively). Fuel up at the gas station (remember to go to the diesel side if your motorhome is of that persuasion) and take a trip to the weigh station to make sure you didn't overpack, something we'll discuss in Chapter 14. As previously stated, every RV has its weight limitations, and a weighing-in is good practice against stuffing your new purchase like a sloppy beef burrito.

> **ROAD SCHOLAR**
>
> Make sure you bring everything needed for hook-ups before you camp out. A sewer hose and shoreline electrical cord should come with a new RV, but many folks lament that neither is ever long enough. A fresh water hose, designed especially for RVers, is usually the responsibility of new owners, as are the various adapters for the different kinds of electrical hook-ups.

License and Registration, Please

One of the great misconceptions about RV travel is that a special driver's license is required. For the vast majority of RV owners, this simply isn't true. Your regular driver's license is good for the operation of nearly every kind of recreational vehicle. However, laws change, which is why you should check with your local DMV (always a fun time!) to see if any special tests or licenses are required to operate your dream machine.

In many states, anything towed or driven (think any kind of RV, big or small) must be titled and registered with the Secretary of State. This usually means you'll need a license plate or two, so plan to pony up the money for those fees. Thankfully, on new RVs, dealers usually take care of this headache, but if you buy a preowned RV, you'll need to do it yourself. Plan to show proof of insurance at some point in the process.

A Little Insurance

Insurance isn't a matter of choice—rather, one of degree. The lending institution that probably made this purchase possible will demand a full-boat policy to protect its investment, which basically makes the discussion of why to insure an RV a moot point. You need insurance, so go and get some. Moreover, a minimum level of insurance is the law, so there's no getting around it—every vehicle must be insured. Besides, it just makes good sense—whether you're involved in an accident or theft, or if liability issues are raised while parked at a campsite, you should be covered.

Buyers of new RVs must show proof of insurance before taking ownership, so get it beforehand. The finance company and state laws say so. Besides, an uninsured wreck on the way home is no way to begin this exciting new way of life. Start comparing quotes when you've settled on a particular make and model, and finalize the policy after you reach a deal.

The good news is that RV insurance isn't usually as expensive as automotive premiums. This is doubly true for less expensive towables, which dodge their fair share of lofty payments. You can thank historically low accident rates among the RVing population for lower premiums, as well as less overall usage and lower incidence of vehicle thefts. Because RVers tend to be older and more experienced drivers, they usually stay out of trouble ... unlike your 16-year-old with that souped-up Camaro. What can I say? We're a safe bunch.

PULL OVER

Carefully read over your policy to ensure that you have coverage for any number of scenarios. Provisions for damage from weather, as well as replacement costs for stolen or damaged personal possessions, can be overlooked. Also avoid doubling up coverage, such as medical costs, already provided by your homeowner's policy.

RV Insurers

Go ahead and talk to your automobile insurance provider on the subject of insuring a new RV. If you reside full time in your RV, chances are insuring it will be a bit more complex. In the case of towables, it may be simple to add a rider to your existing automobile policy. Be sure to call for answers.

The case for enlisting an RV-specific insurance company is obvious. Not only do these companies understand the industry and the lifestyle, but they also can make recommendations based on your level of use, type of vehicle, and specific situation. A couple living full time aboard a fifth-wheel requires a decidedly different batch of insurance than a family taking sporadic trips in a small motorhome. RV insurers excel at these differences, which means they'll be able to craft the best policy for you.

Types of Insurance

Good coverage protects owners both inside and out, while in transit and when camped for extended periods of time. Such policies feature some of the complexities of an auto as well as a home. For instance, an RV traveler is equally liable when a youngster injures herself tripping over your fresh water hose as when bonking into a Honda on Interstate 80. Because an RV is a combination home and vehicle, special care should be taken to protect yourself in each type of situation.

A look through a typical RV policy includes all the usual suspects: liability (bodily injury and property damage), collision, medical payments, comprehensive coverage, and clauses for uninsured motorists. However, replacement costs for interior furnishings, appliances, and personal possessions should also be included, as should living expenses (hotels, rental cars, and so on), in the event you and your rig are sidelined due to an accident. Terms covering you in the event of a breakdown can also be added, including roadside assistance, towing, and rental options. As you can see, there's a lot to think about. Again, we make the case for working with an RV-only insurer. Most RVers would agree that gaps in coverage are less likely to exist when working with someone who has thorough know-how of recreational vehicles.

ONE FOR THE ROAD

In some cases, coverage might fall under an existing policy, with no modifications required. A new pop-up, lightweight travel trailer, or truck camper may require only a rider to your existing auto policy. Check with your auto carrier or policy for answers. Be sure to ask about onboard possessions and whether you're covered when parked or just in transit.

How Much Is Enough?

In the eyes of most carriers, you just can't have too much insurance. Meanwhile, friends might advise carrying the bare-bones amount mandated by your state. As usual, my advice is to take a middle-of-the-road approach, favoring proper coverage somewhere between these two extremes. Again, your lending institution will be very vocal about its coverage demands, establishing a starting point to work from. Your state's insurance laws play a role in this decision, too. After that, it's up to you to decide how deep you want to go in the insurance barrel. Factor in the age, value, and usage of your RV; your financial situation; and peace of mind (or lack thereof) associated with different policy levels.

Border Crossings

Aside from hungry grizzlies and those funny Mountie uniforms, there's nothing unusual involved when crossing Canada's borders if you're looking for a little vay-cay up north. Pull up to the border, answer their questions, politely hand them your passport, and make tracks to the nearest Canadian bacon outlet. The same insurance that's good enough for American soil is honored (and appreciated) in those parts as well. Ask your insurance agent for a proof of insurance for Canada before you head out. Heading down south—really far south—is another matter. A sojourn into Mexico requires specific documentation stating in no short order that your coverage extends within this country. Unfortunately, a quick call to your insurer may reveal that it doesn't, forcing you to buy insurance from one of a number of near-the-border businesses offering insurance help.

The Price Is Right

By now, you know the drill of getting a good deal. Comparison-shopping is what separates the inflated-price-know-nothings from a company built to serve you well during both good times and bad. Start by calling around or let your fingers do the work online to separate the proverbial wheat from the chaff.

Owners willing to assume more of the risk receive lower premiums by carrying a higher deductible. True, if something goes wrong, you'll be asked to chip in more moolah. However, the monthly savings can add up to a pleasing sum. Choose a dollar amount that you can live with, provided this figure ever comes a-calling. Determine the cost savings by switching the payment schedule from monthly to bi-monthly, quarterly, or semiannually. Reducing coverage during periods of nonuse, such as RV storage, is also a good idea. This practice is referred to as *suspension coverage.*

RVOCABULARY

Suspension coverage is a type of insurance policy that allows you to cancel or reduce vehicle coverage during periods of dormancy, including storage.

Rate Adjustments

Even the best rates have some flexibility, based on a number of eligible factors. Here are a few:

- Graduation from a defensive driving course or school
- Onboard safety features, such as air bags or antilock brakes
- Antitheft devices
- Good driving record
- Special senior rates
- Rural versus urban residency
- Low annual mileage

ONE FOR THE ROAD

The RV Driving School (530-878-0111; www.rvschool.com) is the oldest and most comprehensive of its kind. Participants can receive behind-the-wheel training at various locations throughout the country. Graduates of the two-day course learn and/or reinforce their driving skills and may benefit from lower insurance rates for their matriculation. I strongly recommend the school for even the most experienced drivers.

Full-Timer Policies

Full-time RVers fall under a different class of RV owners. Because their RV serves as a permanent home and they spend a majority of their time there, an insurance company assumes more risks. Some insurers deem participants "full-timers" if they live in the vehicle for more than 150 days per year. Qualifications vary, so ask around. Of course, this status means you'll pay higher premiums, something a few folks are unwilling to do. A little white lie to Mr. Insurer won't hurt anyone, they believe, as they claim to use the RV only sporadically. However, if an accident should occur and it's proven that you do indeed fit their definition of a full-time RVer, your coverage might be voided, leaving you a big (and potentially expensive) problem.

> **PULL OVER**
>
> Your current auto club may not cover your new RV, even for routine saves for such misfires as a dead battery or lockouts. For those unwilling to switch or add on to their regular auto club, be sure of what is and isn't covered ahead of time.

Roadside Assistance

You're headed down a deserted stretch of road when the cautionary lights on the dashboard start glowing like a Christmas tree. Or perhaps a tire blows or another calamity transpires, such as steam from the engine or a horrendous sound coming from underneath. It's late and there's no one around. Best-case scenario, you dial for help on the cell phone and wait for a tow or on-the-spot fix-it from a qualified RV service technician. Worst case, you're stranded, baffled at how to fix things or unable to do so, without a clue of whom to call. This is why roadside assistance was created—to shield you and your family from potentially dangerous situations like these.

Think changing your SUV's tire was tough? Wait until you try grappling with one twice that size, in the rain, with all your earthly possessions onboard, without a jack. A better idea is to let the pros handle it. Because a breakdown now strands the family's home as well as its transportation, it's doubly important to have a good service waiting on the speed dial. Anyone doing any RVing at all should have *some* form of roadside assistance, designed to meet the specific needs of these kinds of vehicles. End of story.

Helping Hand

Do you know the old saying, "Don't send a donkey to do the work of a buffalo"? No? Well, I might have made it up. How about, "Don't send a boy to do a man's job," which is what you're doing when you call the local gas station or auto mechanic for help for a stranded rig. Conventional tow trucks are powerless against large motorhomes; transporting the fifth-wheel to safety is beyond the grasp of most dispatched trucks from the local towing company. And then who's going to fix it? The mechanic at the Shell station? Not likely. Trouble, in this case, is best left to a certified RV service technician, not to the same guy who's a whiz working on 1970s muscle cars (although these folks are my heroes, nonetheless).

In addition to heavy-duty towing equipment and a knowledge of RV mechanisms, RV roadside assistance companies usually belong to a large network of troubleshooters. If they can't do the job, they should be able to locate someone who can, saving you a lot of grief when you're phoning frantically for help, stuck at the side of the road.

PULL OVER

Beware of hidden charges, most likely found within the towing section. Watch for mileage and cost restrictions. A 10-mile towing limit might get you only to the nearest town, not to a qualified RV repair center. It might be worth spending a little more in membership costs to avoid getting underserved during crunch time.

What's the Plan, Stan?

A good service plan offers heavy-duty towing equipment for both motorhomes and trailers, as well as provisions for ancillary vehicles, such as the car you're towing behind your Class A. Affiliation with a comprehensive network of RV service centers is also warranted, with locations throughout the country. Subscribing to a company that lacks West Coast towing services does you little good when you're watching the steam pour from the radiator outside Reno. Nationwide plans are better than regional providers; regional plans are better than local ones. Tire changing, lockout service, and the traditional battery jumping and gas filling should be included.

Lemon Aid

That citrus smell onboard was a dead giveaway. Far be it from me to dash the good feelings of any new RV owner, but a frank discussion on what to do in the rare event your RV is defective—okay, a lemon—is in order. This fruity label is slapped on any vehicle that fails to live up to the warranty after repeated attempts to remedy a problem(s). In the eyes of the law, declaring a vehicle a lemon is the scarlet letter, a nasty brand for all the world to see. A busted radiator cap won't garner much sympathy from the courts, but a chronically underperforming engine, leaky roof, or uncorrectable brakes are good examples. (Well, not really *good*, but *appropriate* candidates.) Invoke your state's lemon laws when reasonable steps have failed to correct a problem with the manufacturer.

Gasp! Is My RV a Lemon?

Laws vary from state to state concerning the definition of a "lemon." However, many share similar legal themes, including the number of repairs within a 12- to 24-month period, number of days confined to the service center within a period of time, and defects that are deemed a threat to safety that remain unfixed. The more serious and debilitating the problem is, the more leverage you have to slap a lemon tag on any particular vehicle. Determine your state's laws by contacting either the Department of Transportation or Consumer Protection Office. The Better Business Bureau (www. bbb.org) features a searchable database of lemon laws organized by state. My hope is that you never have to experience a lemon, except in lemonade. If you do, don't procrastinate getting the help you deserve. Problems don't fix themselves, and the sooner, the better in the case of a lemon RV.

The Write Stuff

That X#%@% transmission has been in the shop three times in six months, and you've had enough. Proper documentation is the key to either resolving a dispute or championing your case as hard evidence if the matter goes to the courts. Always start with the dealer that sold you the vehicle, regardless of the problem. Although they didn't build the unit, dealers can be powerful advocates when lobbying a manufacturer for justice. An unhappy customer—a yelling one, at that—can be quite damaging to a small dealer's reputation, so involve your dealer in your fight.

Record all the events that transpired in detail: when you purchased the vehicle, when and where it was repaired, mileage, and days spent in the shop. Get names and include those whenever you can. Be sure to save all copies of work receipts and any correspondence about the problems in question. To many manufacturers, an angry customer armed with a paper trail is as formidable as Darth Vader wielding a lightsaber.

> **ROAD SCHOLAR**
>
> Send complaints and important correspondence via certified mail with a return receipt. This makes absolutely sure the participant receives each document and moves these letters to the top of the mail bin, which should expedite matters. It also sends a message that you're serious about getting satisfaction.

Any phone calls should be backed up with a letter restating the points of the conversation. As the old saying goes, "A verbal agreement isn't worth the paper it's written on." Don't rely solely on verbal correspondence. List the actions you want taken. Keep the tone professional. Whether deemed a nuisance or, better yet, an important customer, you are much more likely to get issues resolved by talking to the top people. And always, always get the names of all people you speak with, and involve them in your fight. The more people are aware of your problem and working on your behalf, the better.

BBB AUTO LINE

Repeated correspondence and calls go unanswered, or the manufacturer's attempts at appeasement are far from satisfactory. Going to court should be your last resort. In case you haven't heard, lawyers are costly (news flash). A better alternative is to invoke the aid of the BBB AUTO LINE (1-800-955-5100; www. bbb.org). This national Better Business Bureau service has been helping resolve warranty and lemon law disputes for 30 years. If both parties are willing, a neutral arbitrator oversees the case and provides a ruling. Technical experts may also be involved in the process, if needed. The arbitrator calls a hearing to determine fault, rules on a settlement, and oversees that the decisions are carried out. Of course, the mere act of involving the Better Business Bureau might be enough to garner a quick settlement.

The Verdict

Like a pair of old ski boots, the arbitrator's decision is only partially binding. Both parties must agree to abide by the final ruling ahead of time, usually limited only to covering warranty violations, replacement procedures, and arbitrator costs. No punitive damages or monies for personal injury, fraud, or angst can be awarded.

The Least You Need to Know

- Don't take delivery of a new unit until all your questions are answered and you know how to operate all onboard systems and appliances. Schedule an appointment for a walk-through with the salesperson, and arrange for a follow-up visit within 30 days, after you take the vehicle camping.
- Operating an RV without proper insurance is against the law. Towable and motorized RVs fall under different guidelines, as mandated by your state and the finance company that loaned you the money. Many travelers discover that an insurer specializing in RVs is definitely the way to go.
- Modest costs and a network of qualified RV service professionals make membership in a roadside assistance company a must. Automotive clubs often lack the heavy-duty equipment for towing and the technicians to work on RVs, so join a club that specializes in recreational vehicles.
- Lemon laws vary from state to state but are worded to replace, repair, or repurchase defective vehicles. Meticulous recordkeeping and persistence are how such battles are won. Otherwise, take the matter to the Better Business Bureau or the courts.

Operating and Maintaining Your RV

The moniker of an RV as a home on wheels mostly fits. However, unlike your trusty condo, charming Cape Cod, or stately colonial, a recreational vehicle requires a little assistance in terms of its utilities. For example, flipping a switch doesn't always guarantee that your lights will come on. Opening up the tap doesn't necessarily deliver a fresh and cool supply of water. A little forethought is required to guarantee a steady flow of electricity for the appliances, LP gas to run the furnace, fresh water for showers and drinking, and the like. But it's not rocket science—I get you through it. These chapters break down an RV's various systems and components, with an eye toward demystifying the process of self-sufficient travel. And when it's time to put the rig away for the winter or an extended break (sob), I've even included a chapter with step-by-step instructions for preparing your dream machine for dormancy.

Electrical Systems

In This Chapter

- Knowing the sources of your RV's electricity
- Staying powered up, no matter where you go
- Learning tips for safe and efficient operation of systems and appliances

Repeat after me: all RVs are self-contained. In short, your RV should offer fresh water, LP gas, and, for the purposes of this chapter, electricity. All that onboard lighting and those temperature controls, cooking appliances, and entertaining options aren't just for show. There's real, bona fide electricity flowing though those outlets, just looking for something to do.

If powering up all these electrical doodads was as easy as it is at home, this chapter wouldn't be necessary. You'd just flip a switch and expect the lights to come on. You'd run all the appliances at once without giving a single thought to consumption or limits. You'd fall asleep with the TV on, wrapped in your electric blanket, while your vacuum hummed and the kids stared longingly at the burritos sizzling away in the microwave. RVing is pretty happy-go-lucky, but it's not *that* happy-go-lucky. The laws of cause and effect are still in play, and every RV has its limits. Here's how to keep that sweet, wonderful current humming, no matter where your travels take you.

Straight to the Source

Before you learn to wield your electrical know-how, it's important to know where the stuff comes from—or, better yet, how electricity is generated. Onboard electricity is available through three basic sources: engine power, coach power, and shore power.

Engine Power

This is also known as the 12-volt DC (direct current) automotive system. Like "the Force" within a young Luke Skywalker, engine power rests inside, in this case, your motorhome or tow vehicle's engine (accomplished for towable owners via wiring connections made during hitch-up or through the trailer electrical connector cable). The dynamics at work here are basically the same witnessed in your automobile. Start the ignition and what happens? Power. Not only power to drive, but power for the interior components as well. The dashboard lights up. The radio belts out your favorite Beatles song. Interior and exterior lights are ready for action. Windshield wipers, the lovely horn, even the cigarette lighter are all ready to go. The same is true with your RV. Turn the key in the motorhome's cockpit or inside the tow vehicle, and a number of things come to life.

Equipment controlled by engine power includes:

- Engine
- Windshield wipers
- Horn
- Dashboard lights
- Headlights
- AM/FM radio and CD player
- Power doors, mirrors, and locks
- Dash-mounted heat and air-conditioning
- 12-volt appliances plugged into the cigarette lighter or separate 12-volt outlets or power points
- Electric brakes (towables only)

The heart of this system rests in the *automotive battery*, which sparks the engine into action upon ignition. An *alternator* is responsible for maintaining the battery's charge and, as revealed momentarily, is the core between the two DC battery systems (engine power and coach power).

> **RVOCABULARY**
>
> The **automotive battery** provides the power to start the RV or tow vehicle's engine and keeps the 12-volt equipment running. The **alternator** works in conjunction with the automotive and coach battery systems to maintain a positive charge whenever the engine is running. The condition and the state of charge in each of the batteries determine how hard the alternator must work.

Coach Power

The second source of power for the RV's other assorted 12-volt equipment is called the coach power, or the auxiliary battery system, because its range extends far beyond the simple dashboard delights provided by engine power. This is also referred to as the 12-volt DC coach system.

Equipment controlled by coach power includes:

- Interior lights
- Water pump
- Exhaust vans
- Furnace fan
- Roof vent fan
- Exterior lamps
- Power awnings
- Alarm systems
- LP and CO leak detectors
- Roof-mounted evaporative cooler
- Radio/CD player
- Monitor panels

- TV antenna booster

- Slide-outs

- Leveling jacks, hydraulic or electric

- 12-volt appliances

- Inverter

In this case, a *deep-cycle battery* is used, one capable of supplying a greater amount of current and holding its charge longer than the smallish battery residing in the engine. The alternator is enlisted here as well, but this time it works feverishly (okay, maybe not *that* hard) to recharge both sets of batteries, meaning more current to go around.

> **RVOCABULARY**
>
> Your RV's **deep-cycle battery,** also known as a marine-style battery, provides a greater supply of power for the coach's 12-volt electrical system. These larger batteries are capable of withstanding multiple "deeper" discharges than their automotive counterparts.

Coach/RV Batteries

Coach/RV batteries come in different sizes, each limited in the available current it can store, which is measured in amps. Obviously, the greater the amp rating, the more power is available to run your onboard systems—and the less often it must be recharged. Two 6-volt golf cart batteries are usually included in larger RVs. When wired in a series configuration, the two heavy-duty 6-volters combine to yield approximately 250 total amps of storage capacity but are delivered at the user-friendly 12 volts.

Automotive and deep-cycle batteries are separate and very unequal. Automotive models are designed for a high-current output, but for a short duration, such as when starting the engine. Deep-cycles are designed for a low current rate, but for a longer duration. These batteries should never be swapped, but should be replaced with only another similar battery capable of doing the job.

The Most Common Examples of Deep-Cycle Batteries

Group 24	70 to 85 amps
Group 27	90 to 105 amps
4D	180 amps
8D	250 amps
Golf cart	250 amps at 6 volts

Hey, That's My Power

Just what prevents the automotive battery from draining the reserves of the deep-cycle batteries, and vice versa? Is it the honor system? This type of electrical embezzlement between the two batteries is thwarted by an *isolator,* which effectively splits the alternator output to each battery system and never allows them to be connected together.

RVOCABULARY

The **isolator** maintains battery separation, to prevent one battery from taxing the reserves of the other.

Shore Power

Don't be confused by the nautical terminology—you won't need a boat, and no awkward docking is required. Shore power works the other side of the proverbial street, in the form of AC (alternating current), found at electrical hook-ups at campsites or even from an old outlet found in a home or garage. Your RV ain't choosy. In a pinch, an onboard or portable generator can do the trick if no electrical hook-ups are available, allowing for use of the full range of appliances (depending on the size of the generator) when camped in remote locations, where electrical hook-ups are elusive.

This electrical system, also known as the 120-volt AC electrical system, powers all the big-time consumers of electricity onboard. The 12-volt systems previously mentioned simply don't possess the necessary muscle to power larger appliances, such as the air conditioner or microwave oven. If the equipment plugs into an outlet, chances are, it falls under the umbrella of the 120-volt system.

Equipment controlled by shore power includes:

- Roof-mounted air conditioner
- Microwave oven
- Hair dryer
- Vacuum cleaner
- TVs (unless 12-volt)
- Computer
- Toaster
- Coffee maker
- Converter
- Refrigerator (runs on more than one power source)
- DVD player
- Washer/dryer
- Portable heaters
- Ice maker
- Anything that plugs into a typical house receptacle

Is a piece of equipment 12-volt or 120-volt? Following the previous lists should help determine what equipment falls under what power source onboard your RV. However, in the cases of some appliances, it's not always clear, such as TVs, commonly available in either 12-volt DC and 120-volt AC versions. Check the label or the owner's manual, which should reveal the exact voltage.

Rating Electrical Hook-Ups

Available current from a campground electrical hook-up comes in several forms: 15-, 20-, 30-, or 50-amp service. As you can see by the accompanying figure, the outlets' shapes reveal the extent of their electrical output. Although the process for hooking up is the same (connecting the electrical cord to the outlet within the campsite's pedestal box), an adapter plug might be needed to secure a proper fit, assuming your power cord doesn't match.

A 15-amp connection means, you guessed it, there are only 15 amps of electricity to supply current for your onboard goodies. The vast majority of campgrounds deliver 30- and 50-amp service, which is usually plenty for most onboard equipment.

Left to right: a 15-amp outlet, 20-amp outlet, 30-amp outlet, and 50-amp outlet.

What Do I Have?

Most new RVs should come with a power cord suited for 30- or 50-amp hook-ups. Bigger units almost exclusively favor 50-amp service. What happens when you plug a 30-amp cord (with adapter) into 15- or 20-amp service? Connections work on the theory of the lowest link in the chain. In this case, you can expect 15- or 20-amp service. Conversely, attaching to 50 amps when you're rated for only 30 amps yields just 30 amps of power.

The Trickle-Down (and -Up) Theory

Plug into a 120-volt receptacle (such as that found at the campsite), and all your equipment will thank you. Not only are your larger appliances working stead-fastly, but the smaller, 12-volt components are feeding off the same electrical source, thanks to a converter. The name almost says it all. A converter transforms (okay, converts) existing 120-volt AC power into 12-volt DC, thus getting the RV's 12-volt system in on the act. Now everything's powered. The coach's deep-cycle receives a boost via an integrated battery charger, which helps to eliminate drain. A converter is standard equipment onboard most RVs.

Not one for charity, the 12-volt system also does its part by aiding the 120-volt system. Some larger luxury RVs also have inverters installed. An inverter says "Right back at ya," allowing for larger appliances to be run off the 12-volt system. Who needs a generator when there's an inverter to be had? Indeed. Some folks forego the generator route all together, relying on an inverter to summon up the energy to heat that pot of coffee, microwave a couple of spuds, or cool off (thank you, air conditioner) in desert climes. Like generators, inverters have their limits, listed as watts. Exceed these ratings, and your RV will do its best impression of a prehistoric cave after the circuits are tripped. The downside of this amassed power is that an inverter really taxes the battery, so be prudent with its usage. This is part of the reason they're usually listed as options and are more common in the aftermarket sector.

ROAD SCHOLAR

The wise RVer carries adapters to fit each kind of outlet, as electrical hook-ups vary from campground to campground. Adapters are inexpensive and can mean the difference between powering up and petering out.

Generators

As the secondary means to infuse 120-volt power to your RV, a generator can be your best friend when camped off the beaten path. If you're one of those who likes remote locations while maintaining your more civilized equipment, make sure you have one at your disposal. When camped away from hook-ups and without an onboard inverter, a generator is the only way to activate larger equipment, such as the air conditioner, hair dryer, and microwave oven. As mentioned in our RV round-ups in Chapters 2 and 3, generators are fairly standard on motorized vehicles and less common in towables, particularly smaller models lacking the necessary space, fuel source, and big-ticket appliances (in some cases) for which they are used. Portable generators are available in the aftermarket.

Most generators run on gas, but diesel and propane models are available. In the majority of cases, installed generators tap into your motorized RV's fuel supply, making for a steady fuel source. Most onboard models are designed to quit running when the motorhome's fuel dips below a certain level. A generator's power is measured in watts. Just how many watts are needed for all your stuff is really up to you, based on your appliance needs. The very largest of the onboard models can now put out between 12,500 and 15,000 watts, generally found on only the biggest rigs. Expect a typical generator to come in at approximately half that wattage. These ratings are important: exceed them, and you'll trip the breakers and the flow of energy will be interrupted. This then involves putting on that raggedy robe that you should have donated to the Salvation Army years ago, turning off all the 120-volt appliances, resetting the breaker, waiting a fair amount of time, stewing over your mistake, and starting it all again, now a much more power-savvy traveler. We'll talk about knowing your power limits in the following sections.

ONE FOR THE ROAD

Would you rather have a 3,000-watt (W) generator or a 3.0-kilowatt (kW) version? Trick question! They're the same, as 1kW equals 1,000W. For example, a 4.0kW generator is another way of saying its output is 4,000W; 4.5kW is 4,500W. This is just another way the metric system inches ever closer to mainstream America.

A typical generator, found on most motorhomes and higher-end towables.

Is It for Me?

Generators aren't cheap, so consider their possible role in your camping adventures before you plunk down extra money for one. Staying at traditional campgrounds means constant access to electrical hook-ups, so you won't need a secondary power source there. If you're a less-is-more kind of family and you want to leave the computers, blow dryers, and such at home, you probably won't need it. Generators best serve those who boondock or have heavy power requirements. Otherwise, you may not miss it.

Camped or On the Go

Don't think there won't occasionally be energy needs while in transit. Larger motorhomes are nearly impossible to cool down on a hot day utilizing just the dashboard air conditioner. Generators work equally well when you're on the go, whether the coach's cool AC is in order or someone wants to heat up leftovers in the microwave.

Peak Performance

Generators are like Beagles: they need attention. Run them at least once a month (generators, that is; Beagles like daily exercise) under a substantial load (a few appliances at a time), whether you need to or not. This action helps recirculate stagnant fuel while cleaning the lines, the carburetor, or fuel injectors. Try to run the generator at heavier loads instead of just on and off to warm a cup of coffee or some other small chore. Allow even new models to warm up at least a few minutes before you activate any 120-volt equipment. Repeat this courtesy when the task is completed, letting it "cool down" without any load before you turn it off. Routine maintenance such as changing the spark plugs, filters, and oil should be performed based on the operating instructions of the particular unit.

Generator Courtesy

Although any normal flow of electricity features a slight, pleasing hum, generating power fills the air with a noisy racket and some carbon monoxide (CO), to boot (expelled through an exterior exhaust vent). Take special care to make sure you're not annoying your neighbors—or blasting lethal byproducts through a vent into an open window. If you are purchasing a generator, spend the additional dollars to get a quiet unit so you don't disturb anyone. Many campgrounds prohibit generator use during quiet hours or disallow them altogether. It's generally bad form to excessively run a generator, which parallels a chronically barking dog or loud reruns of Barney. Be a good campsite neighbor.

PULL OVER

Carbon monoxide is one passenger you don't want along for the ride. As stated, a generator produces enough of it to merit attention. Make sure that the unit's exhaust vent is clear and that wind isn't blowing the gas back inside the RV. Every new RV comes with a CO detector. Make sure it works and test it often. Although these steps should avert trouble, I also recommend never sleeping with the generator running.

Monitor Panels

Your RV will no doubt feature the electronic equivalent of the Magic 8-ball found somewhere inside in the form of a *monitor panel*. Want to know how much fresh water is left in your fresh water tanks? Need to gauge how soon the wastewater tanks need to be emptied? For the purposes of this chapter, a monitor panel also displays the state of the charge within the deep-cycle battery(ies). Nicer versions deliver even more information than Scotty gave Captain Kirk, with readouts devoted to the state of the water heater (on/off) or the fresh water pump (on/off), as well as information regarding the slide-outs and thermostat controls. Monitor panels usually reside in very conspicuous places, such as the kitchen or bathroom wall, with a quick examination relaying all this information (usually in a cool-looking LED light display) so you always know the status of the onboard systems.

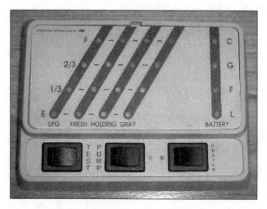

An interior monitor panel displays important information concerning the levels of your RV's holding tanks, LP gas container, and battery voltage.

Be forewarned: most monitor panels still offer only ranges, not exact levels. This is especially true on lower-priced units. Use them only as a guide, and don't let important items such as battery charges drain or holding tanks exceed capacity. However, on the whole, today's panels are much more accurate than the shot-in-the-dark versions of the past. Newer, more expensive models can be terrifically precise. With sensors now often mounted on the exterior of the tank (rather than the interior, where, ahem, debris and such can affect the readings), these units use, well, who knows, some kind of NASA technology, presumably, to provide the most correct measurements the industry's ever seen.

Electrical Requirements

As you can see, recreational vehicles are electrical dynamos, capable of powering lots of complex equipment through different electrical systems. A combination of engine, coach, and shore power, teamed with an understanding of what is responsible for what, should keep you from sitting in the dark wondering why the lights won't come on. Still, everything has its limits. You've experienced this fact at home when you've blown a fuse, sending you scurrying to the basement to fumble with the circuit breakers. A recreational vehicle is no exception. Generally, when you plug into the campsite's electrical pedestal, all is good. Those camping off the grid need to conserve their juice. The key to determining exactly how much power you'll need is to calculate the total current (listed as either amps or watts) required to make each necessary product go. For instance, the standard RV light draws about 2 amps (see the following table). Five lights shining brightly at once use 10 amps. Add to this mix the sporadic use of the TV, the furnace fan, and the water pump left in the on position, and that number grows. Can your RV handle it?

Estimated Electrical Requirements of Typical 12-Volt RV Accessories

Lamp bulb	1 to 2 amps
Water pump	5 to 8 amps
Small 12-volt appliance	2 to 8 amps
Forced-air furnace	5 to 8 amps
Powered vent	1 to 7 amps

Estimated Electrical Requirements of Typical 120-Volt RV Accessories

Curling iron	60 watts
Laptop computer	120 watts
Small power tool	450 to 500 watts
Blender	300 watts
Roof-mounted air conditioner	2,000 watts
Coffee maker	1,000 watts
Medium-size microwave	900 watts
Toaster oven	1,200 watts
19-inch flat-screen LCD TV	50 watts

Again, these ratings are all approximate. Amp or watt draw is usually listed on the product's decal or within the specs of the user's manual.

And returning to lights for a moment, light-emitting diode (LED) lights are popular and draw one seventh of the energy of standard 60-watt incandescent bulbs. A compact fluorescent light (CFL) uses one fourth of the energy of the same bulb. The initial cost for LED is more, but LEDs last much longer, too. The average life span for an LED is 50,000 hours, a CFL follows at 8,000 hours, and the incandescent lags way behind at 1,200 hours.

Running Out of Juice

Will your batteries run dry when you least expect it? Can the generator or inverter save the day when hook-ups are miles away? Is there any limit to the flow of current at the campsite? For answers to these questions, read on.

Hooking Up

Connecting to a shore power source (campsite, home, and so on) means a constant source of electricity. However, you're limited in *how much* electricity you have to work with. Connecting to 30-amp service means you have, you guessed it, 30 amps of electricity at any one time. That's probably enough to run the air conditioner and the microwave at once, as well as a number of smaller items—but don't push it. Of course, you can add up the total amps required so you know for sure. Tripping the circuit breaker lets you know that you're asking too much and you'd better turn something off. The same theorem is true in the case of 15-, 20-, or 50-amp power, with these limits governing how much electricity you have to work with at any given moment.

Generators and Inverters

Both generators and inverters work when void of hook-ups. Both help run larger appliances, and both have their limits. A small generator or inverter producing 3,000 watts of electricity (check the decal or owner's manual for the model's rating) will struggle like a driver's ed student at the Brickyard 400 to power a number of power-hungry appliances all running at once. Get a larger unit if your plans call for hot-and-heavy power usage.

ONE FOR THE ROAD

As mentioned in Chapter 2, the EFOY (Energy For You) fuel cell is an emerging technology designed to cover all of your power needs. These devices are still fairly expensive, but are host to many advantages over generators (www.efoy.ca).

Drain in Vain

Most monitor panels update users on their battery's approximate status, or you can do a little simple math to gauge how long it can go. For example, a battery rated for 100 amp-hours means just that. Assuming that it's at full strength, it will provide 100 hours of service at 1 amp per hour. Of course, nobody uses just 1 amp. Add all devices that will be utilized and multiply that by the number of hours each device will be used. Leave a little extra room for current "leaks" or "drain" that can and will occur, a sort of electrical subversion. This number gives you an idea of how long your fully charged battery can go until it begins to cry out for help. Sure signs of fading include dimming lights and a grumbling water pump.

Keeping batteries charged is a top priority when away from shore power. Driving is the easiest way to recharge all batteries. In drastic cases, it may take a few hours behind the wheel to bring the automotive and coach batteries back from the dead. For most people with schedules of driving one day and camping the next, you already have a good system of depleting and recharging. Connecting to shore power also energizes a depleted system, as does running the generator for at least 30 minutes every so often.

PULL OVER

Leaving on even the tiniest exterior compartment light can slowly drain a battery over time. Avoiding unknown battery drains is important to keep the charge at respectable levels. Periodically inspect the entire RV, both inside and out, to see if there's any unbeknownst battery drain going on.

Solar Power

Solar power, or photovoltaics, provides a legitimate means of keeping RV batteries charged and appliances humming. In this case, energy from the sun is trapped in solar panels affixed to the roof of the RV and is converted into DC power. The more solar panels, the more watts produced. A voltage regulator automatically monitors things, making sure the 12-volt battery is charged but not overcharged. If your RV is equipped with an inverter, the 12-volt DC is transformed for use in the 120-volt equipment, meaning that you might not have to run the generator except usually for the largest of appliances (for example, the air conditioner). This is especially nice when it's just a cup of hot coffee you're after and it's not really worth the effort of warming up the generator or taxing the inverter. Several companies sell all-inclusive kits, with everything needed to get started.

Solar energy is quiet, is virtually maintenance free, and can last and last and last. True, the less sunlight, the less power, but panels trap energy even on overcast days—even when covered in snow. Besides, you didn't take up RVing to hang around the Midwest in December, did you? You're probably not going to struggle to find Ole Sol very often. Starter kits (without inverter and deep-cycle batteries) run between $300 and $1,000. A 20-year warranty is not unusual. The sunlight—for now, anyway—is free.

PULL OVER

Not all deep-cycle batteries are compatible with solar energy. Be sure your existing batteries are equipped to handle the charge before you invest in an expensive series of panels. Fortunately, more battery manufacturers are producing versions to support solar applications.

Blackout!

"I knew I shouldn't have started up my 120-volt chainsaw," you say to yourself just moments after the RV goes dark. You've tripped the breaker. Now what? Immediately turn off all 120-volt AC devices that were in operation. Now to find the problem. It may be the 30-amp breaker at the campsite pedestal, but it's most likely the main 30-amp circuit breaker in the coach that trips. Check them both and reset the tripped breaker (just like at home) to get back on track. You've exceeded your RV's limits, and you might want to find out why. If you're not sure why this happened, recalculate your amp/watt numbers. Perhaps your daughter sneakily plugged in the hair straighteners, skewing the numbers slightly. It won't take long before you know your limits and learn not to exceed them.

Important Add-Ons

Here are some suggestions for useful accessories to add safety and convenience to your electrical systems.

Shoreline Power Cord

All new RV purchases come with a 30- or 50-amp shoreline power cord for hooking up to 120-volt electricity at the campsite or wherever. Unfortunately, it never seems to be long enough, particularly when asked to snake around the picnic table, under the lawn chairs, around the maple tree, and to the electrical outlet 25 feet away. It's a good idea to make sure you have 50 feet of cord, in two cords of 25 feet each. Keep in mind that not all shoreline cord is created equal. Use only types of the heavy-duty RV persuasion, made specifically for the rigors of outdoor use. Be sure to match any additional cord's amperage with that of the original (for example, 30-amp with 30-amp). Choose cords with bright colors to avoid tripping over them when walking around the campsite at night.

Surge Protectors

When plugged into a campsite's electrical supply, the system is always at the mercy of potential power spikes and surges. Lightning, faulty wiring at the pedestal outlet, and an overtaxed campground can all contribute to a shocking experience for your RV's sensitive components. Spend a little money for a high-grade surge protector, one with the ability to shut down an incoming power flux before any damage is done. At a minimum, be certain that the protector actually protects with the proper circuitry and isn't just a power strip providing extra outlets. Most good protectors implement some form of circuit-breaking technology and have a specific joule rating.

Testers and Meters

A polarity tester is cheap insurance against a faulty or potentially dangerous electrical campsite hook-up. A polarity tester plugs into a 120-volt AC receptacle and tracks the three legs—hot, neutral, and ground. If all three wires are in the right place, the correct LEDs will light up. If any two are reversed or open, the telltale indicators will reveal the problem. For RVers, this means that if the polarity tester doesn't like the outlet, avoid it. Consider this a handy and inexpensive necessity before plugging into the campground pedestal.

I also recommend a good, accurate digital voltage meter, or voltmeter. Useful for measuring the AC voltage at the campsite's electrical pedestal, this device helps travelers avoid subpar voltage situations, which are damaging to appliances, particularly the roof-top air conditioner. Anything near 120 volts is okay. Too high (above 130 volts) or low (below 105 volts), and it's best to ask the campground owner for another site. Don't leave home without one.

Last but not least, get an ammeter. This handheld device measures your RV's total power draw, in amps. Want to know just how many amps all your onboard equipment is using? An ammeter will tell you, although spending $150 to $200 is a pricey alternative to tripping the occasional breaker.

The Least You Need to Know

- RVs rely on three distinct electrical systems: engine power, coach power, and shore power. The engine and coach systems are responsible for 12-volt DC equipment; shore power, typically harnessed by plugging into a campsite's electrical outlet or produced via generator or inverter, powers 120-volt appliances.

- Like your home, an RV has its electrical limits, based on the electrical needs of the RV's equipment and how much electricity is available, either stored in the batteries or generated through shore power.

- Electrical hook-ups offered at campgrounds vary but include 15-, 20-, 30-, or 50-amp service. Consider this number the limit for your RV's electrical consumption.

- Appliances such as generators, solar power systems, and inverters are capable of creating or transforming electricity to your RV's batteries while you're away from a typical energy source.

LP Systems

In This Chapter

- Using LP gas (propane) as a power source
- Refilling, safety, and storage tips
- Operating tips for LP gas-powered appliances

Like electricity, your RV's LP system is a very good thing, especially when you know how to wield it. Without LP gas there to work its wonderful magic, you and your crew would be mostly out of luck, come mealtime, with the burners and oven sitting there in a most useless fashion. When the temperature dips, the thermostat would be powerless to stop it without old, reliable LP gas to save you. And forget about that hot shower you relish every morning; that'd be gone, too. Your LP system is the key to much of an RV's better functions. With that said, it's important to understand how and why it works so you're never left out in the cold.

LP: It's a Gas

There's no real mystery to LP (liquefied petroleum), otherwise known as propane. Like Jumping Jack Flash, it's a gas, gas, gas—but it doesn't start off that way. LP is sold in liquid form and stored in a container (or two) outside the RV. When released, the vapor trapped inside the tanks works its way through the lines to fuel components onboard. LP gas is inexpensive to buy, clean burning, fuel efficient, and relied upon by each and every RV on the road today. Like its fellow electrical system, LP gas is the wind beneath the proverbial wings of many of the wouldn't-want-to-live-without-it stuff onboard. However, unlike electricity, sewer, and fresh water, you can't simply "hook up" to LP at a campsite. Sorry, it must be stored in containers, or tanks, and carried with you. When it's empty, fill it up, and continue on your merry way.

When you think propane, think heat. Love your gas grill working wonders out on the patio back home? Good, because it provides the perfect working example of the role of LP gas as it relates to life aboard your RV. Check it out the next time you throw a few T-bones on the grill or that mango-encrusted halibut that gets the neighborhood all a-flutter. LP gas, stored in a small tank, meanders up through the supply line to fuel the burning flame beneath that culinary delight. LP gas + flame = a steady heat source. This is an RV's propane system in a nutshell. Unfortunately for us grilling purists, there are no charcoal-burning RV's in existence … yet.

Here are the LP appliances onboard your RV:

- Refrigerator (may operate from electricity, too)
- Furnace
- Range/oven
- Stove/cook top
- Water heater (also electric on some models)

The following is a rundown of each LP appliance and how to make it sing.

Refrigerator Madness

Because the RV's refrigerator is the one appliance that necessitates constant operation (unless you want green mayonnaise), newer models were designed to be powered by multiple sources, namely 12-volt, 120-volt, and LP gas. A digital mode selector enables owners to switch among the three settings easily; just press a button or turn a knob to make the change. You'll probably find yourself splitting time among the power sources, depending on the situation. Or just sit back and let the fridge's autoselect function (if so equipped) do all the work for you. A preset priority list switches from 120-volt, LP gas, and 12-volt. (The engine must be running for the 12-volt selection.)

ONE FOR THE ROAD

Absorption refrigerators must be level to work properly. The complex mix of hydrogen, ammonia, and water utilized for the cooling process mustn't be allowed to settle in one end or the other, which risks damage and/or subpar cooling. Some RVers mount a bubble level when parked to know if their fridge is on the up-and-up. Even on unlevel terrain when driving, refrigerators work fine, thanks to the rocking motion that adequately moves the fluids back and forth.

Refrigerators can come in high-end versions, boasting double doors and up to 20 cubic feet of storage—with a freezer and ice maker thrown in just for kicks. An older RV may be capable of delivering "only" a bi-modal power source (usually propane and 120-volt). On the smaller end, as observed in pop-ups and truck campers, the fridges probably resemble a dorm room–size model similar to the one that held bottles of … soft drinks (yeah, right) during your beloved college days.

Chill Out

Here are a few tips for selecting the proper refrigerator mode. Use the 12-volt electricity, created in abundance by the constantly recharging automotive and coach batteries (thanks, alternator) when heading down the road. Twelve-volt can drain the batteries quickly when parked, however, so switch to one of the other power sources as soon as you reach your destination. If camped away from shore power, conserve the batteries and switch to propane mode. Otherwise, go with the 120-volt source when plugged in at the local campground, which is free and provides virtually limitless amounts of electricity.

The Heat Is On

Two things determine the comfort level onboard during slipping temps: the power and efficiency of your heating system (measured in BTUs) and the quality of your insulation. You can't do much about the latter (although insulation package upgrades are sometimes offered), so it's good to know how the heating system works when it's cold outside. And yes, your mother was right—put on a sweater and keep the door closed. What, were you born in a barn?

Use the Force

Most RVs rely on a forced-air furnace, which is just a fancy way of saying an onboard furnace that uses a fan to funnel warm air through a series of ducts. The furnace is a true team effort between the electrical and LP systems; the furnace itself runs off propane, controlled by a thermostat, while the coach's 12-volt battery powers the fans or blower. When a chill is in the air, go to the thermostat, turn it on, set the temperature, and wait for the warm winds to heat things up. You'll need LP gas in the container to make it go and enough 12-volt battery power for the fans to do their job.

Although not likely, it is possible that your RV uses hydronic heat, a method that uses water instead of air for radiant and semiconvected heat. This heat source is still fairly rare, as only the big boys have them due to their high costs and effects on vehicle weight.

Spaced Out

If the furnace is weak, the night is freezing, or you just have ice water in your veins, feel free to plug in a space heater. This is especially nice when your sleep-walking spouse makes off with all the blankets. True, it won't defrost the entire vehicle, but a well-aimed model can keep you plenty warm and save on LP costs. Space heaters should never be left unattended.

ROAD SCHOLAR

A constantly burning pilot light is an unnecessary waste of propane. Extinguish them when not needed, to spare you unnecessary LP costs. They also launch onboard temperatures during the hot summer months, so it's best to keep the flame going only during mealtime.

Home on the Range

It's lunchtime and the natives are restless. Surely there's nothing better than cooking over a campfire, but fancier meals (like mac 'n' cheese!) benefit from the sweet precision of the RV's range. Expect anywhere from two to four gas burners to be awaiting your command in the RV's kitchen, each propane reliant and similar to those found at home. Turn the cooking dial to release the gas, light the flame, or utilize a spark-ignition button (the most common method), and you're in business. Otherwise, the stoic pilot light burns brightly, eliminating the need for a light.

You might toil cooking a 25-pound Thanksgiving bird, but an RV oven works well with most creations. Again, there's nothing too out of the ordinary here to get going. Locate the pilot light (inside and usually at the bottom center of the oven). Turn the oven dial to pilot light, strike a match, and fire it up. Select the appropriate heat setting and get going. Check the manual if the pilot's location proves elusive. Spark ignitors can be found on most ovens as well.

Water Heater

LP-fueled with push-button activation, the water heater is the difference between a warm shower and a cold one. An electronic ignition switch (or DSI, direct spark ignition) is common, saving you a trip outside with a lighter. Expect the typical 6- or 10-gallon water heater (still the two most common varieties, although the 12-gallon version is becoming more popular) to be fully heated within 30 to 45 minutes. (Leave this on when camped or just activate it when needed.)

Some water heaters are LP/120-volt electric, giving you a couple of options when washing the pooch. (Propane seems to do a faster job warming things up, however.) Some water heaters found on motorhomes may boast a motor-aid feature, with hoses running from the engine through the water heater and back. In this setup, hot engine water heats the water in the tank, resulting in hot water as soon as you arrive and shut off the engine.

A typical RV water heater, mounted on the outside but controlled on the inside.

LP Containers

Let's start our discussion of how the LP system works at the heart of the matter: the LP containers themselves. Containers are always stored outside and vary in size and shape, depending on what type matches to the RV. Larger vehicles will probably offer two containers, with larger capacities to match. (See "Typical Specs" in Chapters 2 and 3 for a range of sizes per RV.) In these cases, with special devices to do so, the first one automatically switches over to the secondary container when it runs out of LP.

Turning the tank's valve to the open position unleashes a flow of propane through the lines of the coach and awaiting appliances (see the list earlier in the chapter). As the supply of LP gas within the containers starts to diminish, the pressure with which it's dispensed could decrease as well. This is the reason behind a pressure regulator—to maintain a steady level of LP gas through the lines at all times. While the valve is open, the regulator maintains the proper pressure of gas running through the lines, so everything inside keeps firing away without a hitch while you're parked. The valve should remain closed, or in the off position, during travel.

PULL OVER

LP containers are mounted horizontally (ASME) or vertically (DOT) for a reason. Reinstalling the tanks in a different position can cause the liquid LP (instead of their vapors) to pour into the lines, creating a dangerous situation onboard. The same rule should be honored during transport and refilling. Keep the containers in the same position as they are mounted at all times.

Container Types

Not all RVs share the same kind of containers. Two types are used in the RV industry: DOT and ASME. Who cares, right? It's just a lousy container. Ah, not true. The distinction is significant, affecting how they are filled, stored, and handled. It's prudent to learn the differences between the two because there might be a quiz later.

DOT

DOT (Department of Transportation) cylinders are usually mounted vertically and installed most often on fold-down campers, truck campers, and travel trailers, both big and small. In most cases, you'll find them mounted to the trailer's tongue. DOT cylinders can usually be unscrewed and removed, so you can take the tanks in for a refill without having to bring the whole RV along with you.

A pair of DOT LP gas containers, which stores the fuel responsible for much of an RV's heating and cooking elements.

ASME

Nope, the American Society of Magazine Editors isn't in the propane business. The American Society of Mechanical Engineers, now that's more like it. ASME containers, or tanks, as we like to call them, are always affixed horizontally, within an accessible exterior storage compartment of most motorhomes and usually located in a front storage area under the gooseneck of fifth-wheel trailers.

An ASME LP gas container, affixed horizontally to the RV.

Who Needs a Refill?

Your RV's LP gas container(s) will periodically (shock!) run empty. This is a finite resource, after all, and unlike the ice cube trays in the freezer, you're definitely going to want to refill them. Expect to use a couple gallons of the stuff per week during warm weather, more during colder climes, when the furnace is working overtime. This, however, is just an approximation. A gauge on the cylinder lets you know when the supply is running low.

The nice thing about propane is that it's cheap and available all over the place. Most campgrounds sell it, as do propane dealers and outlets, hardware stores, and some service stations. Because you must be licensed to dispense the stuff, all the consumer needs to do is sit back and let the attendant handle it. It's still a good idea to know a little something about it, just to look smart.

What Do I Do?

Okay, here's a job for you before you fill up. Extinguish all pilot lights—water heater, stove, and range (if so equipped). Turn off all LP appliances, including the furnace, and switch the refrigerator to 12- or 120-volt—anything but the propane setting. Finally, make sure the container's valve is in the off, or closed, position. And please, don't smoke.

Gas Crisis

It's not unusual for some LP appliances to act a little goofy after a new batch of propane is added or during initial start-up after periods of dormancy. Your refrigerator might struggle to switch over to the propane mode; the water heater may simply mock you. The usual culprit is air trapped inside the lines, caused by a left-open container valve, in most cases. Turn on the stove burners to purge the lines, then attempt to light each one. This is an easy way to correct the problem. It might take a few moments, but they'll eventually ignite, signaling the triumphant return of your LP system.

If it fails to light, double-check the system. Is the valve open far enough to release an adequate supply of gas into the lines? Do you have enough propane in the container? During one deep-woods pilgrimage, I was minutes away from fleeing back to town when I couldn't get the furnace to kick on. It was 30°F outside and falling fast. The crew had murderous looks in their eyes for me and the $100K motorhome with everything but heat. And then I remembered, oh yes, I actually have to turn the valve on, don't I? Not one of my better days.

Safety First

Like gasoline, propane is highly flammable, which is what makes it such a desirable fuel source. Think of it like the Godfather—treat it with respect, and it will do you plenty of favors. Capeche? Care must be taken not only when replenishing the supply, but also while driving down the road minding your own business. Learn these few rules—and learn them well.

Handling the Tanks

As mentioned before, the biggest mistake is manhandling the containers like some drunken bouncer. Don't jostle or invert containers when removing or installing them before, during, or after a refill. This is really only the case for removable types, which some folks treat as a sack of potatoes. Again, vertical containers should stay vertical; horizontal ones should stay horizontal at all times. Shaking, improper mounting, and general mistreatment might invert the liquid supply, which should rest at the bottom of the tank. Always treat tanks with care.

LP tanks are located outside for a reason: the gas and subsequent vapors are harmful in the event of a leak and are better left outside. Never bring containers inside the RV or store them in unventilated areas.

PULL OVER

Traveling with container valve(s) open is a bad idea. In the case of an accident or fire, propane-filled lines won't help the situation very much. In fact, the results could be disastrous. Make doubly sure the containers are closed before you pull into a gas station, and turn off all LP appliances as well.

Happy Trails

Here are a few propane-related steps to add to your pretrip routine:

- Turn off all LP appliances.

- Switch the refrigerator to 12-volt or 120-volt, or leave it off. (The unit's insulation will keep it cool for a reasonable length of time, provided the door remains closed.)

- Extinguish all pilot lights.

- Close valves on all tanks (turn to the off position).

- Don't use the furnace to warm the RV in transit.

Consider an onboard LP detector a true must-have. Fortunately, it's standard equipment on all new RVs. Don't look to the ceiling for its locations—look to the baseboards. LP gas is heavy and stays close to the floor, exactly where the detector should be, blasting an alarm when it senses trouble. Check it often, and replace batteries as needed. Some aerosol sprays can mistakenly trip the alarms, too. Go outside to spray on suntan lotion if you don't want to jump out of your skin at the sound of the alarm.

That Rotten Smell

Some describe it as rotten eggs; others say it's more like onions or garlic. In either case, it's an odd smell because you're making peanut butter and jelly sandwiches. Such an odor signifies a gas leak. Put down the white bread; it's time to vacate.

Leave the coach immediately, propping open the door behind you to air things out. Again, smoking or any spark-producing activity is a no-no. Don't return until the RV is aired out completely. Shut off the LP valve, extinguish pilot lights, and keep LP appliances turned off until a trained service professional finds the source of the problem.

The nasty smell was added to make the naturally odorless LP gas detectable for situations like these. Every coach also should have an LP gas detector as standard equipment. Check this and other alarms often to guarantee they're in working order. More on this in Chapter 19.

The Least You Need to Know

- LP gas, or propane, is a liquid fuel source, with gas vapors delivering fuel to your RV's furnace, stove, oven, water heater, and refrigerator. Exterior containers are mounted, supplying onboard appliances through a series of gas lines.

- Propane powers many of the appliances onboard. Newer refrigerators usually offer trimodular settings, meaning they can be powered by 12-volt, 120-volt, or propane. A forced-air furnace uses a fan to circulate the heated air through ducts inside the coach. Operating the range, oven, and water heater is similar to operating these at home, requiring manual lighting or electronic ignition of pilot lights.

- For safety reasons, propane containers should be turned off while in transit. Extinguish all pilot lights and discontinue the use of LP appliances. Handle tanks with care, always keeping them in the same position they were mounted in, to avoid inverting the liquid and vapors inside.

Plumbing Systems

In This Chapter

- Explaining the fresh, gray, and black water systems
- Learning the how and why of connecting to fresh water and purging holding tanks
- Maintaining and troubleshooting the various water systems

It isn't enough that a bed, electricity, heat, air-conditioning, and a working kitchen are all at your disposal, but some crazy engineer began installing water systems as well. Just think, a cool drink of agua on a hot day. Brushing your teeth without that walk to the campground's bathroom. And just for you, a warm shower, water for cooking, a private bathroom—all onboard and without needing a degree from your local community college to operate. Hooray, clean dishes for everybody!

Still, this chapter is about more than just turning on the faucet and filling your Batman mug. It's about using the self-sufficient capability of an RV to your advantage and understanding the complex (but easy-to-use) series of fresh and wastewater systems. On top of that, it's nice to have an answer for junior when he asks where the water comes from.

Water World

Essentially, the watery world onboard an RV isn't much different than life at home. Hot and cold water pours from faucets, the showerhead delivers a steady (albeit limited) stream every morning, toilets flush, and awaiting drains send it all away. The main difference, however, is that (1) unless connected to a constant source, your fresh water supply is finite and must be periodically refilled; and (2) used water, or wastewater, is collected in tanks and must be emptied.

All but the smallest recreational vehicles come with onboard plumbing and holding tanks to facilitate all these functions, which can be divided into two basic systems: fresh water and wastewater. Let's take a closer look at each.

Fresh Water System

The fresh water system consists of all faucets, including sinks and showers (both inside and out), as well as the water heater and the toilet's water level. As the name implies, the fresh water onboard is the good stuff, ready for drinking, cooking, cleaning, or loading up the squirt gun and having it out with a grumpy co-pilot.

Water Sources

Because the world is comprised of 70 percent water, finding an adequate supply for fill-ups isn't too much of a challenge. (However, leave the saltwater to the tropical fish.) Fresh water is either supplied via a water inlet (most readily available as part of a campsite hook-up) or stored in your RV's fresh water storage tanks, available for when you need it. Although the water in both cases is basically the same, the manner in which each is accessed is different.

Tapping into a campsite's fresh water hook-up means a sweet, uninterrupted flow of H_2O. As long as you're connected, it's always on, with RVers enjoying a steady flow.

Connecting to fresh water is facilitated through a special drinking water hose (supplied by you) that runs from the campsite's water outlet to the RV's water inlet. The connection on your RV is often referred to as the city-water hook-up and is found on the driver's side (street side) of the vehicle. To activate, simply connect and twist the campsite's faucet to start the flow. All the water faucets inside are now ready to go.

Using the Right Hose

When it comes to the fresh water supply, a hose is most definitely not a hose. Don't use the same garden-variety hose you use to water the lawn; only a specially labeled and manufactured "drinking water" version, designed for RVers, will do.

Usually white and available in a variety of lengths, these hoses are made to better protect the drinking water while abolishing that stubborn rubbery taste.

> **PULL OVER**
>
> How nice, the campsite comes with its own fresh water hose. I'll just use that one. Never! Remember, the hose is the conduit for the water you'll be drinking, showering in, and brushing your teeth with. Is that hose clean? Relying on your own equipment guarantees a source you can trust. And heed the 25-foot rule. Toting along a single 25-foot water hose is not always long enough; a 50-foot version is overkill and a tripping hazard. Carrying two attachable 25-foot hoses is considered the best defense against coming up short when attempting to reach an elusive water outlet.

Treat the drinking water hose with the respect it deserves as the pipeline of your fresh water supply. Store it in a clean, dry place. Connect both ends when not in use to seal the inside against dirt and debris. Storing it in a plastic bag adds yet another layer of protection, especially if you're of the Felix Unger mind-set in regard to cleanliness. Purchase a new hose at the first sign of wear.

Handling the Pressure

Not all water pressure was created equal. Surely you've noticed this fact at home when the pressure dips as Grandma does the dishes while you're taking a shower. Unfortunately, water pressure can be unpredictable, a fact of life for RVers relying on a campground's reserve. Although too little pressure can be annoying, too much can be problematic for the plastic piping throughout the vehicle. It may seem hard to believe (someone call Ripley's!), but that innocent-looking water valve is capable of unleashing potentially damaging force.

Just as a surge protector squashes electrical spikes, a *water pressure regulator* overrides dramatic changes in pressure to establish a steadier stream. The cost is about $10 for this small device that runs interference between the water outlet and the end of the hose.

> **RVOCABULARY**
>
> A **water pressure regulator** combats the elusive and sometimes volatile water pressure when connected to water hook-ups. Attached to the drinking water hose to regulate water flow into the RV, such devices help protect delicate piping onboard. The item is relatively inexpensive and available at most RV stores.

Keeping It Fresh

Many RVers tap into a fresh water supply and never give it another thought. Water is water, right? I, on the other hand, take a more cautious approach, preferring a diet free of as many pesticides, bacteria, and lousy-tasting water as I can. Again, it's up to you.

If water purity is a concern, filters are available for both the inside faucets and exterior connections. Even the most deluxe purifiers, with promises of water quality rarely seen since the times of melting glaciers, are usually fairly inexpensive. Such add-ons are good insurance in an overly polluted world as filters keep contaminants out of you and from damaging the water heater and onboard plumbing.

ROAD SCHOLAR

All this talk of water cleanliness making you worry? It's still true that quality water is not the exception in North America, it's the norm. But why take chances? A modestly priced water purifier should eliminate most concerns. Other folks stock the fridge with bottled water, a bulky, albeit comforting addition to any packing list. And always use a water filter to safeguard the connection between your fresh water tank and water pump.

Going to the Store

Sailing down the road and dying of thirst? Don't like the looks of the campground's water supply? Parked in the boonies and desperately need to boil water for spaghetti? In any of these situations, water is available by tapping into your very own ready water supply, compliments of the fresh water storage tank. The name says it all—the tank acts as a sort of giant canteen for the passengers onboard. Unlike the limitless supply accomplished by connecting to a fresh water source at the campsite, carrying your own reserve has its limits. After you consume the last drop, it's time for a refill, best facilitated at the campground, a backyard faucet, or another safe and sanitary source.

An RV's fresh water–holding capacity, like most things, varies from unit to unit, vehicle class to vehicle class. A high-end motorhome or fifth-wheel trailer can reach 100 gallons, granting a more than reasonable period of time between fill-ups. Smaller fold-downs or camper vans require more diligent visits to the water fairy, with each probably storing less than 20 gallons total. Review the "Typical

Specs" section of each kind of RV in Chapters 2 and 3 for a range of fresh water storage tank sizes.

Fill 'Er Up

Replenishing the water supply isn't too challenging. Fresh water is pretty common at most any campsite, the in-laws' house, rest stops, some gas stations, and the like. In the meantime, you can always use bottled water for drinking or a shower at the campground's facilities, so it's not the end of the world if you run out. The connection to the fresh water storage tank varies among the types of RVs. Most have a simple gravity fill on the side of the vehicle, allowing for easy attachment of the hose. You're now ready to fill. (Remember, this is a different inlet than what you use for the water hook-ups.) When full, the water simply overflows down the side, signaling that your job is complete. Other larger units and high-end coaches might employ a "quick fill" valve that the owner opens while connected to city water, thus filling the tank. This is certainly a convenient alternative to reconnecting the hose directly to the fresh water tank.

If you are going to a location with water, there's no need to completely fill the water tank. This water is just extra weight that you will dump at the end of the trip. Fill enough to meet your rest area needs on the road.

Pumping Up

Possessing a full tank of water means you're only halfway there to a tall glass of refreshment. Hah, I knew it couldn't be that easy, you say. Actually, it's easier. A 12-volt *water pump* must first be activated to actually propel the water up through the pipes in a gravity-defying feat. You must use a pump whenever you take water from the fresh water tank. Switch the pump to the on position before showering, washing hands, or performing whatever watery function is needed.

 RVOCABULARY

A **water pump** is the difference between carrying fresh water and actually dispensing it. Flip the water pump to the on position, and the 12-volt appliance forces water from the fresh water storage compartment up through the twists and turns of your RV's plumbing, to the faucets, shower, and marine-style toilet—wherever it's needed.

The water pump is usually found in a fairly conspicuous place, often near the kitchen or bathroom, most likely on or near the monitor panel. After a few trips, you should begin to decipher the pump's status by listening for changes in its sounds, kind of like distinguishing the various cries of a newborn. But unlike junior, the pump won't keep you up at night or spit up on your favorite shirt. A steady hum signals that the pump is activated and functioning correctly. Hiccuplike patterns probably occur as a result of not turning off a faucet completely. Changes in tone occur as the fresh water levels sink, reaching a more frantic pace when the tank nears empty.

The RV's coach battery is responsible for powering the 12-volt pump, an act that will slowly drain the deep-cycle battery over time—that is, unless you're connected to shore power (campsite electrical outlet, generator, or inverter), in which case, there's probably enough power to go around. Revisit Chapter 9 if you have no idea what I'm talking about.

It's a good idea to turn off the pump whenever you leave the RV. In the event of a leak or watery mishap while you're away, the pump will keep chugging along, doing its job of pushing water through the lines. Only this time, the workaholic pump will send water through the leak and onto the floor, causing a slippery mess.

Of course, it's not necessary to activate the water pump when you've connected to an outside water source.

The Heat Is On

Although you've probably been told to go take a cold shower from time to time, it's not really something you want to make a habit of (I speak from experience). A water heater is the difference between a warm shower and the more displeasing, icy variety. Thankfully, nearly every RV has one.

PULL OVER

The water heater must be allowed to fill up with water prior to activation. Failure to do so could harm the unit. Turn on the hot water faucets before turning on the heater. A spurting or foamy discharge from the pipes signals that it's not yet filled; a free-flowing water supply suggests the heater is sufficiently topped off and ready to light.

Available in 6-, 10-, or 12-gallon capacities, most water heaters are large enough to warm a reasonable-length shower—but don't push it. You might need to hustle some with a hair full of suds to avoid a chilly reception. This is especially true if morning rituals include a soapy rendition of *The Phantom of the Opera*. It may be a strange adjustment, not having the enormous residential water heaters you've grown used to at home, but you'll get used to it … in time.

A flip of the water heater's switch, or lighting of the pilot flame, is all it takes to get things heated up. Water heaters most often run on LP gas, but electric/LP models are becoming more common. It's then just a matter of allowing enough advance time to let the heater do its thing. An hour's head start will suffice to heat the 10-gallon models. Like the water pump, some folks leave the water heater on whenever they're around, creating a warm water reserve at all times. After all, you never know when you might want to shower, need warm water for dishes, or whatever. Again, this taxes your resources, in the form of propane (although at a minimal rate), so keep that in mind. We'll talk more about conserving water and propane in Chapter 18, when we cover roughing it. As with most things, it's a good idea to shut it off when leaving the RV for extended periods. A showerhead equipped with an on/off switch is the easiest way to conserve water. Your RV may or may not have one, but never fear, showerheads are easy add-ons found in the aftermarket.

Bathroom Talk

Some mothers insist that if you're going to talk bathroom talk, you go sit in the bathroom. It's for that reason that I'm typing this chapter in the bathtub, so as not to offend any maternal sensibilities. All but the smallest fold-down campers and camper vans are outfitted with a marine-style toilet, similar to what's found on an airplane. Water levels and flushing are operated through floor pedals, a back lever, or a combination of the two.

PULL OVER

Be especially careful about what goes into the RV's toilet. Just like a James Taylor song, they can be somewhat sensitive. As a rule, don't add anything to the basin besides, well, you know. Cigarettes, hygiene products, and Legos (don't ask) are no-nos. Rely on biodegradable toilet paper, which is more easily dissolved than regular kinds. Regular tissue paper can clog the system.

Unlike the "head" at home, travelers can add to the existing water levels of the marine-style toilet via one of the pedals after each use. How much more is up to you, but remember that the water supply is limited, and all such wastewater must eventually be emptied from the black water tank. You do want the contents of the black water holding tank to be covered with water to assist with odors and to safely jettison waste materials throughout the pipes, so there's really no excuse to play with water levels. In some models, the user needs to hold the flush handle partially down to allow water to get into bowl. When not in use, there should be enough water to keep seals lubricated but not enough to spill out during transit; 2 to 3 inches should do.

In the absence of a marine-style toilet, expect a small porta-potty in its place. Porta-potties function independently from your RV's plumbing. The water is manually filled; all waste materials are captured in its own portable holding tank basin and must be emptied. These are more common in small towables and Class Bs.

Wastewater Systems

The question still remains: Where does all that fresh water go, anyway? Down the drain and off into oblivion? Does a flush of the toilet dispatch waste straight to the landfill? Well, not exactly—but I'm sure some energetic engineer is working on that. In the case of the RV's plumbing system, the old saying is true: "What goes in, must come out." The same is true with "used" fresh water, now suddenly transformed into "wastewater."

Wastewater takes two distinctly different forms: gray water holding tanks and black water holding tanks. A look at each is provided next, along with what to do with them.

ONE FOR THE ROAD

Although we advise using the onboard monitor panel only as a guide, many RVers report wildly goofy readings coming from their black water holding tank. In-tank probes report the status of the RV's tanks, which can be corrupted by debris that has adhered to these sensors. A good cleaning should remedy the problem and restore mostly accurate readings.

Water Colors

Gray water is what empties down the drain from the faucets and shower. Black water is the water and material waste from your RV's marine-style toilet. A network of pipes delivers each to a specific holding tank, all the while keeping them oh-so-separate from the fresh water supply and piping. Gray water empties into the gray water holding tank; black water goes straight into the black water holding tank. When these tanks reach capacity, they must be emptied. Sounds reasonable, right?

RVers have a choice in where and how they choose to empty the gray and black water tanks, but in either case, they must be emptied. Exactly when to empty these tanks depends on the holding capacities of each and your water usage. Review the "Typical Specs" section in Chapters 2 and 3 for a range of holding-tank capacities by RV.

Runnin' on Empty

Like a Beagle barking to go out in the early dawn hours, your monitor panel will tell you when the holding tanks are nearing capacity. After a while, you'll just sort of know when it's time. In extreme cases, severely full tanks scream "no vacancy" when water refuses to drain. It's time to dump the tanks—and do it now.

When it's time to purge the gray and black water holding tanks, RVers have two choices: through a campsite sewer hook-up or at a dump station. The locations are different, but the process for each location is basically the same.

ROAD SCHOLAR

There's no way to sugarcoat it. Dumping the tanks is a dirty business. With this in mind, I strongly recommend wearing rubber gloves when engaged in all sewer-related duties. Keep a box of disposable surgical gloves in an exterior compartment, along with a bottle of soap for washing up afterward. Store the sewer hose in its own compartment, to prevent possible contamination of other essentials. Many people store the hose in the hollow rear bumper of the RV. And be sure to keep it far away from your fresh water hose.

Sewer Hook-Ups

Camping at a site that offers a sewer hook-up gives you the chance to empty the tanks without the long lines of impatient RVers or a special trip to the dump station. The connecting task is performed through a sewer hose (yours), running from the singular sewer outlet underneath the RV to the in-ground sewer opening at the campsite. Be sure to stick the hose a good ways into the sewer opening to prevent it from slipping out unexpectedly. There are sewer hose connectors and adapters designed to get a good seal at the campground sewer connection. Also, you can place some weight on the hose to prevent it from jumping back while draining.

ONE FOR THE ROAD

Water and electric hook-ups are plainly visible and easy to find. Sewer outlets, on the other hand, may be more elusive because they're sometimes off by themselves at the corner of the campsite. Their in-ground location only complicates matters, occasionally hidden by tall grasses or piles of leaves. An appropriately marked metal cover or a twist-cap lets you know you've hit pay dirt.

You'll notice that the gray and black water holding tanks each have their own individual dump release valves for emptying tanks. When pulled, the contents of the tank empty, running through the hose and down the sewer drain. *Warning:* opening these valves without a sewer hook-up and awaiting sewer hose causes the contents to pour out all over your campsite. I guarantee you won't make that mistake more than once (but try never to make it in the first place).

With a secure sewer connection (always double-check before dumping) and full tanks a-callin', it's time to dump. Follow this exact process every time for best results. Open the black water tank's valve first (the large valve handle), allowing it to empty completely down the sewer drain. It's a good idea to give the toilet a couple of flushes here (more, if necessary) to clear out the tank with extra water to remove any accumulated materials. Close the black water tank's valve and then pull the gray water's release (the smaller valve handle), allowing it to empty out completely. Why this order? This method allows the gray water to push any accumulated heavier black water materials out through the hose. Remember, although there are two valves, the contents of each are going down the same sewer hose. Close the gray water valve. Lift the hose starting at the trailer to expel any remaining water. Congratulations. Empty tanks. At this point, add some water to the black holding tank. (I know what you're thinking—I just emptied the darn thing!—but some water and some holding tank chemicals make it smell pretty.)

> **PULL OVER**
>
> Get in the habit of periodically inspecting your various hoses for damage and leaks. Replace as needed. Also double-check hook-up connections (water, electric, sewer) every day. With all these cords and hoses lying around, one may come unplugged or be pulled out of place. Dragging the hose on the ground can lead to pin holes, causing leaks in the hose.

With a constant sewer hook-up, why not just leave both tank valves open all the time, to empty each tank as you go? Certainly, that's a fair and obvious question. Although empty tanks leave your RV light and lively, a totally empty gray or black water tank isn't really a good thing. Leaving both valves constantly open may drain all the water while keeping materials behind. This can result in an odiferous situation and a costly tank repair if the buildup is large enough. Soap, dirt, and oil remains from showers and handwashings can cling to the tank walls and hose lining long after the liquid is gone. The same is true in the black water tank, although the materials in question are, well, different—but just as potentially damaging. In both cases, having a steady base of water in the holding tanks is a good thing.

Down in the Dumps

Dump stations are clearly marked, usually off by their lonesome at most campgrounds (both public and private), rest stops, RV stores, RV service facilities, and a few gas stations along the way. Most campgrounds offer this as a free service for guests and may allow nonguest dumping, if you're in dire need, for a modest fee. True, dump stations are not the most pleasant spots on earth, but their availability is a godsend to travelers with bulging tanks.

In the absence of a sewer hook-up, most travelers prefer to visit the dump station before hitting the road on the way to their next adventure. Again, good riddance to that extra weight. It's for this reason that you might wait in line for one, particularly on a Sunday afternoon, a popular checkout time at many campgrounds. Pay special attention to pull up to the dump station correctly so that the tanks match the corresponding side, just as you would match your fuel tanks to a gas pump. Also park close enough that the sewer hose can reach the sewer drain.

It's always a good idea to visit the dump station to empty wastewater tanks before you leave the campground. The sign by this one politely reminds everyone to use the hose when dumping.

PULL OVER

This may sound like an oxymoron, but make sure the dump station is clean before departing. Most offer a water hose for cleaning any spilled residue, to aim toward the sewer drain for disposal. Hoses are also there to wash hands and clean off sewer hoses, both good habits. *Do not* use this hose for drinking or to fill up your fresh water holding tanks, for obvious reasons.

Basically, the procedure is the same as the one outlined earlier. If you forget, instructions are usually posted somewhere near the dump station for a quick review. Grab your rubber gloves and locate the sewer opening at the dump station. You'll probably be able to slide open the sewer drain's cap with your foot. Stick one end of the sewer hose down the opening and attach the other end to the tank inlet underneath the RV. Release the black water tank valve until it's empty, as demonstrated by a slowing sound of the black water. Have the co-pilot flush the toilet (sans those dirty gloves!) a couple of times for an additional rinse of the black water tank.

Close the black water valve and pull the gray water's release to let those contents through. When empty, close its valve and disconnect the sewer hose from the RV. Hold the hose up high as you walk back toward the dump station, giving gravity a chance to drain any remaining excess fluids down the drain. Give the sewer hose a quick wash with the dump station's hose (definitely don't use your own) and store it back in its own private compartment. Close the sewer inlet on the RV and slide back the drain cover. Tidy up the dump station if you've made a mess (the true purpose of the aforementioned affixed hose) and get out of Dodge. Don't forget, add some water to the holding tank and treat with holding tank chemicals.

Mr. Clean

Even the best-kept holding tanks must be routinely cleaned, for different reasons. Clean and sanitize the fresh water storage tank so your drinking water is bacteria free and safe for drinking, cooking, and making that scary gargling sound you do when brushing your teeth. Although it's true that gray and black water tanks will never be "clean," a little preventative work eliminates clogs, bad smells, and potential repairs. Here are some ways to keep these tanks as nice as possible.

Fresh Water Tank

Avoid icky water with periodic purges and cleaning of the fresh water tank. This is also a good idea before long periods of storage and when the current batch isn't your best. The best time for this is when fresh water levels are low. Either let the fresh water tank reach empty or find the tank's drain, usually a simple plastic drain cock at the side of the RV or a full-way gate valve that must be opened, and empty the tank. Most coaches 10 years old and newer have two low-level drain valves, one each in the hot and cold lines, supposedly at their lowest point somewhere in the coach. Opening the low-level drain valves, the fresh water container valve, and the water heater drain will quickly empty all the fresh water from the system. Just be sure the city water is not connected and running, or you'll never finish the job.

With an empty (or near-empty) tank, concoct a bleach cocktail to rid the tank and pipes of mold and other evildoers. One cup's worth of bleach to every 15 gallons of water is a proven winner. Let the bleached water stand for a while, or better yet, take the RV out for a spin. The sloshing motion should add a little extra muscle to your sanitizing efforts and coat all those hard-to-reach areas within the tanks. Run the faucets and showerhead and flush the toilet to clear out the pipes. Rinse the tank, refill, and repeat. Harder-hitting chemicals and cleaning agents are available in the aftermarket, making this chore somewhat easier.

Wastewater Tank

No matter how hard you try, the black and gray water tanks will never sparkle. However, taking steps to combat odors and sediment should make for more pleasant and less odiferous travels. Even the most diligent dumping practices create clogs and buildup over time, which must be removed. To do this, attach a "water wand" (found at RV supply stores) to the end of a hose to blast residue throughout the hidden areas of your black water tanks via the toilet. The safest way to protect and treat the holding tanks and to eliminate odors is to then use a nonchemical, enzyme-based product, preferably one that contains live bacteria. The live bacteria actually digest the odor-causing molecules and break down the solid waste. This type of bacteria was used after the Alaskan oil spill to help digest the oil and to aid in the cleanup efforts, so it's more than good enough to be used here. Note that some RVs have a built-in black water flushing system.

The Least You Need to Know

- An RV contains two different water systems, with two distinct purposes: fresh water and wastewater.
- Wastewater comes in two forms: gray water (from sink and shower drains) and black water (water and materials from the toilet). Wastewater relies on a different network of plumbing, and each kind empties into its own holding tank.
- RVers can connect to water hook-ups at campgrounds for a steady supply or carry water with them in the fresh water holding tank. When relying on one's own reserves, a water pump must be activated to force the water up through the pipes.
- Keeping tanks clean is important. Fresh water tanks should be occasionally drained and sanitized with specially made cleaners. An effort should be made to eliminate buildup in wastewater tanks through regular cleanings and additives to prevent smells and buildup.

Basic Care

In This Chapter

- Learning procedures for storing your RV
- Getting your RV ready for spring travel
- Cleaning and preventive maintenance tips

Sadly, for many of us, RVing is only a seasonal exercise. That nasty foe known as winter often puts a cap on our adventures just when things are getting interesting. Sure, at the onset of those little black storm clouds and sinking temperatures, full-timers and snowbirds can simply point their rigs south. Alas, for the rest of us, it's time to prepare our RVs for a long winter's nap.

Long-term storage isn't as easy as unhitching the trailer and placing a "Do Not Disturb" sign on the door. There's a little more to it than that. And after spring does eventually roll around, getting the rig back into fighting shape requires some diligence on your part as well. Of course, basic care is warranted year-round. In between trips visiting long-lost relatives, caravans, rallies, and lazy days camped beachside, a little preventive maintenance goes a long way to keeping things running as they should. But don't worry, we're talking pretty simple stuff here. Even those who don't know a crescent wrench from a croissant should have no trouble following along. Your RV will thank you.

Time for Storage

The onset of winter acts as the proverbial wet blanket for most RV adventures. Cold, snow, ice, campground closures, fear of frostbite—take your pick—all serve to dampen most folks' enthusiasm for life on the road. Hypothermia instead of a suntan? A snowsuit instead of a swimsuit? No thanks, say most of us, we'll see you in the spring. Warm-weather residents, too, may subject their vehicles to long periods of nonuse. Maybe work's been crazy and you can't get away for months at a time. Or a family crisis keeps everyone at home when normally they'd be out and about. Maybe you parked the rig in the Rose Bowl parking lot and it takes you two months to find it. Whatever the reason, periods of dormancy come with the territory.

An Idle World

Like their automobile brethren, RVs weren't meant to sit; they were designed to go and go and go. An idle vehicle gets old before its time—kind of like us. Tires distort under the unmoving pressure. Batteries discharge and corrode. Engine components clog, fluids go stale, and hoses crack. Pests and critters build abodes inside, seeing a nice place to live rent free. Oxidation and damage from the sun can ravage a docile RV's once good looks, while winter may freeze pipes, leading to costly repairs. Before you know it, that once fine investment isn't looking—or acting—so fine. Whatever one's reasons for putting the RV away for a while, fortunately, an afternoon of elbow grease is about all it takes to tuck in your home on wheels for an uneventful rest. The biggest challenge is probably finding a place to put it.

Where Do You Want It?

Where your RV goes during periods of nonuse depends primarily on its size and your given situation. Ideally, vehicles should be shielded from the elements, temperature extremes, pollution, blowing sand, salty air, and other troublemakers. Storing your RV inside is preferable to storing it outside. Homeowners may be able to devote some or all of the garage to pop-ups, truck campers, van campers, and maybe some low-profile Class Cs and trailers. With enough room in the driveway or yard—provided neighbors or local ordinances won't be irked—an RV might fit there nicely. In cases of outdoor storage, some kind of covering is strongly recommended. (A number of companies produce specially designed canopies and covers to fit the contours of any size RV.) Otherwise, seek the aid of a professional storage facility. Some campgrounds, RV dealerships, and service centers rent space for such occasions. The best of the best will do the necessary prep work (as outlined in the following section) for a fee to get the vehicle ready, if you'd rather skip the work.

Winterizing

After finding a comfy spot for the RV, the task becomes how to negate the possible damaging effects of such inactivity on one's vehicle. This practice is usually referred to as winterizing, regardless of the temperatures the unit faces during its downtime. At this point, industrious owners roll up their sleeves and prepare the vehicle, both inside and out. Although slightly more involved for those vehicles facing cold-weather climates, the process is basically the same for everyone. A few extra steps are required for motorized vehicles.

Everybody Out

Start by removing all food, even nonperishables. For one thing, the inside of a closed-up RV can get very hot or cold, depending on the season, and items can surely spoil, become stale, attract bugs, and so on. Also, anything canned or bottled could potentially freeze and burst. Few sights are more disheartening than an exploded 2-liter bottle of root beer inside your RV.

Remove clothes, blankets, and linens for laundering. Unless the vehicle remains on your premises, there's no reason to leave any valuables aboard, so take home any key items or anything you'll need while the RV is away. Because dirt and debris only get more stubborn over time, a good cleaning—both inside and out— is recommended before storing. Follow the tips in the following "Clean Machine" section to keep your RV looking its best.

Plumbing

A lengthy sabbatical is harder on the pipes and holding tanks than any other system onboard. Stagnant water turns nasty and pollutes holding tanks. Remaining liquids can freeze and burst the pipes during frigid temperatures. The end result is the same: unnecessary costs and a headache come spring. Fortunately, a few simple steps eliminate this mess. Start by emptying both the fresh and wastewater tanks at a nearby dump station or during the last campout of the year. You won't get out every drop, but it's a good place to start. Unlatch tank drains to purge any remaining fluids and turn on faucets and the shower to clear the lines as much as possible. (Refer to the exact procedures in Chapter 11.) Don't forget any water left in the toilet and the water heater, which must both be emptied.

Empty holding tanks provide a great opportunity for a thorough scrub-down. Remember our mantra: clean is good. Close any opened faucets and drain plugs before beginning. A water wand (an attachment that delivers high-volume water pressure) is best for rinsing black water tanks, allowing users to access the inner reaches of the tank via the toilet and blast tough nooks free of any accumulated materials. Gray and fresh water tanks require a more subtle approach because there's no straight shot inside as with most black water models. Although a few cleaning agents can do the job (most RV supply stores are full of remedies), it's just as easy to fill the emptied tank with fresh water, add some baking soda or bleach (1 cup per 15 gallons of water), and drive down the bumpiest road in town for a few miles. The sloshing motion will coat the tank walls and do the dirty work for you. When accomplished, drain the tanks completely and close all water escape points (faucets, valves, and so on) before signing off.

Using Antifreeze

Of course, you and I both know that you didn't get *every* bit of water out of the lines and tanks, a problem if your storage location experiences a yearly deep freeze in January. What to do, what to do?

One option is to blow out any collected water in the lines with compressed air. RV supply stores offer numerous devices up to the task. Although the pipes will most definitely be void of water, this high-pressure procedure could damage weaker plumbing and more antiquated systems. A better solution might be to add a few gallons of RV antifreeze (yes, RV antifreeze) to the fresh water tank. Activate the water pump, open the various faucets, and let the stuff work its magic through the plumbing system. Like its name suggests, antifreeze won't go cold on you; it acts as an overzealous babysitter for the plumbing system while you're away. As a further precaution, add an additional cup to each drain afterward, including the sinks, shower, and toilet.

ONE FOR THE ROAD

No, it's not a misprint—RV antifreeze goes down the drains. This stuff isn't the lethal, automotive type you're accustomed to, but rather a product designed for use throughout the RV's water systems. It's specially formulated, nontoxic, and cheaper than a plumber, come springtime.

A water heater bypass kit eliminates the middleman—in this case, the water heater, which would otherwise require having to add 6 or 10 gallons of RV antifreeze to the unit as well. Pricier RVs probably already have such a device. Otherwise, it's a cheap alternative to excessive antifreeze.

Impenetrable Fortress

The biggest precaution concerning your LP gas system isn't so much the appliances, propane containers, or fuel lines, but rather the vents used for many of the LP appliances. Various members of the animal kingdom have been known to use such open avenues as intake and exhaust vents to set up a homestead onboard. And you thought your nephews were annoying! Mesh screens should already be in place for everyday use to keep out birds and varmints, but we're talking total lockdown here. To ward off potential freeloaders, cover any vents and openings with cardboard, aluminum foil, or the material *du jour*. A little duct tape here goes a long way, too. Mice are particularly partial to a dormant RV, making their home via unchecked openings and sometimes bringing along the spouse and kids. Meanwhile, birds favor exposed roof vents; ants and spiders are attracted to sweet smells onboard. Spray the perimeter with bug spray for an added layer of protection.

Remember, you're not going for style points here, so shore up the exterior by any means necessary. This includes going underneath the RV and making the chassis impenetrable. Visit the roof and cover the air conditioner (special covers are made for this very purpose) and repair any exposed seams with sealant (available at RV supply stores). Go inside and turn off the dashboard temperature controls and close vents, thus shutting off a potential rodent freeway in the making. Keep windows closed. If things get a tad buggy onboard, call an exterminator or use conventional pest-ridders.

LP Gas

Propane containers should be topped off before storage; a fuller tank weathers dissipation better than a half-empty version. Shut off the LP supply completely and cover the tanks to prevent dust, debris, and the elements from causing premature wear. Removable tanks can be taken off, covered, and stored, but should never be placed in the RV, which is the very last place you want LP gas fumes.

If you take off the fitting to remove a DOT LP cylinder, be sure to cover the open end with a bag and rubber band to keep critters from intruding. Also, always plug the fitting on the tank outlet with the appropriate plug. Finally, all LP appliances (ranges, oven, refrigerator, furnace, water heater, and so on) should be turned off during times of storage.

Prop open the refrigerator door, empty the contents (yes, even the mustard), and, if equipped with a freezer, allow it to completely thaw out. Enlist a few pots and pans to catch any drippings. This is a golden opportunity for a quick fridge scrub-down with warm, sudsy water to remove the memory (and odor) of a hot dog goulash lunch. Leave the door open for the remainder of the storage, unless you have a penchant for mold. An open box of baking soda tucked away inside gives smells the boot.

PULL OVER

RV refrigerators are less tolerant of heat than residential models. Avoid the old blow-drying trick to hasten the thawing-out process, which could damage components.

Assault and Battery

During storage, the 12-volt battery system is like a mobster in the witness protection program—it's safe, but not particularly happy. It misses the high-rolling action of the old days, and there's little you can do to improve its mood. However, a fully charged battery handles this incarceration best, most easily accomplished by connecting to shore power (a weekend camping trip, for example) prior to storage. Top off the battery's water levels, which dissipate over time. In colder climes, it's best to remove the battery altogether, storing it in a dry, warm location for its protection. Otherwise, disconnect the cables (negative cable first) to safeguard them electrically during storage. All this may seem like a lot of work, but remember, these batteries are the heart of the 12-volt electrical system. Flip the off switch on the RV's main breaker panel (see the owner's manual for the location) to safeguard the 120-volt system. Unplug all electrical appliances and remove dry cell batteries, which can corrode over time, from alarms, detectors, and any devices inside. Follow the manufacturer's directions for the onboard or portable generator (if so equipped). At the very least, clean the unit and cover the exhaust pipe to prevent unwanted intruders. Draining the fuel filter, changing the oil, and adding a rust inhibitor are also advisable.

Tired Out

Anyone who's ever tended bar, worked retail, or suffered through an afternoon as a store mannequin at Bloomingdale's (it's a long story) knows how hard it is to stand on your feet all day. Take this lesson to heart and consider the plight of your RV's poor tires, which endure thousands of pounds of pressure all day, every day. Storage worsens the effects considerably because the weight is stationary, resting squarely on one rubbery spot. After a few months of this torture, even the finest treads may begin to resemble a donut with a Homer Simpson–sized bite out of it.

Those lucky dogs with leveling systems should consider using them to support the vehicle's weight on the jacks instead of the tires. Always consult the device manufacturer and review the owner's manual regarding long-term jack use. Otherwise, incorporate a set of outside jacks or blocks for each axle—money well spent, considering the expense of replacing messed-up tires. A cost-free but more doting method is to periodically move the RV a half-revolution (once or twice over the winter should do it) to distribute the weight over other portions of the tire's surface.

ROAD SCHOLAR

Storage time is the best time for you to take inventory of necessary work onboard. Do any hoses, cords, or seals need replacing? When was the last time curtains, fabrics, clothes, and blankets were laundered? Spray for pests, deep-clean the carpet, and add a new showerhead if the old one leaks. A little extra work now reduces would-be annoyances later.

Engine Care

That taunt you're hearing is probably from the towable owner relaxing in the shade as the motorized community contemplates a few more steps. Because we want our motorhomes to act just as sprightly when we call on them again, a little work must still be done to the engine. As previously mentioned, inactivity is hard on any vehicle, but most taxing on the motor—particularly in harsh climates. Start by protecting the fuel source by topping off the gasoline or diesel tanks.

A fuel stabilizer, found at nearly any automotive or RV supply store, is a must. Just be sure to add the right one for your engine type (gasoline or diesel). Idle the engine to allow the additive to make its rounds throughout the system.

As always, strive for full tanks and fluid compartments in the engine, to lessen the chances of them freezing or drying out. Top off the radiator with antifreeze matched for your climate; flush and replace with a batch suited for Siberia-like temperatures if that is indeed the case. Inspect levels throughout the engine (windshield wiper fluid, oil, brake fluid, and so on) and refill as needed.

Spring Shakedown

Those of us still making snow angels in March call it a spring shakedown. However, run these drills whenever you're reuniting with your RV after a period of storage. The primary goal when prepping the vehicle back into service is to undo everything you did to get it ready for hibernation in the first place. When that's done, a few added steps are needed to get the vehicle back into the swing of things.

A Quick Look Around

Like a third-grader on the first day of school, there's plenty of work to be done to get ready for the new season. For starters, the interior might be a tad musty from being cooped up. Open windows to air things out. Check for any signs of leaks or trouble or just anything amiss. Assuming everything is as it should be, start by rectifying the paste-up job you should have done on the vents and various openings throughout the coach. Start on the roof and work your way down, ending things underneath the chassis. Put on your inspector's hat and tear away any makeshift blockades installed last time to ward off bugs and varmints.

Check seals around doors and windows for leaks or wear. Reinstall new ones at the first signs of trouble; these are popular avenues for water to slip inside. How are the seams on the roof? Check around the air conditioner, vents, antennas, and so on. Reseal with aftermarket products, if necessary, to dissuade a season's worth of weather from sneaking around onboard. Crawl underneath the unit, looking for any irregularities. Colorful puddles, dangling wires, and gremlins asleep in the wheel wells are all red flags. Inspect the tires for wear and air up as necessary.

Take in the unit for service if you detect problems underneath. Nip concerns in the bud now before you're a thousand miles from home.

Systems Check

Reinstall and/or reconnect the 12-volt battery terminals and top off water levels. Plug the electric cord into an electrical outlet to revamp the coach batteries while you work. Despite their inactivity, voltages probably dropped fairly dramatically while you were away. Plug in all needed appliances; add dry cell batteries to alarms, detectors, and any devices onboard. Inspect safety devices (smoke alarm, LP and CO detectors) to guarantee their working condition. Follow the owner's manual for a yearly checkup of the RV's generator (if so equipped). Let motorized RVs warm up for a few minutes. Test appliances one at a time and follow their various owner's manuals for yearly preventive maintenance while you're at it. Now is as good a time as any to undertake these procedures. Contact the specific appliance or component manufacturer if you're unsure how to proceed.

Uncover and/or reattach any propane containers. If LP container(s) were removed, quickly open and close each tank valve just before reconnecting them, to expel any contaminants that may have settled in the throat of the valve, where it can definitely block an orifice. And you know what it's like to have a blocked orifice. Like your boss, the fuel lines will probably be full of air, so a quick purge of them is in order. Turn on the stove burners to expel air out of the fuel lines; take turns lighting each one. Assuming that the refrigerator is level (and many RV storage yards are not), close the refrigerator door and set it to either 120-volt or LP operation.

Attach your fresh water hose and connect to city water, if possible. Otherwise, take the rig someplace where you can fill and drain the tanks. Although nontoxic, the RV antifreeze in the line isn't quite as refreshing as your favorite cocktail. It's best to drain, refill, and repeat. Fill the fresh water tank and water heater, activate the water pump, and open up the faucets, including the shower. This should clear out the lines. Flush the toilet, too. Repeat these steps as necessary to guarantee proper cleansing. Look carefully for any possible leaks. Freshen tanks with cleansers, as detailed in Chapter 11.

ROAD SCHOLAR

A shakedown trip, such as the one recommended in Chapter 8, is the best way to test out all the appliances and systems. Secure a full–hook-up campsite close to home; spend one day operating off the park's utilities and the next day using the RV's self-contained features. Rely on the coach batteries, generator, inverter, and/or solar panels for electricity; use the storage tank for the water supply. Be satisfied that everything is working before you embark on a longer trip.

Motor City

Anything with an engine requires periods of TLC. If you're of the Type A persuasion, you probably know the exact intervals of when to change oil and flush the radiator, as well as the harmful effects of a dirty air filter, by heart. The rest of us have a tendency to let these things slide. Unfortunately, an RV has a long memory and may penalize you in the form of a needless breakdown later. As with spring training for ballplayers, consider this the time to tune up your RV's mechanical prowess. It's a long season ahead. Again, manufacturer recommendations reign supreme here, but here are a few to get you started. Some tips won't apply for owners of diesel engines.

RV Tune-Up Checklist

❑ Check fluids and change, if necessary
❑ Check oil levels
❑ Check brake fluid
❑ Check transmission fluid
❑ Check radiator fluid
❑ Check power-steering fluid
❑ Check windshield wipers
❑ Check windshield washer fluid
❑ Check hoses and belts for wear
❑ Inspect air filter
❑ Change spark plugs

Trailers

Although spared the extra work underneath the hood, towable owners also have some work to do. Carefully eyeball the hitch, the trailer tongue, wiring, safety chains, and all accessories used to facilitate connections for any signs of distress. This is especially true of any places undergoing metal-on-metal contact, which promotes rust, scratches, and dents. Look for defects in the spring bar assembly, coupler, receiver, and ball mount. Tighten bolts and lube components, as suggested by the manufacturer. A few rodents like to cleanse their palates by munching through electrical wires, so pay special attention to their condition.

Drive-Through

When you're satisfied that things are as they should be, hitch up the trailer or start up the motorhome for a quick fact-finding mission. Start by checking all exterior lights (brakes, headlights, turn signals, and so on) before throwing it into gear. Have a pal jump out and give you the thumbs-up on the light situation behind you, spot-checking that everything is in working order. Test the brakes on a motorhome or tow vehicle before departing to ensure that you can stop smoothly without chatter or slippage. If you're pulling a trailer with a brake controller, this is the time to check that it is set properly—that is, achieving a balance between the braking of the trailer and the braking of the vehicle.

Take a trip through the area, paying special consideration to any unusual sounds, smells, and quirks picked up since you last drove it. How are the brakes, steering, and acceleration? Operate the full gamut of dashboard controls and doodads. A jaunt on the expressway reveals any problems at higher speeds. Book an appointment with a qualified service center if things aren't as they should be or if recommended preventive maintenance is more than you can (or want to) handle.

Clean Machine

I'm not your mother, but a clean RV yields many advantages. For starters, it just looks nice, and you won't be embarrassed when the neighbors lobby for an impromptu tour. Keeping the roof and exterior washed makes it easier to spot subtle damage topside, minimizes the potential oxidizing effects of the sun, and turns heads when you pull into camp. But washing, drying, and waxing a 35-foot fifth-wheel probably isn't your idea of a great day off. Thankfully, it takes only a few days' worth of work during a season to keep things looking nice. In between scrub-downs, park the vehicle under a tarp or canopy to ward off salt, sand, dust, and debris.

Exterior Care

The first step when cleaning up is to identify what kind of materials you're dealing with. The roof is generally made of a different composite than the sidewalls, so adjust your cleaning agents accordingly. The needs of a rubber roof are considerably different than those of an aluminum version, and vice versa. Always use products designed for the material in question. Most RVers agree that RV-specific cleaners are usually better than automotive or household products. A hose with a large extension and/or brush is warranted to take the strain out of washing taller, wider, and longer vehicles. Again, the aftermarket is full of products to help you. Tough sap, tar, black dirt streaks, and bird droppings (why do they always find me?) usually require additional muscle to remove. Overachievers should finish the job with a wax made especially for their type of sidewalls.

Survey the roof and exterior for signs of rust, scratches, dents, or (gasp!) holes as you go. Low-hanging branches are likely to blame for roof damage; that picnic table you ran over probably explains the dent in the bumper. Nip body damage early before it saps resale dollars from the unit. A faded appearance is generally indicative of sun damage, which may or may not be remedied by oxidation fighters. Find a quality body shop to restore lost luster. Backyard mechanics find plenty of help in the aftermarket sector with roof repair kits and other godsends. Tighten screws and check seals around doors and windows as you go. Lube joints on outside storage compartments, awnings, entry steps, doors, and the like periodically for easy motion.

It's worth stating again that tires are the most forgotten aspect of any RV. And they are among the most crucial. Like Rodney Dangerfield, they get no respect. Too bad, considering the heavy loads we ask them to carry with rarely a second thought. Check for uneven wear, tread, cuts, and so on. Using a tire gauge always lets you know where you stand, so take pressure readings before any trip. (Pressure readings must be taken when the tire is "cold" or anytime when driven less than a half-mile.) Know how much pressure should go in each by weight. Dealers have charts to help you. Keep tires clean and use protectants to repel ozone and UV damage, which can damage them over time.

Interior Care

Vacuum often to deter dirt from settling. Larger house vacuums just aren't practical to bring along; they take up useful space and electricity. A small 12-volt model should work okay, especially if you run it often to prevent dirty buildups. A deep-down industrial vacuum (a.k.a. Rug Doctor), available for rent at numerous places, gets the original color and charm back in a hurry. Launder curtains and removable upholstery annually. Always follow cleaning directions to avoid inadvertently creating fabrics now useful only for Barbie's Dream House. As with the exterior, pay special mind to the materials used for countertops, cabinets, sinks, and throughout the interior. You'd be surprised at the variety. Make sure the cleansers jive with where each is applied. Review the appliances' owner's manuals for care and cleaning instructions.

I could write another book just on preventive maintenance, cleaning tips, and basic care. This is just the tip of the proverbial iceberg, depending on your mechanical aptitude and willingness to give up a Sunday or two to do the work. I'm always surprised at the numbers of RVers who do many of these jobs themselves, but you may fall out of that category. Don't feel bad—I'm not much with a socket wrench, either. Follow guidelines in manuals for routine care, troubleshooting, and checkups. Seek the services of a quality RV service center or dealership if you're uncomfortable working on the vehicle yourself.

The Least You Need to Know

- Recreational vehicles must be properly stored during longer periods of nonuse. Turn off all systems and appliances, and patch any openings to keep out pests. Take special precautions against freezing temperatures, including prepping the battery, draining the tanks, and adding RV antifreeze to the drains and plumbing fixtures.

- Undo the work you did prior to storage to get the RV back into shape. Reconnect and recharge batteries, drain and refill the water supply, and take the vehicle out for a test-drive.

- Always use RV-specific products, being careful to match cleansers to the appropriate materials. Clean roofs, sidewalls, and tires ward off oxidation and enhance their appearance. Routine vacuuming, laundering, and tidying up inside eliminates stains and buildup of dirt.

Start Your Engines

You're almost there. You've found an ideal RV (either purchased, rented, or borrowed from that neighbor who owed you a favor), learned the basics of life onboard, and are now ready to hit the road. Whoa, Nelly! Hold those horses for a minute. I know you've got a bad case of itchy wheels and all, but spending some time getting acquainted with the various driving/towing techniques is probably a good idea. Fortunately, in the following chapters, you'll learn the basics of RV driving and the importance of weights (the RV's, not yours), along with how and what to pack.

Towin' the Line

In This Chapter

- Matching tow vehicles to trailers and vice versa
- Towing trailers, fifth-wheels, and secondary vehicles
- Operating tips and must-have accessories

You may have already decided, after reading the earlier chapters on the subject, that a trailer is the best choice for your family right now. Whether it's the lower cost, variety of floorplans, available living space, or something else that appeals to you, towable RVs offer many distinct and wonderful advantages. This chapter is for you. But you motorized fans, listen up, too. Just because you're riding high in a camper van, truck camper, or mega motorhome doesn't mean your towing days are necessarily over. Install a hitch on your motorhome, and you now have the option of taking a car, boat, or even small trailer with you. This can add a whole new dimension to an already exciting lifestyle.

This chapter deals with all things towing, from towing a full range of trailers and secondary vehicles to toting the smallest fold-down trailer, from towing enormous fifth-wheels to bringing along a compact car or even a pair of snowmobiles or four-wheelers. Got an existing car, truck, or SUV you want to pair with a shiny new towable? I tell you how to make a match made in heaven (or, at least, the nearest dealer's lot). Found that great fifth-wheel, travel trailer, or fold-down camper you can't live without? I help you narrow the field to find the right tow vehicle for the job. I demystify the confusing towing terminology, break down how to transport most any type of vehicle, and provide a host of tips and accessories to make this task safer and easier. Read on—your chariot awaits.

How Much Can My Vehicle Tow?

This is the million-dollar question. Well, maybe not a million dollars, but one can easily spend tens of thousands of dollars on a tow vehicle/towable combination, only to find out too late that they're incompatible. Not to sound like your mother or anything, but this is one situation when you really need to do your homework before you plunk down all that hard-earned cash. If you haven't yet purchased either a tow vehicle or a towable, great! You have the most options available to you.

What Do You Mean, Homework?

Maybe you already have an existing car or truck and you need to know just what—or how much—it can safely tow. I can help. Even if you've put the proverbial cart before the horse, so to speak, and have already purchased a towable, I can help you choose the right tow vehicle for the job. Regardless of where you are in the process, the first step is to determine the *tow rating* of the vehicle you own or are considering. Basically, the tow rating is how much the vehicle can safely pull. Every vehicle has its limits, and yours is no exception.

RVOCABULARY

Listed in pounds, the **tow rating** measures the maximum weight a vehicle can safely tow. The larger the tow rating, the heavier the towable a vehicle can safely transport. Most manufacturers now list the tow rating as part of the standard vehicle specifications.

Obtaining That Rate

Every vehicle has a tow rating. Even the tiniest compact car has one, although it might be embarrassingly low. Just don't count on a two-door coupe to haul around that 40-foot travel trailer you've been eyeing. A number of factors combine to affect tow ratings, including engine size, rear axle differential ratio, type of transmission, and so on. And unless these inherent qualities of the vehicle are somehow altered (adding a new engine, for instance), the tow rating will not change. The manufacturer determines this rating, and it can change from year to year. For example, a newer Ford F350 delivers a higher tow rating than an F350 that is several years old, due to recent changes in the vehicle's specifications. For a vehicle you already own, check the owner's manual or contact the manufacturer for this crucial bit of information. *Trailer Life* magazine and its companion website, www.trailerlife.com, compile an annual listing of tow ratings for a wide variety of vehicles. Current-year ratings, as well as those from past years, are available online. It's important to look for the rating of the specific year's model you're considering.

The Big Three

Congratulations, you're halfway there. With your tow vehicle's tow rating in hand, you now know exactly how much it can safely pull. The next step is to determine the weight of the trailer that you hope to haul around. Makes sense, right? Although trailer weights are also readily available, finding the exact figure in the brochures can be confusing. Here it's boiled down to three important terms to help you match a tow vehicle with a towable.

Unloaded Vehicle Weight

Also listed as the UVW, or dry weight, this figure describes the weight of just the towable—no cargo, no fresh water or propane, and definitely no passengers toting heavy fruitcakes—just the *actual* weight of the trailer and nothing else. Provided by the manufacturer, consider this weight somewhat of an approximate number. Why? Because add-ons (sometimes installed after the unit leaves the factory) in the forms of slide-outs, an extra air conditioner, awnings, or other upgrades may not be included in that number, serving only to escalate this figure. Pulling onto a truck scale is the only way to know the towable's true UVW, which I discuss in Chapter 14. Savvy RV shoppers make it a point to weigh their towable before they purchase it so there are no surprises after the fact.

Gross Vehicle Weight Rating

Sometimes shortened to GVWR, this is the *maximum* carrying capacity of the fully loaded vehicle. The UVW is what it actually weighs; the GVWR is how much extra weight it can safely carry—or, rather, its maximum weight limit.

This rating includes everything onboard—water, propane, food, all passengers (including the 15 pounds you gained over the holidays), and the gear. Consider this figure non-negotiable. Exceed it, and you're asking for trouble. The GVWR is the towable's absolute limit and the magic number for tow vehicle/towable matchmaking.

Gross Combined Weight Rating

Commonly seen as the GCWR, this rating applies to the maximum weight limit for the tow vehicle, the towed object (trailer or secondary vehicle), and all passengers and cargo inside each. Why is this term necessary when we have the GVWR? Because the tow vehicle itself is carrying gear and passengers, which affects its towing abilities as well. Basically, this number serves as the maximum *combined* weight of what the tow vehicle can safely handle, hence the name.

> **ONE FOR THE ROAD**
>
> Make buying decisions based on hard facts, not on what someone tells you that you can handle. Images in brochures and advertisements are sometimes misleading, with pictures of undersized vehicles pulling towables way out of their league. And don't believe everything that RV salesperson tells you: he's there to sell RVs. It's ultimately your job to do the appropriate homework.

Making the Match

All this brings us back to the original question: how do you know what you can safely tow? Look at the tow rating for the tow vehicle you have (or plan to purchase). Compare this number to the GVWR of the trailer you are considering or already own. If the GVWR of the towable is *less* than your vehicle's tow rating, you're in business. Hallelujah, the tow vehicle is up to the job. However, if the trailer's GVWR is greater than the tow vehicle's tow rating, you have two choices: find a lighter towable or find a tow vehicle with a higher tow rating. Don't be tempted to push the envelope here. Always heed these ratings, and don't ask a tow vehicle to do more than it can. It will reward you in the form of lower maintenance costs and fewer frustrating breakdowns along the way, not to mention safer travels. More on the perils of overloading in Chapter 14.

Come on, the numbers are close enough, you say. That awesome travel trailer with that cool floorplan, a bevy of slide-outs, a gas fireplace (yes, there is such a thing), and sliding French doors is just a couple of hundred pounds more than your vehicle can handle. So what's the big deal? Besides, your neighbor has a trailer just like it, and his pickup can pull it, no problem. Remember, every tow vehicle has its own tow rating, and every towable its own GVWR. You can't tell what those numbers are just by looking. And it's very possible that your neighbor simply made an uninformed choice, as some new RVers do. The moral of the story is, don't listen to your heart or your ego on this one. Make the safe, smart choice, and rest easy knowing you have done everything to ensure the safety of your loved ones.

PULL OVER

Some first-time RV buyers make the mistake of plunking down their hard-earned cash for a trailer on impulse, without doing proper research. Regrettably, some salespeople are occasionally misleading or uninformed in their assurances that your tow vehicle can do the job. And then it's too late. You discover that you have a mismatch—a towable too heavy for the vehicle to tow. A costly mistake.

The Hitching Post

The trailer hitch is the vital link in the towing system. Its purpose is to connect the trailer to the tow vehicle, attached either to the bumper or frame (for conventional trailers) or within the bed of the truck (for fifth-wheels). As seen in the following table, there are different hitches for different trailer weights, with each rated according to the load it is designed to handle.

Hitch Classes

Class	Weight Limits
Class I (weight carrying)	Trailers up to 2,000 lb.
Class II (weight carrying)	Trailers from 2,001 to 3,500 lb.
Class III (weight distributing)	Trailers from 3,501 to 5,000 lb.
Class IV (weight distributing)	Trailers from 5,001 to 10,000 lb.
Class V (weight distributing)	Trailers from 10,001 to 15,000 lb.

Take the Fifth

Unlike conventional bumper- or frame-mounted versions, fifth-wheel hitches aren't divided into traditional weight classes (Class I, Class II, and so on). In the case of fifth-wheels, hitches are segregated and labeled by weight capacity (for example, a 15,000-pound hitch, a 20,000-pound hitch, and so on). Furthermore, ratings vary from manufacturer to manufacturer.

Which Hitch?

A dealer specializing in towable RVs is the most likely place to obtain the right hitch. The dealer should be able to advise you on the correct type for your towable and install it as well. If you prefer not to go this route, aftermarket service centers and hitch shops specialize in matching tow vehicles to trailers and make their living installing hitches. Prepare to answer questions about what you're towing and its GVWR. Search online under "Trailer Hitches" for businesses near you.

ONE FOR THE ROAD

Different towing packages are available in the aftermarket or may be equipped on a tow vehicle with an integrated towing system, to save you a few steps. A tow vehicle that comes from the manufacturer set to tow will already have the ideal gear ratio, a sufficiently powerful engine, an engine brake, the wiring, and perhaps even the hitch already installed.

Choosing the right hitch, like most things related to towing, boils down to weight. Again, the hitch must be able to handle the load of your trailer. For instance, a trailer with a GVWR of 7,000 pounds requires a Class IV hitch rated for the job, which, as seen in the preceding hitch class's table, can handle that load and then some. The hitch and the tow vehicle's tow rating must work together, and you're only as strong as your weakest link. If your truck is rated to tow 10,000 pounds but you find yourself with only a Class II hitch, consider the vehicle's limit now reduced to 3,500 pounds. You'll need a new hitch if you want to tow more. Conversely, a Class V hitch on a small tow vehicle makes little sense because the tow vehicle could never, ever pull such a load.

As stated earlier, most conventional trailers have a uniquely different hitch configuration than fifth-wheels. These hitch types are mutually exclusive and can never be substituted for one another. A closer look at each type is provided in the following sections.

Conventional Trailers

Let's start with the hitches found on conventional trailers, namely on travel trailers and pop-ups, and for some secondary vehicles towed behind motorhomes. For any one of these scenarios, one of two standard hitches is required: a weight-carrying hitch or a weight-distributing hitch.

Weight-Carrying Hitch

Take another look at the hitch classes table. You'll see that the Class I and II types are of the weight-carrying persuasion. (In a few cases, Class IIs are sometimes a receive-type hitch.) Here the hitch is forced to support the brunt of the trailer's hitch weight. Usually mounted to the bumper, these hitches are useful only for smaller loads less than 3,500 pounds, limiting the user to very lightweight trailers and pop-ups. However, for those pulling a secondary vehicle behind the motorhome, this allows for a fairly decent selection of automobiles.

Those towing smaller loads, usually less than 3,500 pounds, can rely on a weight-carrying hitch to do the job.
(Courtesy of Draw-Tite)

Weight-Distributing Hitch

Question: Would you rather carry Aunt Gertrude's pool table yourself or have three other people help you? Unless you're Superman looking for a workout, you'd surely rather enlist the help of some buddies. That's exactly the rationale behind a weight-distributing hitch, sometimes referred to as a load-equalizing hitch. Attached to the frame of the tow vehicle, these hitches are designed to spread the weight to both axles of the tow vehicle instead of relying only on the back end. With the weight properly distributed, larger trailers can be towed with greater ease and stability.

A weight-distributing hitch, specially designed to distribute the load of the towable among the tow vehicle's axles, is the only type of hitch suitable for larger towables.
(Courtesy of Draw-Tite)

What's What—Hitches

Although the dynamics at work in a weight-carrying hitch are barely more than a ball attached to the vehicle's bumper, the weight-distributing hitch is somewhat more complex and comprised of several important parts. A basic understanding of the purpose of each should help eliminate confusion when the fella at the hitch shop is "talkin' the talk." And because we'll be dropping a few of these terms when it's time to hitch up, better learn them now.

The typical trailer hitch is made up of three important parts: the *hitch receiver, ball mount,* and *spring bars.*

RVOCABULARY

The **hitch receiver** acts as the hitch's overall foundation, bolted or welded to the frame of the tow vehicle. The **ball mount** serves as the connection point between trailer and tow vehicle, sliding into the receiver hitch and pinned in place. Proper height and tilt are important for a snug fit, which is best left up to a professional installer to dictate. The ball mount on weight-distributing hitches is removable when not towing, to avoid becoming a knee-basher. The **spring bars** are designed to disperse the towable's weight among the tow vehicle's axles for better handling and steering. These are sometimes referred to as tension bars.

Getting Hitched

Getting hitched doesn't have to be difficult. We're still talking about trailers, right? Anyway, don't be intimidated by this part. Even if you have zero experience, anyone can learn how to connect the faithful tow vehicle with a dream towable. It's best to find a place where you can practice without the pressure of an audience. And don't ever let anyone rush you—this is when mistakes are often made.

The first step in hooking up a trailer is to raise the trailer's *tongue* (the metal A-frame portion that connects to the tow vehicle) above the level of the ball hitch on the tow vehicle. This is accomplished via a jack found on the tongue, which has the dual purpose of helping level your trailer after you arrive at your destination (so you don't roll out of bed at night). You can easily adjust the height of the trailer by moving this jack up or down, either manually or with the aid of a power jack, if available.

After you have the trailer's tongue in position above the level of the ball hitch on the back of the tow vehicle, back up the tow vehicle until its hitch is positioned just below the *coupler* on the end of the tongue. It might take you a couple of tries, but be patient. Take your time, and just pull forward a bit and try again, watching the hitch and trailer tongue as you ease in. If possible, enlist the help of another person to guide you back via a series of hand gestures (no, not *that* one) and voice commands. You're halfway home.

> **RVOCABULARY**
>
> The **tongue** is the "A"-shaped portion of the trailer frame responsible for hitching up to the tow vehicle and securing the LP containers, and it's the location for the tongue jack that raises and lowers the front end. The **coupler** is the forward-most component of the trailer's tongue, which fits snugly over the ball hitch to make a tight towing connection.

When in position, use the jack to lower the coupler onto the ball of the hitch, and lock it into position. (Those using a weight-distributing hitch should put the spring bars in before lowering the jack.) Raise the tongue jack slightly to put the weight of the trailer onto the hitch. (The tow vehicle should "drop" a little if a good connection has been made.) Because you won't need the tongue jack anymore (not until you unhook the trailer later, that is), raise it or fold it up against the tongue of the trailer so it's safely out of the way. Well done. At this point, a basic connection has been made. With a few finishing touches, you'll be on your way.

Wiring It Up

Regardless of the type of hitch you use, you will need a wiring harness to go with it. This is usually included in the hitch installation. In simplest terms, it involves running wires from the brakes and lights on the trailer to the brakes and lights on your tow vehicle. The goal here is perfect symmetry between the two, in terms of running lights, turn signals, and brakes. The wires should be bundled together in a neatly accessible manner near the hitch, and the same goes for the trailer. When it's time to hit the road, the wires are easily connected or disconnected near the hitch by simply plugging them together or pulling them apart. (When not in use, make sure both ends of the wiring are tucked up out of the way so they don't become frayed or dirty.) When connected, a magical thing happens. The trailer's lights and braking system mimic the actions of the tow vehicle. Not only is this cool, but it'll keep the local police force happy (it's the law)—and it's a vital step before towing a trailer of any size.

ROAD SCHOLAR

Ball hitches come in a few sizes, so you need to ensure that you have the right size for your towable. Again, your dealer or hitch shop should help here. If it's too big or small for the trailer's coupler, you must replace the hitch with the correct size. Most hitches allow you to swap out the ball portion for another size, a versatile option for towing different trailers. The correct ball size is usually stamped on the top portion of the coupler.

Draw Bar   Hitch Receiver   Weight Distributing Hitch
Safety Chains   Electrical Wiring

A closer look at all the players involved in a standard hitch-up for conventional towables.
(Courtesy of Blue Ox)

Brake Time

Remember Newton's First Law of Motion? Probably not, unless you teach physics, so here's a recap: every object in a state of uniform motion tends to stay that way unless an external force is applied to it. A tow vehicle's brakes are designed to stop you and a decent-sized payload—and that's about it. But where does this leave your trailer chugging along behind you? Fortunately, most trailers come equipped with brakes of their own. This way, you're not dependent on the tow vehicle's brakes to stop the entire load. Now it's up to you to connect the towable's brakes to that of the tow vehicle, as documented in the previous section.

To match both sets of brakes (the tow vehicle's and the trailer's), wiring must be installed when the hitch is installed. After doing this, simply plug both connections together after hitching up to ensure that both braking systems work in tandem. The trailer brakes should engage automatically when you step on the tow vehicle's brakes. However, they can also be applied by hand through a device known as a *brake controller*, mounted near the steering wheel of the tow vehicle.

RVOCABULARY

The **brake controller** is a device mounted within the tow vehicle to activate the trailer's brakes independently or in conjunction with the tow vehicle's brakes.

A brake controller is a must on all tow vehicles towing a travel trailer or fifth-wheel with electric brakes. (Most trailers feature electric brakes.) The brake controller is added to the tow vehicle at the time all other wiring is done. Some newer tow vehicles have brake controllers as an option at manufacture. The brake circuit terminates in the same plug as the lights and charge line, and so on. Most controllers have an independent method of activating the trailer brakes without activating the tow vehicle brakes, such as when descending a hill or stopping a slight sway situation. The device is installed in the cockpit, usually near the steering wheel.

Safety Chaining

Safety chains are a must to keep your trailer from "running away" in the unlikely event it becomes unhooked. As part of the hitch installation, two short chains are attached to the trailer near the tongue. The crossed chains form a basket of sorts—a safety net, really—to catch the tongue in case the trailer ever tries to part company with the tow vehicle. The chains are welded to the coupler and connect to rings welded to the hitch receiver on the tow vehicle. Instead of "S" ends, universal chain links with a threaded nut are used. The chains should be long enough to hang loosely but not touch the ground, to prevent an ongoing spark-fest. When not in use, the chains simply hang under the coupler because they remain welded at that end. Wrap them along the trailer tongue to keep them up and out of the way. Again, the trailer dealer or hitch shop is the best source for getting and applying safety chains.

Breaking Up Is Hard to Do

In the unlikely but potentially catastrophic event that the trailer and the vehicle decide to part ways, a *break-away switch* keeps you covered. Not only does it add further peace of mind in case the trailer and tow vehicle no longer want to see each other, but the guy behind you certainly will appreciate it if it's ever called upon. Mounted on or near the tongue, the device is equipped with a pin attached to a cable, which, in turn, is attached to the ball mount. The connection is wired from the trailer's battery and to the electric brake circuit on the trailer. If the trailer and tow vehicle ever disconnect from one another during transit, the separation pulls the pin, and the trailer's brakes are automatically activated to help slow the runaway trailer. It's kinda like pulling the pin on a hand grenade. It's important to have a charged battery on the trailer so this feature won't let you down in this unlikely but potentially very dangerous event. No battery, no break-away switch, no brakes, no stopping the runaway trailer, no good.

 RVOCABULARY

The **break-away switch** is a pin-activated safety device mounted near the trailer's tongue that automatically activates the braking system in case of separation from the tow vehicle.

Conventional Trailer Checklist

- ❏ Coupler and hitch locked into position
- ❏ Safety chains crossed under trailer tongue and attached to bumper of truck
- ❏ Spring bars and sway control (if added) adjusted properly
- ❏ Wiring connected
- ❏ Break-away switch cable connected
- ❏ Running lights, turn signals, and backup lights tested
- ❏ Trailer brakes checked/adjusted

Fifth-Wheels

With their unique gooseneck design, fifth-wheel trailers require a different kind of hitch, which is mounted in the bed of the truck doing the towing duties. Unlike regular trailers, which rely partially on gravity to help reinforce the connection, fifth-wheels use a locking hitch mechanism. Here, the *kingpin* on the front of the fifth-wheel slides and locks into the hitch mounted in the bed of the truck. Again, the weight of the fifth-wheel determines the type of hitch required. Opt for a fifth-wheel hitch that "flexes," as it will allow you to hitch up on uneven ground more easily and will take stress off the hitch when driving over uneven terrain. Air ride hitches reduce road vibration and trailer sway. All these configurations are available at RV dealerships or hitch shops.

RVOCABULARY

The **kingpin** is the part of the fifth-wheel that slides and locks into the truck-mounted hitch. It is cylindrical and sticks down a few inches below the underside of the front of the fifth-wheel, near the nose of the trailer. Incidentally, this is a common place to bump your head while rummaging through outside storage compartments while parked, so be careful.

One of the benefits of a fifth-wheel hitch is that it can be removed, thereby freeing up the bed of the truck for other things. Different fifth-wheel hitch makers have their own methods of attachment, but most are removed fairly easily by removing the pins that hold them in place. Others require unbolting the hitch in several places before lifting it out of the back of the truck. Most RVers do this only when they will not be towing their fifth-wheel for a while.

The Big Hitch

Hooking up a fifth-wheel is a little different, but there's more than a little common ground compared to conventional trailers. First, you must use the fifth-wheel's jacks in the front of the trailer to raise or lower the kingpin to the same level as the hitch. (Smaller models might require a hand crank.) This part is easy—just access the switch inside the small compartment on the driver's side of the trailer (right near the front) and press the switch in the desired direction. This is also a good job for Junior, by the way.

Instead of the bumper- or frame-mounted hitch used for conventional towables, a fifth-wheel hitch such as this one is installed within the cargo bed of the tow vehicle.
(Courtesy of Draw-Tite)

Drop the truck's tailgate and slowly back up the truck, aimed right at the kingpin. With a little practice, you will probably be able to make this connection perfectly using your rearview mirror as you maneuver in or by eyeing the hitch through the back window. Use side mirrors or have someone help you, if necessary. When the kingpin is right behind the hitch and properly lined up, simply ease back and lock it into place. Expect a bit of a jolt when this happens. Otherwise, lower or raise the hitch, if necessary, so that it's at just the right level for the kingpin to slide into the hitch. Next, get out and push the *locking pin* through the hole in the kingpin, fastening it into place with the wire clip.

> **RVOCABULARY**
>
> Also known as a safety pin, the **locking pin** secures the connection between the kingpin and fifth-wheel hitch for a tight fit and added safety. Exact methods of locking vary among hitch manufacturers.

Final Steps

Just as we do for conventional trailers, with the hitch connection made, it's time for some final steps to ensure a safe trip. Plug the wiring from the fifth-wheel into the truck connection so that the taillights, turn signals, and brake/reverse lights are in working order. The fifth-wheel's braking system will be activated in this manner as well. Safety chains are a nice precaution but aren't as essential here because you won't be using a ball hitch. Consult your dealer or hitch shop for more information. Finally, lower the trailer until all the weight rests on the hitch of the truck, by raising the trailer's front jacks with the push of a button. Keep raising the jacks until they are fully retracted, then manually slide the jacks up the rest of the way (if necessary). Push the metal pins through the holes in the jacks up near the belly of the trailer so they don't slide out in transit. When disconnecting the two vehicles, be sure to lower the jacks to take the weight off the hitch and make it possible to drive the tow vehicle out from under the trailer. These jacks will support the trailer after the tow vehicle is removed.

Final Checklist

- ❑ Kingpin connected into hitch
- ❑ Locking pin in position
- ❑ Wiring connected
- ❑ Safety chains added (if desired)
- ❑ Braking, lights, and signals checked on trailer
- ❑ Break-away switch cable connected

Towing Behind a Motorhome

I've said all along that one of the advantages of a motorized RV is not having to worry about towing. Now I'm going to eat those words. The truth is, many motorhome owners discover that towing a separate car or small trailer (also known as a *toad*, auxiliary vehicle, or dinghy vehicle) behind their motorhome is very convenient, adding greater ease in getting around after their destination is reached. After all, it's certainly oodles easier commuting back and forth to town in a compact automobile than in a 40-foot motorhome. Take a day trip into a state park without worrying about narrow, winding roads or finding a suitable parking space. Leave the campsite for errands in a secondary vehicle without having to ready the motorhome; unhook the water, sewer, and electric; and pile the whole family onboard. Or just imagine the fun you could have taking along the four-wheelers or jet skis. The advantages are obvious and well worth the effort of mastering a few towing essentials.

RVOCABULARY

Toad is a slang term for the car or truck being "towed" (get it, towed or toad?) behind a motorhome. Another frequently used term for this type of secondary vehicle is a dinghy, as explained in Chapter 1.

What Can My Motorhome Tow?

Your motorhome has its very own tow rating, too. To find it, subtract the motorhome's GVWR from its GCVR (both found in the owner's manual or through the manufacturer). The difference is how much weight your motorhome can safely tow—easy, right? Easier still, the tow ratings might simply be listed separately, so no heady math is required. Choose a secondary vehicle that does not exceed that weight, and you're ready to roll—literally. Those pulling automobiles can learn the toad vehicle's weight from its owner's manual or by contacting the manufacturer. Don't forget to add the weight of the actual device used to transport the towed vehicle (for example, tow bar, dolly, or trailer). When choosing a toad, it makes sense to choose the lightest vehicle that will meet your needs. And remember, don't fill the toad vehicle with gear—this affects the motorhome's tow rating, too.

Towed Vehicles Come in Threes

There are three ways to tow a vehicle behind a motorhome, truck camper, or van camper. Again, a hitch is required—just as the conventional trailers previously mentioned. After all, something must connect the two vehicles, right? Your three basic options include tow bars, tow dollies, and trailers. A look at each attachment follows. The best option for you depends on the vehicle you want to tow, particularly if you already own said vehicle.

PULL OVER

Just as not all frogs become princes, not all vehicles make good toads. Always consult the owner's manual or contact the manufacturer concerning towing instructions and procedures for any vehicle you want to pull behind a motorhome. Although many vehicles can be pulled using any of the three methods described in this chapter, some cannot be towed using a tow bar, the method of choice among RVers.

Tow Bars

Tow bars connect a secondary vehicle to a motorhome while allowing the car or truck to be towed with all four wheels down. This is generally the most convenient option and gives a streamlined appearance. Tow bars are the most popular choice among RVers because they're easier to store and install than the much larger (and heavier) tow dollies or trailers; most models simply fold up when not in use. Tow bars are more expensive than tow dollies, however, and not all vehicles can be towed this way.

There are two types of tow bars—those that remain on the motorhome and those that are attached to the toad (towed vehicle). Although both have their advantages, most RVers prefer the type that remains with the motorhome when not in use, where it's less likely to be stolen. Instead of a ball couple, this type of tow bar utilizes a swivel, which is more secure and less likely to drag when driving over uneven surfaces.

Some manufacturers make vehicles that can be towed with all four wheels down (referred to as four-down); others can't be pulled in this matter. You may also discover that a certain model year gets the green light, whereas an older model does not. It's important to check with the manufacturer of any vehicle you're considering towing behind your motorhome, to find out whether it's rated to be towed with a tow bar. Towing a vehicle with a tow bar if it's not approved for this method can result in big-time damage to the toad's drive train, damage certainly not covered by the warranty. If the intended vehicle is not approved for towing with all four wheels down, it may still be possible to use a tow bar with the help of manufacturer-approved aftermarket products such as transmission uncouplers and lockout devices. Otherwise, a tow dolly or trailer is the answer.

Hooking up with a tow bar is pretty simple. Depending on the type you purchase, you must either align the bar with the motorhome's hitch ball by driving the car forward or line up the baseplate on the toad with the tow bar that is attached to the motorhome. It's simpler if you have a second person directing you while you maneuver the vehicle forward. However, this can be a frustrating process, and self-aligning tow bars are not known as "marriage-savers" for nothing. Many travelers find them well worth the money. They also make it easier for solo RVers to hook up. A wiring harness and safety cables must also be connected. After they're hooked up, set the ignition key of the car to the position recommended by the manufacturer of that vehicle, and put the car in neutral (or whatever setting is recommended in the owner's manual). There is so much difference between manufacturers from one year to the next that it's impossible to dispense specific advice here.

For many folks pulling a vehicle behind their motorhome, a tow bar is a lightweight and easy-to-use product to do the job.
(Courtesy of Roadmaster)

Tow Bar Checklist

❏ Towed vehicle connected to tow bar and motorhome

❏ Towed vehicle's steering and transmission set to tow

❏ Safety cables crossed and wrapped around legs of tow bar to keep them from dragging

❏ Wiring connected

❏ Running lights, turn signals, and auxiliary brake device working on vehicle

❏ Break-away switch cable connected

PULL OVER

Drivers must never attempt to back up the motorhome with a tow bar or tow dolly attached. Doing so could damage the entire set-up, including both vehicles. If you're in a jam, the best remedy is to disconnect the tow bar or dolly and move the towed vehicle separately *before* attempting a backup. Next time, remember to get out and walk it before you drive into a blind alley.

Tow Dolly

A tow dolly (such as the kind you rent from U-Haul) is designed to tow a vehicle with two wheels on the dolly and two wheels riding along the pavement. This option is less expensive than a tow bar and can be used with many different vehicles. No modifications are necessary to the toad, and the dolly may even come with its own braking system. Unfortunately, its size can be a burden, as many campsites lack the dimensions to accommodate a motorhome, a secondary vehicle, *and* a tow dolly. A dolly also adds more weight to your bottom line (GVCR), about 500 to 1,500 pounds' worth. You will have more maintenance, including two extra tires, and in some states, a tow dolly even needs to be licensed separately. As with the tow bar, never back up while a tow dolly is attached to the motorhome.

If you decide to tow with a tow dolly, a ball hitch must be installed to the motorhome. Hooking up with a tow dolly is a little more involved. First, it must be hitched to the motorhome. This can be done manually, by simply wrestling the dolly into position, to save having to back up the motorhome. Next, connect the wiring harness and safety chains between the two. Finally, drive the car up onto the dolly and secure it into position with straps designed for this purpose. Rear-wheel-drive vehicles can be loaded with the rear wheels on the dolly, front-wheel-drive vehicles with the front on the dolly. Set the towed vehicle in neutral, and you're ready to go. Again, always consult the towed vehicle manufacturer for safe towing practices, as they do vary.

Tow dollies are useful to transport vehicles not equipped to ride with all four wheels on the ground.
(Courtesy of Roadmaster)

Tow Dolly Checklist

❑ Coupler and hitch locked into position

❑ Towed vehicle secured into position, with correct axle on dolly

❑ Safety chains crossed under dolly tongue and attached to receiver or frame of motorhome

❑ Wiring connected

❑ Running lights, turn signals, brakes, and backup lights working on vehicle

❑ Break-away switch cable connected

Trailers

Very few motorhome owners choose the trailer option these days. They're now relegated to towing expensive vehicles (such as racecars or vintage autos) or hauling other cargo, such as jet skis, ATVs, motorcycles, or a small boat. In those situations, the extra cost and weight of a separate trailer might be practical. Generally, only the larger motorhomes are capable of handling this much weight. With a trailer, backing up without unhooking is possible, unlike the other two options.

Hooking up a trailer to your motorhome is just like hooking up most towables. Have someone help you back the motorhome into place, aligning the hitch to the coupler on the trailer's tongue. Connect wiring and safety chains before you depart.

Using a supplemental trailer to haul a towed vehicle is a reliable, albeit weighty, method of transport.
(Courtesy of Exiss Aluminum Trailers)

Trailer Checklist

- ❏ Coupler and hitch locked into position
- ❏ Towed vehicle secured on trailer
- ❏ Safety chains crossed under trailer tongue and attached to frame of motorhome
- ❏ Wiring, including break-away switch cable, connected
- ❏ Running lights, turn signals, and backup lights working on vehicle
- ❏ Electric brakes tested and adjusted

Wiring, Chains, and Brakes

As with all towables, proper wiring is a must. Again, this will be part of a professional installation at an RV service center or dealership. They'll do the hard part for you; all you have to do is plug it in. If using a tow bar, you can also use a detachable light bar if you don't want to alter the car's wiring, although this isn't as convenient and is more vulnerable to theft.

Safety chains or cables are also needed, regardless of which method of towing you use—tow bar, dolly, or separate trailer. Some tow bars have the wiring and safety cables inside the frame of the tow bar for a neater appearance.

And keep in mind that adding the extra weight of another vehicle makes your motorhome harder to stop. A secondary braking system is needed to compensate for this fact. If you're towing a trailer, it will generally have its own brakes, and many tow dollies feature independent brakes as well. A separate toad braking system, which activates the brakes in tandem with those in the motorhome's cockpit, is highly recommended for towing with a tow bar. It's required by law in most states, and the limit is as low as 1,000 pounds in a few places. Even though you may get away with not having an independent towed braking system, depending on where you travel and your luck (Irish, are you?), don't skimp in this area. Moreover, a break-away system that activates the brakes if the toad becomes disconnected from the motorhome is a very good idea.

Inspections

Get in the habit of checking your connections before you leave on a trip and periodically during the journey (such as during a rest area stop). A quick walk-around inspection, with special attention to the connections, lights, brakes, and safety chains, is time well spent.

The Least You Need to Know

- A tow vehicle can safely transport a trailer if its tow rating is more than the towable's gross vehicle weight rating. Otherwise, secure either a larger tow vehicle or a lighter trailer.
- A properly installed hitch facilitates the connection between the vehicle and trailer. Conventional trailers utilize either a bumper- or a frame-mounted hitch, with classes based on the weight of the load. Fifth-wheel trailers use a special hitch, mounted in the bed of the truck doing the towing.

- In addition to a suitable tow vehicle and hitch, towing situations mandate safety chains in case of a break-away and extra wiring to control the towed vehicle or trailer's brakes, turn signals, and brake and backup lights.
- Towing a vehicle behind a motorhome offers an easy way to commute back and forth from the campsite. This is accomplished through the use of a tow bar, a tow dolly, or a trailer.

Weight and Packing

In This Chapter

- Learning the importance of your RV's weight limits
- Knowing how and where to weigh your rig
- Implementing packing tips for both you and your RV

Americans are compulsive about their weight. Why did I eat that last slice of pizza? How long must I toil on the treadmill to burn off that chocolate chip cookie? Does my butt look big in these jeans? Fortunately, unlike the grapefruit diet you're on, this chapter delivers some amazing weight-loss tips (not for you, for your RV), as well as weigh-in strategies and the proper way to pack and load vehicles for proper balance and optimum driver control. The result is a leaner, meaner RV and a lifetime of safer transit.

A portly motorhome or towable is trouble on wheels. Like all vehicles, RVs have their limits as far as what they can and cannot safely transport. With new RVs boasting tons of clever storage compartments, enormous holding tanks, room for numerous passengers, and plenty of space for your spouse's drum set, becoming overloaded is almost a foregone conclusion for most newbies. At the very least, an overweight vehicle consistently underperforms, increases the likelihood of needing service and repairs, and might earn owners an expensive ticket from the local constable. Worse still, added pounds compromise the safety factor, something that can never be overstated.

ROAD SCHOLAR

Make the weigh-in the last step in the purchase of a new RV (whether towable or motorhome) before you sign the final papers. This ensures that your shiny new toy on the lot really does weigh what the sticker or brochure claims and helps you determine whether it allows you enough extra payload for your family and all your belongings.

Weighty Concerns

Understanding an RV's weight restrictions is very important for both novice and veteran RVers. Exceeding these ratings can be problematic for you and your family, not to mention others sharing the roadways with you. This added girth can cost you more in repairs and maintenance, because expensive components such as transmissions, brakes, and tires will wear out prematurely. The strain on the chassis, the very foundation of the vehicle, is also cause for concern. It will take a heavier motorhome or trailer-tow vehicle combination longer to stop and more muscle to maneuver, and will otherwise transform a once-roadworthy RV into a sluggish pile if you let it fatten up. Gas mileage suffers, too, costing you plenty of dollars over time.

Here are a few more reasons not to gamble on these weighty odds. In the event of an accident, an overloaded RV screams "liable" at the top of its lungs. A zealous insurance company can and will refuse coverage, warranties may be voided, and the fallout could spill over to a courtroom, costing you more than you ever imagined. Driving an overweight vehicle is also against the law, and for good reason: it's dangerous and easy to remedy. Have I made this point clear? Keep that vehicle underweight and out of trouble.

Does My Rig Look Fat?

In this case, it's not at all about looks, because your RV will have a tendency to wear its weight very well. Routine weigh-ins are the only real way to determine your RV's true weight. Weighing your rig is very important for safety (yours and everyone else's) and should not be neglected. Here's how.

Weight and See

So where does one weigh a recreational vehicle? The nearest certified scale is probably a lot closer than you think. The most likely place is a truck stop (most have scales) or possibly a grain elevator. Your RV dealer should know where the nearest scale is located. Two good sources for weigh stations are Pilot/Flying J Travel Plazas, as most are equipped to weigh trucks and RVs, and allstays.com, which has a listing of weigh station scale locations throughout Canada and the United States.

The beginning of a trip is probably the best time to belly up to the scale, when the volume of provisions (food, particularly), full fuel and fresh water tanks, and LP gas containers are at their greatest. New RVers are especially prone to overpacking. In addition, it's a good idea to weigh an RV regularly. In time, you'll begin to know what things can come along and what must stay behind—such as Grandma and her seven cats.

Tipping the Scales

None of us likes bellying up to the scale, as the results can be a bit dispiriting. But an RV has no such conscience. When you arrive at the scale, simply follow the signs. When prompted by the green light or voice commands, pull ahead very slowly until told to stop, either over the loudspeaker or by the light changing to red. You may have to ease ahead a short distance, because some scales are equipped to weigh your rig at different points to ensure that the weight is properly distributed.

Motorhome owners should learn their vehicle's total weight (separate from any towed vehicle), the weight of each axle (accomplished by pulling only the front or back wheels on the scale), and the weight of the vehicle they're towing (if applicable)—these measurements are performed separately. Those pulling a secondary vehicle definitely want a tally of the motorhome/dinghy vehicle combination as well. Trailer owners' work is similar. Start by weighing the loaded tow vehicle first. Pull the trailer onto the scale and weigh the entire tow vehicle/trailer combination together; then weigh just the trailer alone and, finally, each axle.

When indicated, drive off the scale and park your rig. Go back inside to get your printout and pay the fee (usually nominal, but money well spent). Now, how did you do? No idea what all those numbers mean? Let's take a closer look.

The Tale of the Tape

To start, find the total weight. You're looking for two things here: first, the total weight of each vehicle so you don't overshoot the individual weight limits of each, or the GVWR (see Chapter 13 if you're drawing a blank). Second, you want the combined weight of the towing combination, so as not to exceed the limitations of the vehicle doing the towing, better known as the GCWR (see Chapter 13 again). Compare these numbers with the manufacturer's recommendations. If the scale reports ratings less than the manufacturer's guidelines, you're in good shape. However, if it's greater than your vehicle's weight or towing limit, well, it's time to diet, which we discuss later in this chapter.

The printout should also reveal the various *axle weights*, the recommended limit that each axle can safely support. Compare these figures with your RV's axle recommendations (also known as gross axle weight, or GAW), found in the owner's manual or through the manufacturer. Too much, and you have to redistribute the weight (see how in the following section) inside the RV.

RVOCABULARY

The **axle weight,** also known as the gross axle weight or GAW, is the number of pounds each axle can safely support. Axle ratings are available through the manufacturer or listed in the owner's manual or in brochures. Proper weighing at a truck scale can detail the exact weight for each axle.

The Painful Truth

If these numbers are within the proper limits, you're ready to hit the road. But if not, you need to take out a few things—or redistribute them (in the case of inflated axle ratings). Sometimes you can be within the safe limits overall but overweight in one area, such as over the rear axle. If that's the case, you need to lighten the load in that area. In the case of extreme overloading, it's time for some serious soul searching. How did this happen? What stays and what goes? Take a deep breath. Let's start at the beginning ….

Leader of the Pack

A new RV, a wide-open itinerary, and the call of the open road. It's an exciting time, for sure. Don't let this euphoria corrupt the packing stage, as it always seems to doom bright-eyed first-timers. Overpacking is almost a foregone conclusion for the new RVer. You simply want to bring everything you can because, well, the RV looks big enough to handle it. Again, RVs have space and weight limits, and overzealous packing is the fastest way to exceed them. Modify behavior in the packing stage, and you shouldn't have problems later.

Knowing When to Say When

Let's be scientific about it. Just how much can an RV hold? Actually, someone's already done most of the work for you. The RV's *net carrying capacity* reflects the difference between what the RV actually weighs, or the unloaded vehicle weight (UVW), and the maximum it can safely hold, or the gross vehicle weight rating (GVWR). The net carrying capacity basically refers to the weight of any and all additional items—passengers, gear, fluids, and so on.

 RVOCABULARY

The **net carrying capacity** (a.k.a. NCC or payload) is how much cargo your vehicle can carry, determined by subtracting the RV's unloaded vehicle weight (UVW) from its maximum capacity (GVWR). This number includes passengers, provisions, full tanks, and the bloated cat. The smaller the number, the less you can bring. The larger the number … hey, you catch on fast.

Doing the Math Yourself

Although the NCC is usually common knowledge, most often listed in brochures and the owner's manual, let's double-check that figure. Take the RV to the truck scale and get the honest truth. First weigh the RV completely empty—no gear, empty tanks, and so on—to determine its UVW. Sure, this, too, is listed in your owner's manual, but as belabored in Chapter 13 and previous chapters, consider this rating an estimate. That original number might have ballooned somewhat from the assembly line to the dealer's lot, affected by every add-on and accessory item, including awnings, an extra air conditioner, and/or a slide-out room.

Next, subtract the UVW from the GVWR (a number that never changes, no matter what happens after the vehicle leaves the assembly line). Bingo, the net carrying capacity (NCC) is born. This number may be sizable or quite paltry. In any event, it's the total weight of passengers, their gear, and tanks full of fuel, fresh, black, and gray water. Write down this number—frame it if you like—as it serves as the absolute packing limit.

Here's a brief example of computing the net carrying capacity. Take a look at the equation—in this case, a typical 34-foot motorhome with two slide-out rooms:

GVWR – UVW = Net carrying capacity

20,500 pounds – 18,000 pounds = 2,500 pounds

In this case, you have 2,500 pounds to work with. Of course, it's a good idea not to push this number to the brink, in the event that you load up on supplies or extras along the way (such as those his-and-her Elvis busts from Graceland). Sure, 2,500 pounds sounds like more than enough weight, doesn't it? However, the example that follows should demonstrate just how quickly a typical family can devour that number.

You Weigh How Much?

With the net carrying capacity in hand, it's time to start loading up. Decisions, decisions. Should you bring along the saxophone? How about the holiday turkey with stuffing, cranberry sauce, and a nice pumpkin pie? How about the kids? Okay, let's bring 'em. I'm certainly not advocating putting every single item on the bathroom scale, but it's good to have at least some point of reference for what you're loading onboard. The following exercise should get you thinking about the cause-and-effect relationship of packing and overloading.

Passengers

Start with the weights of all passengers—and not that suspect number appearing on their driver's licenses, either. Use the *real* number.

Net Carrying Capacity for Your RV

Passengers	Weight
Husband	225 lb.
Wife	130 lb.
Child A	100 lb.
Uncle Frank	210 lb.
Family dog	60 lb.
Total	725 lb.

Holding Tanks

Next, add up all the fluids. What does a full tank of gas weigh? How about a fully loaded LP gas container(s) or the fresh water tank filled to capacity? These numbers adversely affect the net carrying capacity, too. Obviously, tank specs vary by the RV type (see Chapters 2 and 3 for typical specs). The following weight table should help you compute these numbers.

Weights of Various Fluids

Fluid	Weight
Water	8.4 lb. per gallon
Gasoline	6 lb. per gallon
Diesel	8 lb. per gallon
LP	4 lb. per gallon

In the case of a 34-foot motorhome, you can see how these full tanks add up.

Net Carrying Capacity of a Typical 34-Foot Motorhome

Fluid	Capacity	Weight
LP gas container(s)	60 gallons × 4	240 lb.
Fresh water system	50 gallons × 8.4	420 lb.
Gasoline	75 gallons × 6	450 lb.
Gray water holding tank*	50 gallons × 8.4	420 lb.
Black water holding tank*	50 gallons × 8.4	420 lb.
Total**		1,950 lb.

Because there's no reason to drive around with full wastewater tanks, subtract this number when applicable. In this scenario, you can easily subtract 840 pounds if you drive with empty tanks (based on the example above).

**Revised total: 1,110 pounds (with empty gray and black water tanks). Note: Total passenger weight is 725 pounds (based on our example).*

Gear

As you can see in the previous example, emptying the tanks really makes a big difference when estimating the weight of what you can pack into the RV.

After passengers (725 pounds) and the revised weight with empty wastewater tanks (1,110 pounds), that leaves 665 pounds for gear, or about 166 pounds per person (not including the pooch) until the RV reaches the bloated stage. This number includes all food, clothes, cooking supplies, plates and dishes, laptop computers, lawn chairs, fishing gear—basically, anything else added onboard. Keep these numbers in mind before your next trip.

Packing Up

Only you can say what you need on your trip. Of course, a lot depends on where you're going, what time of year, and for how long. You'll pack differently for a weekend a few miles away from home than for a two-month sabbatical through the Western states. Full-timers wrangle with different packing criteria than weekend warriors; larger families' things-to-bring list is different than a couple's.

So with grain of salt in hand, allow these recommendations to stimulate a little thought. Consider it the mother of all packing lists. Until you've nailed down your own list, go ahead and use this. And watch those weights!

Cooking

- ❏ Food and drink
- ❏ Skillet
- ❏ Spices and seasonings
- ❏ Oven mitt
- ❏ Silverware
- ❏ Can opener (manual)
- ❏ Plates and dishes
- ❏ Bottle opener
- ❏ Paper towels
- ❏ Baking dish
- ❏ Drinking cups
- ❏ Cooking utensils
- ❏ Cutting knife
- ❏ Recipes
- ❏ Matches
- ❏ Aluminum foil
- ❏ Tupperware
- ❏ Plastic bags
- ❏ Garbage bags
- ❏ Dishwashing detergent
- ❏ Cutting board
- ❏ Coffee maker or percolator
- ❏ Sponge
- ❏ Toaster
- ❏ Pots and pans
- ❏ Dish towels

Sleeping

- ❏ Pillows
- ❏ Blankets
- ❏ Sheets
- ❏ Alarm clock
- ❏ PJs
- ❏ Robe

Bathroom/Shower

- ❏ Towels
- ❏ Soap
- ❏ Shampoo
- ❏ Lotion
- ❏ Prescription medicines
- ❏ First-aid kit
- ❏ Sunscreen
- ❏ Aspirin
- ❏ Comb/brush
- ❏ Toothbrush
- ❏ Toothpaste
- ❏ Hair dryer
- ❏ Curling iron
- ❏ Deodorant
- ❏ Shaving gear
- ❏ Makeup
- ❏ Vitamins
- ❏ Toilet paper

Personal Effects

- ❏ Watch
- ❏ Cell phone
- ❏ Laptop
- ❏ Music
- ❏ Books
- ❏ Maps and GPS unit
- ❏ Cash
- ❏ Campground directory
- ❏ *The Complete Idiot's Guide to RVing, Third Edition* (shameless plug)
- ❏ Eyeglasses/contacts (with solution)
- ❏ Sunglasses
- ❏ Camera
- ❏ Pen and paper
- ❏ Proof of insurance
- ❏ Swiss army knife
- ❏ Pet supplies (leash, toys, bed)
- ❏ Envelopes and stamps
- ❏ Vehicle registration, proof of insurance, roadside assistance
- ❏ RV and appliance manuals
- ❏ Calling card

Clothing

- ❏ Hat
- ❏ Long underwear
- ❏ Rain gear
- ❏ Shoes (for inside and out)
- ❏ Underwear

continues

continued

- ❏ Jeans
- ❏ T-shirts
- ❏ Jacket
- ❏ Socks
- ❏ Belt
- ❏ Dress shirt
- ❏ Hangers
- ❏ Shorts
- ❏ Swimsuit
- ❏ Laundry bag
- ❏ Laundry detergent

Outside Stuff

- ❏ Golf clubs
- ❏ Fishing poles
- ❏ Lawn chairs
- ❏ Portable grill
- ❏ Charcoal
- ❏ Lighter fluid
- ❏ Cooking grate
- ❏ Bug spray
- ❏ Flashlight
- ❏ Emergency kit*
- ❏ Spare parts kit**
- ❏ Basic tool kit***
- ❏ Tablecloth
- ❏ Frisbee
- ❏ Flashlight
- ❏ Jumper cables

❑ Tire pressure gauge

❑ Two 25-foot electrical cords

❑ Two 25-foot fresh water hoses

❑ Sewer hose

❑ Cable for cable TV hook-up

❑ Hand soap

❑ Disposable rubber gloves

❑ Door mat or carpet swatch

❑ Chemicals for tanks

❑ Wheel chocks and leveling boards

❑ Cleaning supplies

❑ Mini-vacuum

An emergency kit is useful in the event of an accident. It should include flares, reflectors, pencil and paper, flashlight, and disposable camera for capturing the scene of an accident. Compile a list of names (doctor, insurance agent, lawyer) and any medications you're currently taking. Then hope there's never a need to open it.

**The spare parts kit should consist of the following items: an extra LP regulator; batteries for CO monitor, smoke alarm, LP gas detector; extra battery terminals; fuses; wire-splicing terminals; running/stop/marker bulbs; water pressure regulator; holding tank patch kit; and water hose repair kit.*

***A basic tool kit should consist of the following items: assorted Phillips and flathead screwdrivers; needle-nose, 8-inch groove joint, standard slip joint, and locking pliers; duct and electrical tape; socket set ($^3/_8$-inch drive); combination wrench set ($^1/_4$ to 1 inch); crescent wrenches (6 and 12 inches); tire gauge; flashlight; eye goggles; and polarity tester.*

Never forget any must-have items again by stocking the RV with its own supply of linens, dishes, nonperishable foods, and supplies. Avoid bringing valuable items that could get lost or dirty "out in the wild."

Common Pitfalls

Unfortunately, an RV can't lift weights, swim laps in a pool, or jump rope to shed unwanted pounds (a funny image, though). The only way to maintain its proper physique is to not overdo it in the first place. Too many of us take the home on wheels thing a little *too* seriously, treating our RVs like an endless reservoir for everything we could ever possibly want or need. Scrutinize packing lists and realize that a lot of little things *do* add up. Weigh the rig or trailer/tow vehicle periodically during the season to ensure that those numbers aren't creeping up, kind of like our waistlines over the holidays. When overpacking does occur, often one of the following is to blame.

Food Follies

How many canned goods does it take to affect an RV? How about endless cases of soda, an unusual attachment to canned hams, and a month's worth of meals? Now, we certainly don't want anybody to go hungry, but food is a popular overindulgence—both eating it and bringing too much along. First-timers especially seem fearful that their family might become stranded without their Eggos. Tote along only enough food for *this* trip; there's no reason to stockpile here. For shorter getaways, create a menu and buy only those items required. An RV galley isn't like the pantry at home—there isn't the space to keep a lot of provisions onboard "just in case." Think light when grocery shopping. Break down the trip into parts and do the shopping when the cupboards are bare and the natives get restless. It's not prudent to attempt one all-inclusive grocery trip for a lengthy vacation. Moreover, an abundance of cooking supplies will get you into trouble. Those space-hugging cookbooks will, too. Again, a weekly menu should help determine what cooking supplies you need and what will just be gathering dust by week's end.

ONE FOR THE ROAD

Drop needless pounds by substituting lighter items for heavier ones. Use paper plates and cups instead of weightier (and more fragile) traditional place settings. Try cans instead of bottles, fast-food–size condiments over bulky containers, single-serving packages instead of bulk goods, stainless steel or aluminum cookware over glass or cast iron. Remove excess packaging and favor dry goods, such as pasta and pancake mix. They keep well and are lighter than canned items.

Storage Pods and Nooks

Smaller RVs, where storage for a growing family is sometimes dicey, can certainly benefit from an extra storage pod, usually attached to the roof of the vehicle. More room, more stuff. Problem solved, right? Well, yes and no. Again, just because you have the space doesn't mean you should always go and fill it. Because pods are generally outside and out of the way, heavier items always make their way there. I don't need to tell you about the trouble with heavy items, do I? They're heavy! Going the pod route is perfectly fine; just keep tabs on what goes in here, and ask yourself just how important these items really are.

Child's Play

Squeezing their whole life into a suitcase is especially traumatic for kids. It starts off innocently enough. Yes, you can bring Mr. Snuffles. Sure, Frankie the Bee can come, too. A library of favorite books riding shotgun is instant poundage. Teenagers, with bulkier gear, may be especially hard to deprogram. Make ground rules known in advance. Start with one bag or allotted compartment onboard per person and see how that works. Remember, the early days of your RV life are a work-in-progress. You may look back and laugh about your former packrat mentality.

The Loading Zone

Yes, there's a right way and a wrong way to load an RV. Too much weight on one side, and your motorhome or trailer might begin to lean like Adam Richman (you know, of *Man V. Food* fame). Too much weight in the rear, and the rear axles might complain or, worse, exceed their ratings. Meanwhile, a proper *hitch weight* is important to keep towables level while reinforcing the connection between the two vehicles. Furthermore, proper placement of gear eliminates breakage and that frantic search for the corkscrew come vino time. A properly loaded RV is more stable and handles better. Gauge hitch weight by lowering just the tongue portion onto a truck scale. A bathroom scale often works here for some lightweight towables.

> **RVOCABULARY**
>
> The **hitch weight,** also known as tongue weight, is a rating specified by towable manufacturers to aid in ride stability. Generally, 10 to 15 percent of the RV's total weight should be placed near the tongue of the trailer to reinforce the hitch connection. Fifth-wheels usually ask for 15 to 20 percent to be placed in the gooseneck portion.

Even Steven

Towable owners should review the hitch weight (found in the usual channels—in the owner's manual or the brochure, or by contacting the manufacturer directly). Distributing approximately 10 to 15 percent of the trailer's GVWR to the front of the trailer is the best thing for the tongue and hitch connection. Fifth-wheel owners should bump that number up to 15 to 20 percent. Too little weight here, and expect a little fishtailing; too much, and the added weight may buckle the hook-up.

Axles, too, have special needs. Don't overload one or the other. You'll notice that the rear axle weight recommendations are usually heavier than the frontal counterparts for most motorhomes. Follow these instructions by placing more gear aft, which lends greater stability to your ride. Most excess tongue-weight issues arise when some RVer decides he wants to bolt a generator onto the "A" frame of the trailer, mount a 27-drawer toolbox up there, or carry three dirt bikes on the rear of the tow vehicle.

> **ROAD SCHOLAR**
>
> Minimize movement and possible breakage of fragile items by wrapping them up during transit. Sheets, pillows, blankets, and coats make terrific buffers around delicate objects to avoid scratches, dings, and impromptu tumbling demonstrations. Place cardboard sleeves between glassware. Add nonskid material to shelves to keep things from sliding.

Double-Duty

The more items that can do double-duty, the better off you are and the more room you'll have left over. A wastebasket doubles as a bucket come cleaning day. A set of stackable drawers also serves as an end table. Agree on one brand of shampoo for everyone to avoid cluttering the shower. Leave the CD/DVD cases at home and store just the CDs/DVDs in a small case. Use decorative pillowcases to store extra blankets or even clothing when they are not in use. Always be on the lookout for innovative, space-saving products for your RV—such as folding dish racks or coffee tables with surfaces that raise up when needed.

The Least You Need to Know

- Exceeding an RV's weight limits leads to sluggish performance, poor stopping and acceleration, unnecessary wear and tear, added maintenance, and generally a dangerous situation for you and fellow travelers. It's also against the law.

- Determine your vehicle's true weight at weigh stations, and compare it against the manufacturer's recommendations. Scales provide key information such as the total weight and axle weight. Too much weight, and it's time to diet.

- Disciplined packing is the best counter to an overloaded vehicle. Passengers and holding tanks comprise the majority of cargo weight onboard. Knowing what these things weigh should keep you and your rig out of trouble.

- A balanced RV performs better and creates a more stable ride. Distribute cargo evenly side to side to prevent leaning; add a little more weight in back than in the front. Towable owners should settle 10 to 15 percent of the weight near the front to support the hitch connection.

Drive Time

In This Chapter

- Learning the ins and outs of RV driving
- Avoiding common driving errors
- Having the accessories to make driving easier

As explained throughout this book, operating an RV is different, not difficult. Those who have never found themselves behind the wheel of a large motorhome or towing even the smallest trailer should expect a brief apprenticeship of sorts in the cockpit. Backing up, motoring around town, pulling into campgrounds, traversing steep grades, and handling highway driving are all obviously not as effortless as manhandling the family Honda. However, with a little practice and experience, it won't be long before it's second nature—or first nature, depending on how seriously you pursue the RV lifestyle. Hopefully, this chapter aids in that goal as well.

The Only Thing to Fear ...

Novice RVers might be somewhat daunted by driving or towing an RV at first. A little apprehension is totally natural, but with enough practice, this should fade over time. The key is to relax. With every new skill comes some doubts. Realize, too, that even veteran RVers occasionally jump a curb, drive too fast for their own good, or fail to back into the campsite in one flawless motion. RVs are much easier to operate than you think. Adjust your mirrors and fasten your seat belts. It's time to learn how to drive.

Getting Started

Whether you're towing a fold-down camper or piloting a mammoth diesel pusher, the basic principles of safe driving still apply. None of the unique characteristics of an RV (increased height, weight, length) adversely affect the way we drive—they just require some adjustments. The biggest difference is to allow more time and distance for stopping and accelerating and more room when turning corners and changing lanes. Hills are a bit more of a challenge—both going up and coming down—because of the added weight. Keep your eyes on the road ahead and try to anticipate the need to stop, slow down, or turn. And always allow a little extra time for any maneuver. You're not in the Corvette, remember.

Take a Brake

Every RV must be driven differently—motorized and towables need to allow more time to brake than any other vehicle you've ever driven. It won't take long to determine how your vehicle stops at different speeds. It will probably take you, oh, I'd say roughly 10 seconds to learn that you're at the command of a pretty big ship. Why do you think they call the driving area the cockpit, after all? Different size loads affect stopping power, too. Coming to a complete stop takes longer with a rig full of passengers and cargo than when transporting a fairly empty unit. Anticipation is the key, but you probably have these instincts well forged from years of driving. Upcoming brake lights, construction, curves and bends, congestion, and so on are all clear signs to begin to slow down.

As discussed in detail in the previous chapter, it is highly recommended that all towables and towed vehicles feature a braking system of their own. You can never have too much stopping power at your disposal. Each kind of towable should have its own independent stopping force. Such braking controls are wired through the tow vehicle and activated at the touch of the brake pad within the cockpit. An additional hand control (brake controller) near the steering wheel is sometimes offered for those who prefer to control things that way.

The largest motorhomes can usually benefit from a secondary braking system in the form of a hydraulic or exhaust brake. Also a popular add-on to tow vehicles hauling larger trailers, an exhaust braking system (or engine braking system) is a big help, especially when staring a deep descent square in the face. They come in real handy when going down hills, helping you to slow down without overtaxing the vehicle's brakes. Primary brakes can overheat and fail on long descents, so it's important not to overuse them. If you can actually smell your brakes working, they're getting overused.

PULL OVER

We've all heard stories about jackknifed trailers. When the smoke clears, the culprit is usually hard braking, in which the tow vehicle stops and the trailer keeps going. Inclement conditions also share the blame. Avoiding this kind of calamity is just another in the long line of reasons why we wire the trailer's or towed vehicle's brakes to those of the lead vehicle's.

Cornering

When cornering, remember to swing wide. The longer the RV, the farther out you need to go to ensure that everything goes where it's supposed to. Seeing how many curbs you can run over isn't the goal here. Ever notice how semi drivers do this? Your RV probably isn't that long, but the principle is the same. Take it wide and slow. Remember, as you turn, your back end will swing out somewhat in the opposite direction. Trailer owners should think about where the towable is headed as they turn—but watch where the front of the tow vehicle is going, too. For motorhomers towing a car, be sure to compensate for the added footage.

Changing Lanes

Allow more time for lane changes. A motorhome requires more room to complete this move than, say, a Toyota Camry. Although you needn't plan a maneuver like a D-Day invasion, a little forethought always pays off. Check the side mirrors for a nice, wide opening. Signal well ahead of time, look in the mirrors again to make sure you have plenty of room, and move on over. Generally, I find other drivers on the road to be quite courteous—either that, or they're terrified of me.

Steep Grades

The extra weight of an RV means more power is required to get you to the top. Anticipate hills and accelerate a bit before you get there. On longer climbs, it is advisable (and courteous) to pull into the far right lane, allowing faster traffic to pass. Don't worry—you'll have plenty of company in the slow lane, such as the big trucks and fellow RVers. Try to use your brakes as little as possible, as they can become hot on long descents. Use the trailer brakes or toad brakes (if pulling a car) instead of the tow vehicle or motorhome brakes, when possible. (See Chapter 13 on towing for more on braking systems.) Downshift in lieu of hard braking. As mentioned, with very heavy RVs, an engine brake can be a real asset.

Park It

Remember the song "Don't Fence Me In"? It most definitely applies when docking the rig. Leave yourself plenty of room to get out, especially with a bigger trailer or motorhome. RVers should forget about getting that parking space close to the main entrance. Concentrate instead on finding a place with plenty of room around you, preferably at the far edge of the parking lot, where you're out of the way. Besides, the extra walking will do you good. When it comes to parking the RV at the grocery store or roadside attraction, think like James Bond and plan your escape ahead of time. Avoid getting into tight spots, forcing an unnecessary backup to free yourself.

Although very doable, backing up is still best avoided whenever possible. Opt for pull-through campsites at RV parks, especially when toting a larger rig or if you are uncomfortable with life in reverse. Travel centers and truck stops are much more convenient for filling up because they're built for larger and longer vehicles. Designed for drive-through traffic, these stopovers are close to highways and enable RVers to fuel up, park, eat lunch, and then leave, all by driving forward. Presto! No backing up required.

Clearance

Knowing your RV's exterior height keeps you out of trouble. Avoid any situations that might call this into question, such as a low overpass, a parking garage, or the sheltered top of a gas station. Your vehicle's exterior height should be listed in the owner's manual or brochures, or is available through the manufacturer. Be sure to factor in the added height of any extra items, such as rooftop air conditioners, storage pods, and antennas. Measure yourself from the ground to the RV's highest point if you're unsure. Always lower the TV antenna before departing, a forgotten act that has left more than a few owners pondering its sudden disappearance during the trip.

ROAD SCHOLAR

Here's a great tip courtesy of veteran RV writers Joe and Vicki Kieva. Write down the RV's exterior height on an index card and attach it to the sun visor. This way, you'll never forget it and can circumvent any chance encounters with low overheads, such as those found at gas stations. It's a good idea also to include the vehicle's GVWR, giving you a number to shoot for during weigh-ins.

What's the Rush?

The cutthroat world of rush-hour traffic can quickly sap the thrill of the open road out of even the most exuberant traveler. Passing through a metropolitan area during the teeth of the daily commute is just begging for a wheel-gripping, fist-shaking situation. The best way to handle such bumper-to-bumper bonding is to skip it altogether. Awake early or leave late in the day to avoid times of gridlock. If there's no way around a congested area, take Goldilocks's approach when choosing a lane: the fast lane is too fast, the slow lane too unpredictable. Pick the middle lane and stay with it. Relax, accept it, watch for sudden stops, give the vehicle in front plenty of room, and take advice from your co-pilot. Leave the chronic lane-jumping for the guy in the Porsche. If things become unbearable, hit the off-ramp, find a spot at a travel plaza or parking lot, and play a game of Go Fish.

Backing Up

The best rule is to avoid backing up whenever possible. However, it's not always possible when the kids freak out after passing the Dairy Queen on the corner. The biggest mistake people make when attempting to back up an RV is being in a hurry. Take your time and don't let anyone rush you. If people are watching, ignore them (well, unless they're screaming and waving fire extinguishers). Motorhomes pulling vehicles connected to tow bars and tow dollies should never, ever attempt a back up—you will damage the connection. If there's no other way around it, unhook the towed vehicle first and scoot it out of the way. You can back up when towing a vehicle on a trailer, but it's more difficult to see behind the motorhome, particularly if you don't have a rearview monitoring system. Travelers towing travel trailers, fifth-wheels, or fold-down campers can back up without harming the towing connection.

Before you attempt to back up, get out of the vehicle and assess the situation. Sometimes you may not be able to tell for sure whether you are able to drive through or are forced to back out unless you get out and survey the scene. Better yet, wake up the co-pilot to help. If someone is there to help guide you back, discuss where you want the RV to end up beforehand. Note any vehicles, mailboxes, or other obstacles you want to avoid. And don't forget to look up—there might be overhead wires or tree branches best left unprovoked. Look for any landmarks— or make one, such as a stick or mark in the gravel—so you know to stop when the object lines up with your wheels. This is especially helpful when backing into an RV site where you want to align the hook-ups with the corresponding points on the RV.

Get back in the driver's seat and put it in reverse. Use your side mirrors religiously. (Remember, the rearview mirror will probably be either blocked or nonexistent.) Lower the windows to hear prompts from anyone helping you back in. Back up very slowly, using small, quick turns of the steering wheel as necessary. Towable owners should focus on where the back of the trailer is going rather than the movements of the tow vehicle. Don't hesitate to stop, get out, and walk back to check if things get goofy. If you get too far off course, just pull forward and try again.

ROAD SCHOLAR

The trickiest part of backing up a trailer is remembering to turn the steering wheel in the opposite direction of where you want the trailer to go. Place one hand on the bottom of the wheel and then move your hand in the direction where you want the trailer to end up. If the trailer starts to veer to one side, turn the steering wheel toward the problem to straighten it out again.

It Takes Two

Backing up is like life. It's a whole lot easier with someone to guide you. (Are we sharing a Hallmark moment?) Screaming, gesturing wildly, and jumping up and down are not particularly helpful to the driver, but this does make for a popular sideshow. It helps to open the front windows. It's also important that the person guiding you back understand exactly where to stand to stay within the driver's sight. If you can't see the guider in the side mirror, he most definitely can't see you. Communicating via a pair of handheld radios is a great assist.

Practice, Practice, Practice

Like any new skill, RV driving must be practiced. Remember all those y-turns you did in the driveway when you were getting ready to get your driver's license? Practice, practice, practice. Before hitting the road, drive the RV around town to improve your skills and increase your confidence. Set up some cones in an empty parking lot and work on accelerating, turning, slowing down, stopping, backing up, and parking. (Don't worry—RVers aren't expected to know how to parallel park.) Notice how much longer it takes you to stop with the added weight behind you and how much wider you need to swing around corners. Work at that backing-up technique until you get the hang of it. It's much easier to perfect this in private than at a campground full of onlookers.

Class Act

Practice makes perfect, but a little instruction along the way doesn't hurt. Although still rare, a few RV dealers take pains to make sure customers know how to operate their new purchase before taking delivery. Take advantage of any driving classes and seminars offered, whether found at a dealership, an RV show, or other types of get-togethers. Driving schools are also a good bet, offering practical and behind-the-wheel instruction, usually in your very own rig. The advantages of certified RV instruction are many. For starters, attendees learn the ins and outs of driving and towing, taught by veteran RVers and professional drivers. The best situation is actual behind-the-wheel instruction in your very own RV with an able teacher there to guide you. Some RV insurers provide discounts for suitable coursework or graduation from an accredited class or school, saving you a few bucks over the lifetime of a policy.

Fillin' Up

I find travel plazas and truck stops along the highway are the best places to fill up. Drivers can count on plenty of room to maneuver, lofty clearances, and a fresh supply of diesel, a concern addressed back in Chapter 4. Of course, no one's limited to just these places to fill 'er up—most anyplace will do.

Fuel costs are among the greatest threats to an RVer's pocketbook. Don't expect more than 20 miles per gallon, no matter what you're driving or towing; a large motorhome easily sinks under 10 mpg. Face it, you're operating a gas-guzzler, and there's not much you can do about it. However, by keeping weights low, the RV will reward you with a little better fuel economy. Join a travel club or gas chain offering discounts on fill-ups, such as the Flying J Travel Plazas. Even a 10¢ discount per gallon shines brightly when topping off a 100-gallon tank. And it's most definitely true that traveling 55 mph is more economical than taking a high-speed odyssey across the country. Steady speeds and highway miles are recommended. And a friendly reminder for diesel motorhome owners: your rig takes diesel, not gas. Big difference, so don't forget.

PULL OVER

Favor gas stations that offer enough room to maneuver, particularly when operating a large RV. Keep an eye on clearances and avoid getting yourself into a tricky driving situation at smaller facilities. Make doubly sure no LP appliances are in use, pilot lights are extinguished, and propane containers are shut off before you pull in.

Must-Have Gear

Assuming there's any money left after the big purchase, a few extra accessories are recommended to make driving a tad easier. Investing in a larger and wider side view mirror offers more than peace of mind; it provides accurate images of what's going on around you. To find out what's going on around your route, some RV GPS systems include points of interest, national and state parks, and private campground information. Using an RV GPS just makes driving any size rig easier. If for no other reason than late night back-ins, the addition of a rear-mounted camera and cockpit monitor is also a solid idea. (Specific gear to make the towable owner's life easier is listed in Chapter 13.)

Side Mirrors

Invest in a pair of extra-wide side mirrors, providing elongated views of the sides and back of the coach or towable. Because the rearview mirror is absent or rendered useless by obstructed views, side mirrors are your lifeline to what's going on behind you. True, all vehicles come with *some* sort of side mirror, but opt for larger, extendable versions found throughout the aftermarket to create bigger, broader sight lines. Having cracked my fair share of extended side mirrors, try to remember to retract them when not in use. Good luck with that.

GPS/Navigation Systems

Because getting lost is that much more traumatic in a large vehicle, many owners need little rationalizing to drop some money on a Global Positioning System (GPS) or other navigational aid. Believe me, you won't miss all those trip-saving U-turns and quick jaunts off the interstate to get directions. There's a full range of products available, all designed to get you where you're going. But it would be considered a dereliction of duty here if I didn't mention my preference for the RV GPS by Rand McNally. Specifically made for RVers and campers, this GPS highlights RV campgrounds, RV dealers and service centers, rest areas, and travel centers. It includes 14 million points of interest, including national and state parks and fun festivals. It even has recommended side trips complete with videos and photos. Best of all, it shows RV-friendly routes, and the 5-inch- or 7-inch-wide screen makes it easy to read. Of course, for the purist in you, nothing beats a road atlas. Rand McNally makes a pretty good one of those, too. Put both on the RVer's gift list.

Rearview Monitoring System

A rear-mounted camera and cockpit monitor take much of the guesswork out of backing up. Although far from essential, such devices are very helpful, particularly if you're backing up alone. It's also a nice way to learn what's going on behind your vehicle when you hear a bump in the night. Consider it an eye in the sky, if you will. Such systems consist of a camera and perhaps a microphone mounted on the rear of the vehicle. The view from the rear is displayed on a monitor inside near the driver's seat, so you can literally watch where you're going as you back up. These devices aren't substitutes for getting out and checking out the scene first. (They may not reveal low-hanging branches or pieces of broken glass.) Find a camera that works at night for late-night back-ins.

The Least You Need to Know

- Driving or towing an RV is different, not difficult. Respect your weight, height, and width, realizing that stopping, cornering, and accelerating demand more time and patience than with your vehicle at home.
- Practicing is the only way to refine your RV driving skills. Be sure to give added attention to key maneuvers such as backing up, switching lanes, highway driving, and motoring through congested areas.
- A number of products (both dealer-installed and aftermarket) make driving easier, including side mirrors, navigational aids, and a rearview camera and cockpit monitor.

Hit the Road

Life on the road is what you make of it. The reason is that—say it with me one more time—RVing is all about choices. And finally, you're ready. But still, questions may linger—for example, what about traveling to Canada and Mexico? Those traveling with pets, small children, or large crews should also give the following pages a peek for a look at the best ways to cater to your specific group.

I also offer troubleshooting tips to keep your RV running smoothly and life in the campground peaceful. Read on to find out the best places to stay and how to set up and break down camp—with a bit of campground etiquette thrown in. Ever wonder what a boondock is? I highlight the how, why, and where of boondocking, which is camping all by your lonesome. Not to worry—I'll help you through it.

Travel Planning

In This Chapter

- Traveling with kids and pets
- Knowing the ins and outs of RV rallies and caravans
- Learning the steps for international RVing
- Deciding whether full-timing is for you

There are many different ways to enjoy RVing. A month-long tour of national parks or a jaunt through Mexico might just be the thing to get your motor running. Some full-timers appreciate the benefits of being able to visit family wherever they live and for as long they can stand, even if that's just a weekend. If you have several members in the family who like hitting the open road together, RVing might just be your only viable option.

Such diversity calls attention to different needs while on the road. Life as a full-timer is decidedly unique when compared to that of a weekend traveler—the RV is now their home, after all. RVing to foreign countries requires a different level of preparation than, say, a jaunt to Mount Rushmore; signing on for an RV caravan, club, or rally dictates new realties as opposed to life as a loner. So many lifestyles, so little time. Fortunately, you've come to the right place.

All in the Family

Sure, that last car vacation with the kids got a little tense at times. It took only a thousand or so cries of "Are we there yet?" to drive you stark-raving mad and vow to never do it again. You may figure a better vacation answer might be to hop the fastest jet airplane you can find and pray for strong tailwinds. Before you book a seat next to the toothbrush salesman from Toledo, imagine the family vacation from the kids' perspective. Crammed in the backseat for hour after eternal hour, one child on top of the other like a Dagwood sandwich, uncomfortable, hot, thirsty, hungry, and bored, wanting attention. However, consider a recreational vehicle the great equalizer for hyperactive passengers. Kids love them because, well, they're pretty cool and probably not like anything they've ever seen before. If you plan it right, everyone should have his own space, bed, and storage for toys, books, and games to turn those frowns upside down. Mealtime is easily accomplished without a stampede to the roadside fast-food joint; a cold drink is always nearby and the gang can melt the miles watching movies or playing video games.

Here are a few more considerations to turn brooding youngsters into happy campers on the next big trip.

ROAD SCHOLAR

The very first family RV trip should be like Shirley Temple: short and sweet. Although the RV has a lot of creature comforts, a cross-country trip might be too much. An extended weekend is a good start, somewhere within a few hours from home. Remember, your kids need to be sold on the RV experience, too, so don't make their first memories those of endless driving. Increase the distance from home and length of stay slowly over time.

Getting Them Situated

There's nothing like settling arguments over who gets to sit where. Render the wrong verdict, and you'll be surprised at how long a kid can hold a grudge. RVs and tow vehicles equipped with air bags shape some of these decisions for you—no kids under 12 in the front seats. The potential bag deployment is simply too powerful for youngsters up front. As for divvying up the rest of the RV or tow vehicle? Well, that's a tad trickier. Alternate first-round picks, kind of like an NBA draft, so everyone gets a chance to be top dog. Otherwise, assign seats and be done with it. Fortunately, for those motorized owners, most of the seats are pretty comfortable and offer plenty of room to avoid hundreds of miles of kicking, hair-pulling, and drawing on their baby brother with a felt-tip pen. Regardless of where the kids sit, remember to enforce the number one rule: seat belts must be worn at all times.

Sleeping arrangements may not be as democratic, depending on the available space. To avoid a logistical situation not seen since the Marines stormed the beaches at Normandy, keep bed-swapping to a minimum. Because the whole brood is now sharing one enclosed area, reflect on the decision of who goes where before assigning bunks. The cab-over bed found in Class C motorhomes might not be appropriate for some kids, because managing the ascent can be tricky. Find a spot for infants guaranteeing the most privacy, most likely with you in the master bedroom. Sequester those who awaken early in the morning away from the late sleepers.

Watching the Mood

Long trips can be hard on everyone, even in an RV. The latent anticipation coupled with the constant confusion over how much farther is doubly hard for kids. If the mood inside turns ugly, take a break. As one RVer put it, "If Junior ain't happy, ain't nobody happy." After extended driving periods, pull off to a rest stop and share a picnic. A little fresh air will do everyone some good, especially if the dog needs a bio-break. Fifteen minutes throwing the Frisbee or taking a quick hike won't affect the E.T.A. too much, and it gives everyone renewed energy. Keep tabs on everyone's comfort level onboard. In larger RVs, the temperature in the rear is often dramatically different than in the cockpit. Set temperature gauges accordingly, and run the air conditioner if necessary. The dashboard A/C is rarely good enough to cool down those in back of a larger motorhome on a hot day.

Rules of the Road

As family-friendly as it is, an RV still has many of the same potential dangers of home. The easiest and most high-strung response is to prohibit children from touching anything. A better alternative is to explain how things work—that the refrigerator is like the one at home, the stove and burners do indeed get hot, and the bathroom operates to keep water works to a minimum. Deep entryway stairwells bear watching as kids come and go, and doors can be difficult to open and shut for smaller folks. Assist with bed conversions to avoid pinching fingers, and under no circumstances are children allowed up from their seats while the vehicle is in motion.

PULL OVER

Take special caution with platform steps in the entryway, used to help minimize the distance between the RV and the ground. A handrail is a good idea, too. Remember to lower manually deployed steps upon arrival to prevent falls. Electric models should deploy whenever the door opens and retract when closed. Watch out for shins, sometimes bruised if standing too close to the entry door. Carry (and use) a sturdy but small step stool to bridge the gap from the bottom step to the ground, if needed.

On Being Pet-Friendly

We love our pets dearly, but the rest of the world isn't always so pet-friendly, which is why RVing is such a great compromise. A bed, food and water bowls, and a toy or two are all that's needed to turn a furry friend into an exuberant (albeit slightly drooly) co-pilot. Planes stick anything but the smaller breeds of dogs in the cargo hold; hotels frown on pets like a Hell's Angels convention. And you know how a couple kids and a cat or two in the car for eight hours goes—a tad feisty, for sure. Heck, your pets might just be one of the main reasons you took up RVing in the first place. For the purposes of this chapter, pets are limited to dogs and cats, but in many cases, this advice is prudent for any animal.

Traveling with the Pack

Fortunately, our pets aren't nearly as materialistic as we are, so you won't go bonkers packing their things. A food and water bowl, a leash, a few toys, a bed, and an adequate supply of chow are almost all they require—oh, and their usual 18 hours of beauty rest. Don't forget plastic bags for poop pick-up. Also, you might talk with your vet about your travel plans, in case any vaccinations are recommended. Keep collars on animals at all times, with your home address and phone number in case they get lost. Also consider microchipping your pet to ensure its safe recovery in case you become separated.

It's a good idea to spend a few days helping pets acclimate to their new RV surroundings prior to the big trip. Let them get accustomed to the sights and smells for a couple hours inside each night as you read a book or pack the RV. Cats are notoriously slow for getting their bearings in a new space, so be patient with them. Add a litter box, a bed, and a few new toys to make the transition easier.

A few sniffs is all it takes most dogs to get up to speed. Make life onboard as similar to home life as possible. If they sleep in a crate or carrier, have one onboard. If they have a favorite blanket to cuddle up on, make sure that's available for a little extra security. It might help to even feed them inside the vehicle a couple nights before you leave to set up a routine.

Creature Comforts

Once in the swing of things, most pets have few complaints with their roving bed, with the exception of maybe your being a little tight with that extra cookie or wad of catnip. The biggest concerns for them are adequate hydration and general comfort. A few water bowls on the market stay full without sloshing onto the floor of an ever-shaking vehicle. Make sure that the bowl stays full and that there's plenty of circulating air to keep animals cool. Those fur coats get hot—and remember, animals tend to get overheated when they're excited.

ROAD SCHOLAR

Pets can get carsick just as some travel-intolerant humans do. As a rule, it's best not to feed them immediately before a long drive. Overfeeding and frequent cookie breaks only worsen matters. As they get more roadworthy, pets should settle down. Taking frequent breaks with plenty of fresh air should help, too. See your veterinarian for medication to ease their queasiness if problems persist.

Keep this in mind when parked, too. There's a reason dogs break out the ole puppy-dog eyes trick whenever you leave them—they don't like it. Given their druthers, they'd much rather socialize with you than that squeaky toy that looks like a miniature mailman. Cats aren't likely to get too worked up, but leaving any animal alone in the RV for any length of time can be problematic. The best thing to do is to take the animals with you. However, if you can't, take steps to keep them safe and comfortable. Temperature is the first thing to consider. Even on mild days, make sure windows and vents are open. Warmer temperatures require air-conditioning. A word of warning: dogs get overheated quickly. Just because you don't think it's too warm doesn't mean your animal agrees. Be sure to leave out plenty of water and toys as well. Keep time spent away to a minimum. Again, those with busy itineraries outside of camp should consider boarding their animals instead. If you board your pet, be prepared to show that all shots, licenses, and vaccines are current. Think before bringing your pets on your RV vacation.

There are plenty of places they're allowed, but still plenty of places they're not allowed, or allowed with restrictions.

Campground Behavior

Dogs and cats are welcome at most public and private campgrounds. However, always call ahead and double-check before you make a reservation. Some owners are wary of certain breeds, such as pit bulls, while others might prohibit animals exceeding a certain weight. It's not unusual for pet owners to be assessed an extra fee for the privilege, usually $1 or $2 more a night. Nearly everyone admits cats, although they, too, may be subject to additional costs.

The fastest way to turn Mr. and Mrs. Campground Owner against animals is to violate their rules. Most are adamant about not leaving dogs unattended, so where you go, so does your pooch. This is for the animal's protection (see the following section), as well as to cut down on the inevitable barking that seems to accompany a lonely dog. Leash policies are another big one. Truth is, not everyone likes animals (cute or not), which is why the leash rule is enforced just about everyplace you go. Furthermore, a cavalier response to picking up after your pets all but guarantees campgrounds won't be so pet-friendly in the future.

ROAD SCHOLAR

Here are a few extra items to consider for pets. Medicine to ward off fleas and ticks is a good idea. Make sure pets wear a collar with identification and a home or cell number at all times, in case they get lost. Proof of rabies vaccination is worth toting along, as you might be asked to show it from time to time. This could come into play when visiting other countries, such as Mexico and Canada. Again, consider microchipping your pet in case of separation.

The Group Mentality

Although goin' solo is common among the RV community, many travelers find comfort and solidarity in the group setting. RV clubs are extremely popular for novices and experienced journeymen alike. Memberships can open up a world of regular outings, insightful publications, a network of affiliated campgrounds and resorts, and tremendous group buying power, with discounts on everything from insurance to mail-forwarding services to roadside assistance for its members.

The Good Sam Club, for example, boasts a membership base of more than one million members. Other group benefits are more specific, such as Coast to Coast, which offers a network of membership campgrounds. Camping World's President's Club treats members to heavily discounted camping and RV supplies, while the Family Motor Coaching Association (FMCA) was created and run for motorhome owners only. Chances are good that there's a local RV chapter near you. See Appendix A for a list of clubs.

Whether big or small, local or national, enrollment in one or more RV clubs is a great idea, especially for beginners. You should never pass up an opportunity to learn from experienced travelers, and the discounts alone can easily eclipse the annual dues. Of course, it's the intangibles that seem most worth it—making friends, sharing tips and resources, and uniting in a similar RV passion.

Rally Ho

Most clubs feature regional or nationwide events, or rallies, giving the various state and local chapters a few days to meet and mingle. Activities such as these invoke the rare opportunity to share ideas, experiences, and practical know-how not always found in the pages of your favorite publication, book, or website. And they can be plenty fun, too. Rallygoers represent different lifestyles and backgrounds, but all are united in their affection for RVing and the desire to improve their pastime. For some, rallies are the best and most anticipated reason to join an RV club.

If you've never attended such an event, you're missing out on a memorable experience. Just imagine hundreds or thousands of RVers camped out for a week's worth of bonding and fellowship. Food, entertainment, bathrooms, dump service, plenty of campfire chatter—and, of course, a spot to spend the night (with or without hook-ups)—are usually included in entry costs. You can also probably count on a few seminars, led by industry experts and lifestyle mavens, to help you get the most out of all your adventures. Exhibitors are sometimes on hand to showcase the latest products, ranging from the newest $300,000 diesel pusher to that $2 item that might prove indispensable onboard your rig. Hopefully, everyone departs a little wiser and thankful that they made the decision to buy an RV in the first place.

Check out the Good Sam extravaganza rallies for 2012 (http://therally.com). RV publications such as *Motor Home, Trailer Life*, and *Woodall's* also list rallies, and you can find some great websites as well, including RVEducation101.com. The rallies feature great entertainment, classes, and a look at some of the industry's hottest new vehicles and products. This is a great way for RVers to bond and learn. The rallies are held at different locations throughout the country.

> **ROAD SCHOLAR**
>
> Audition prospective tour companies as you would any trip provider. Have they organized trips to these locales before? Exactly what is and isn't included in the price? How many years have they been in business? Are the guides experienced RVers? Have they led previous tours to the area? Does the company have references? Remember, you're paying for their experience and expertise.

Tours and Caravans

An RV tour or caravan is a hoot. If you've never done one, you definitely should, because it's one of those great throwback experiences of a lifetime. Like the wagon trains of old that once meandered their way through the Old West, RV caravans are designed to deliver safe, organized, and enjoyable trips to a host of intriguing destinations. Tame Alaska, follow the NASCAR circuit, journey to South America, or take a trip northeast to experience some amazing fall foliage. A number of companies specialize in planning and guiding such journeys, with packages as simple or complex, lavish or bare-bones as you demand. Trips range from a few days to a couple months. Of course, there's nothing stopping you from forming a caravan of your own, with some close friends tagging along for the ride.

Such trips aren't cheap, but they can be a good deal in lieu of doing all the planning yourself. After the check clears, all you need to do is tag along and enjoy, knowing that everything is taken care of. Meals, admission costs, and campsites are usually included in the price. (Fuel and spending money is up to you.) Tour-goers meet at a designated location, which serves as the springboard for the journey. Experienced guides, sometimes under the manly moniker of "wagon masters," lead the group, make the arrangements, and double as cheery activities directors in the process. Expect plenty of side trips along the way. Nights are usually spent in preselected campgrounds and offer a nice setting for everyone to get acquainted and reflect on the day's events. Quality companies work diligently to load up trips with as much entertainment and novel experiences as possible. You'll find a list of tour and caravan operators in Appendix A.

Crossing America's Borders

It's safe to say you could travel a lifetime and never hit all of America's truly interesting hot spots. Consider it another one of the benefits of living and touring in a country as diverse and dynamic as ours (cue "The Star Spangled Banner"). But over time, you might be tempted to play the role of tourist in another country, fraught with new languages, customs, and perhaps the dreaded metric system. Yikes! "How many kilometers to the Queen Mum's palace, honey?" Space prohibits us from discussing the individual laws and RVing practices of every single country on the globe (it's a big world, don't you know?), so we'll stick to trips to the most popular border crossings, Canada and Mexico.

ONE FOR THE ROAD

Is there such a thing as a recreational vehicle in other countries? Sure there is, with a few differences. Although chiefly an American art form, RVs are found throughout the world, in some form or another. Building practices, size restrictions, and many interior systems are different, meaning the RV that rolled out of the Indiana assembly line might puzzle our European, Australian, or Asian counterparts. Contact an overseas tour company for help arranging trips abroad.

Oh, Canada ... and Mexico!

The United States and its neighbors, Canada and Mexico, have long enjoyed symbiotic relationships. Canada exports a steady supply of hockey stars, stand-up comics, and singers. We reciprocate with Mountie jokes and tourists wondering just how many polar bears there are in Churchill, Manitoba. Mexico gives us our second favorite cuisine, brilliant artists, and year-round sunshine and beach destinations for our holidays.

Both countries are willing hosts, and crossing the borders is rarely much of an event but should be taken seriously.

Canada and Mexico both require visitors to carry proof of citizenship and proof of identity. A valid U.S. passport is required for U.S. citizens. If the family pet is onboard, be prepared to present current rabies certification.

Always travel with a valid driver's license, proof of RV and vehicle insurance, and vehicle registration papers. When returning to the United States, all adult U.S. citizens need to present a valid U.S. passport.

Taking the kids? Under 16? Before any international travel, visit the U.S. Customs and Border Control website to read the most current "Know Before You Go" report: www.cbp.gov/xp/cgov/travel/vacation/kbyg/.

Second opinion? Log on to the U.S. Department of State's website (http://travel.state.gov/travel/).

Other Things to Ponder

For novice RV travelers to Mexico, taking part in an established RV tour is highly recommended. The tour operator will walk participants through the paperwork required to drive vehicles beyond the Rio Grande. This includes paperwork like additional auto insurance. Only auto insurance policies issued by Mexican companies are recognized in Mexico. At the border, be prepared to purchase short-term liability insurance from a Mexican insurance company. Fortunately, these offices lace many border towns for just this event. In addition to aforementioned personal proofs, here's a checklist of other paperwork you'll need. All are available at U.S. points of entry.

- ❏ Temporary Vehicle Importation Permit, plus a processing fee. One permit covers any motorized RVs or a tow vehicle and a towable RV. Cost is based on the year of the vehicle.
- ❏ A refundable bond secured for the duration of your stay in Mexico. It will be refunded only if you leave through the same Mexican Customs point as you entered.
- ❏ Promise to Return Vehicle form, also available at the border.
- ❏ Mexican Tourist Card, approximately $25. Keep this with you at all times and surrender it when departing, or face a fine.

When leaving Mexico, remember that, to recover the bond, you must return to the same border crossing that you entered. There the process reverses: relinquish your Mexican Tourist Card, vehicle permit, Promise to Return Vehicle form, and the windshield sticker to a Mexican Customs official on or before the expiration date, or be subject to a fine.

Safety is a concern in the border towns and some outlying areas, especially in remote parts of the country or throughout areas of unrest. Check the state department's website prior to traveling into Mexico.

Drink bottled water when out and about. Keep your mouth closed when showering, avoid ice, and wash off fruits and vegetables (with bottled water) to avoid a trip-altering encounter with a vengeful Mr. Montezuma. The ceaseless hot weather requires other adjustments. Take it slow, drink lots of bottled water, and wear plenty of sunscreen. And enjoy your visit across the U.S. borders.

The Full-Timing Life

It's not clear whether RVing is up there with baseball and apple pie, but it's truly an American concept. We created it, we perfected it, and our citizenry continues to explore this way of life in record numbers. Recent estimates put those who RV full time, or live year-round in their recreational vehicles, at approximately 1.5 million. Come on, admit it. You're just a tad curious what the year-round life would be like, aren't you?

It may be too early in your RV career to be talking about this level of commitment, but a little chat can't hurt. Surely full-timing is the biggest plunge of them all, but is it right for you? On one side, there's no yard to mow, no house payments, and no laborious commute to work. Every day yields a new view, a new town, and plenty of sights unseen to propel adventures even further. On the other side, it's a radical change. Are you ready for this kind of wanderlust, residing in a home on wheels, traveling the byways like a modern-day gypsy? The full-timing experience has been met with praise and disaster alike. Couples believing they were ready for such ultra simplicity and take-charge freedom have quickly wilted under the strain of tight quarters, money troubles, and lack of purpose, as any viewer of the comedy *Lost in America* can attest to. The flip side reveals couples lamenting that they should have tried it sooner, rejoicing in the new vigor that only a wide-open itinerary provides.

> **ONE FOR THE ROAD**
>
> There are lots of ways to full-time, and none has to be a permanent solution. Many full-timers spend a few years traveling until they find a spot to retire. Others RV year-round "just to get it out of their systems" and then return to their "normal" lives. And for some, this is it—the way they want to live as long as they are able.

Can I Afford It?

The carefree life sounds inexpensive, but it isn't necessarily. Living on the go can be a pricey proposition. Just how expensive things get is up to you. If you're the type who moves around constantly, expect to pay a decent premium for these nonstop adventures. Fuel, campgrounds, and life as a perpetual tourist can add up. However, those who spend months in one location—such as at a sunny seasonal campground off a Florida beach—reap considerable long-term savings and avoid much of the heart-stopping fuel costs.

Some people sell all their worldly possessions—home, cars, and collection of shot glasses from every state—with that cash influx going straight into the travel fund. For them, full-timing means goodbye to mortgages, property taxes, maintenance, and the usual costs of the sedentary life. Others maintain a residence, holding on to the mortgage or lease for when they decide to return to their previous lives.

Just because your home shrinks from a 3,000-square-foot colonial in the suburbs to a 35-foot trailer and tow vehicle doesn't necessarily mean an escape from the high costs of living. A smaller kitchen might not equate to smaller food bills. A month's worth of $30 campsites can sting as badly as some mortgages. Eight miles per gallon goes fast when motorhoming across the country. Tolls, insurance, phone bills, entertainment, and the ongoing costs of owning and operating a recreational vehicle all add up. Of course, there are some breaks. Little space for superfluous possessions means you won't buy them. The budget-breaking vacations of the past are assimilated into everyday expenses, so subtract those as well. And if you do it right, you'll be surprised at how far you can stretch a dollar. Only you know how long you can milk a buck and what type of full-timer you might be. Crunch the numbers and make sure you have a decent nest egg before proceeding. Otherwise, think about ways to make money as you travel.

ROAD SCHOLAR

One of the most popular employment opportunities for RVers is as work-campers, with positions available at many larger private campgrounds. In exchange for a salary and a free campsite, work-campers assist in the campground operation, such as with maintenance, construction, or desk help. The work is usually seasonal. It's not unusual for workers to return to the same campground every year.

Many RVers supplement their savings by working on the road. Thankfully, earning a living out of the office is easier than ever with fully equipped laptops, smart phones, and tablets. Perhaps the best solution is to keep working your regular job, taking advantage of telecommuting and consulting opportunities. Despite being camped 3,000 miles from the office, with the right setup you're really only a phone call or mouse click away. Freelancing is another great gig and a perfect match to the RV lifestyle. Plenty of writers, artists, photographers, and graphic designers get along smashingly in a roving office. And there's certainly nothing stopping you from finding employment wherever you land, whether seasonal, full time, or part time.

What Is My Purpose?

The fastest way to hate what you're doing is to lack a reason for doing it. Full-timing is no different. Traveling around from mountains to beaches, in-laws to grandkids is great—but is it enough for you? At the end of the day, is this a satisfying way to live? What, if anything, do you hope to accomplish out there? Do you plan to keep on working, taking advantage of telecommuting, freelancing, or finding employment to supplement savings? Are you looking for a place to retire, hoping to catch a baseball game in every Major League Baseball park, or driven to tour the sights in every state? Can too much recreation be a bad thing? Think about a schedule and how you'll fill your day. Is this full-time experience a brief interlude or something you might want to pursue in the long term?

Can I Give It All Up?

If you can afford to RV and keep your house, this process is much less traumatic. However, for most, it's one way of life or the other. There's no room to bring along a den full of bowling trophies. Your favorite easy chair, power tools, and precious art must be stored, given away, or sold. Loads of family heirlooms and keepsakes can't make the trip; closets full of clothes shrink down to a suitcase or two. Still, some people can't part with these possessions fast enough. Many have gone online to extol the true freedom this streamlined approach provides. And it's not as if you are disconnected by doing so. Online banking, auto bill paying, emailing, texting, social networking, and Skype-ing with friends and loved ones has never been easier and makes keeping in touch a breeze.

What RV Do I Need?

The short answer is, the biggest one possible. Believe me, you'll find use for every inch of available space, for you and your stuff. Sure, some full-timers make smaller towables, truck campers, and van campers work, but realistically, consider 30 feet the minimum-size vehicle for year-round living. A slide-out or two won't go to waste, either. Remember, this is now your home—where you'll spend most every day and night—so don't skimp on size, floorplan, or features. Gravitate toward vehicles with higher NCC (net carrying capacity, remember?) ratings, meaning more weight left over for you, full tanks, and cargo. Workstations or office-type add-ons found on some models are useful for those keeping a day job. A secondary vehicle is a must for commuting to work and running errands. Towable owners can simply use the tow vehicle; motorhomers should seriously consider towing a car.

The Least You Need to Know

- Appreciate the needs and concerns of children and younger passengers. Be especially careful to pack items that are important to them. Explain the rules of the campground and set a good example of conduct for them to follow.

- Allow pets to adjust to the RV before you bring them along. Help them acclimate by setting up beds, food and water bowls, litter boxes, and toys, just like at home. Set temperatures for their comfort, and avoid leaving them unattended. Most campgrounds accept cats and dogs, assuming that they're quiet, on a leash, and picked up after.

- RV clubs offer a great way to learn about the lifestyle and make friends with those with similar interests.

- A few lengthy journeys and a careful self-examination should help you decide whether full-time RVing is for you.

Campground Life

In This Chapter

- Determining the best places to stay
- Setting up and breaking camp
- Following campground rules and etiquette

Campgrounds are a vital part of the RV experience. Without them, we'd have to beach our rigs in a hodgepodge of locales—most of them well off the beaten path, lacking the recreation, safety, and facilities most of us enjoy as part of travel. When examining the differences between private and public parks, plush resorts, and more rustic accommodations, the most important thing to remember is that the choice of campground dictates much of the outcome of any particular trip. So as the saying goes, "Let's choose wisely."

Home Away from Home

With a fully self-contained vehicle, the spouse, the kids, the family pet, and a week's worth of grub in the fridge, it's hard to go wrong. Unlike the campgrounds themselves, the spaciousness and comforts aboard an RV are constants, a steady environment in an ever-changing world. Touring in such a livable shell, there's not much to be done except decide where to park it. Obviously, RVers sift through all sorts of criteria when planning a trip and choosing their accommodations, and only you know what's most important for you and yours. However, let's look at some of the major decision-making factors to stimulate the thought process.

Location, Location, Location

Most campground stays fall into one of two categories: stopovers and destinations. A stopover is just that—usually just a quick overnight stay on the way to your *real* destination. On a long trip—say, from Chicago to the Alamo—expect to spend a couple of nights along the way. And because these stopovers are relatively short— usually just one day or a night's sleep and then away you go—whether or not the place has a swimming pool, minigolf, or a 7:30 A.M. aerobics class may not be all that important. Rather, as long as it's safe, quiet, and not nestled at the base of a toxic waste dump, everyone is happy enough. Many folks, eager to make time and get a move-on, look for a quick stopover near the interstate and then leave in the morning.

Destination stays are entirely different. First of all, we hold them to a higher standard because this is the spot we've been traveling all those miles to reach. These campgrounds are usually near the attraction we've come to see (for example, Disney World, the Grand Canyon, Graceland), and thus serve as a launching pad for each day's activities. Sometimes the campground itself is the main attraction, especially in the case of deluxe RV resorts or that mountain retreat with the splendid trout fishing. The conditions and offerings of these accommodations therefore become hugely important because this is where you'll be spending much of your time.

Money Matters

Whereas hotels eat precious dollars from a vacationer's budget, campgrounds are far more forgiving. You can expect to pay $25 to $50 for a well-run RV resort with a stocked list of things to do. Even the nicest digs probably won't ever exceed $100—and that's for the finest accommodations in the best places, offering everything a weary RVer could want. On the flip side, a number of federally run facilities are free—yes, free—sparing pocketbooks even further. But most campsites' costs lie somewhere in between, with rates based on amenities, number of passengers, campsite location (pretty views might cost more), season, and any discounts/affiliations you might be toting along.

ONE FOR THE ROAD

Join one or more of the nation's larger RV clubs and perhaps knock as much as 10 percent off your accommodations bill. Many places honor such affiliations. Seniors, AAA members, and large groups may also earn cheaper rates. Those loyal to national chains such as KOA or Jellystone Parks should obtain a membership card for nightly discounts. See Appendix A for various club information.

Special Needs

If you're one of the 54 million Americans with some form of mobility issue or handicap, it stands to reason that you favor more accessible RV parks. Ramps, user-friendly bathrooms and showers, and paved campsites and roads can make all the difference. Of course, special needs come in many forms. Families traveling with pets prefer more animal-friendly settings with dog runs, walking trails, and hosts quick to dish out a dog biscuit or two. If a pull-through site is paramount, make sure the campground offers these and that one is available for you. Kids are bored stiff at "adult-oriented" parks, just as some couples quickly tire of the controlled chaos of "family-friendly" campgrounds. Determine your needs, locate accommodating facilities, and make them known when you make reservations.

Fun, Fun, Fun

Recreation comes in many forms (see Chapter 3 for a list of possible offerings). One person's pastime is another person's snoozefest, so make sure there's plenty of stuff for everyone to do. Again, if you're only staying the night, this probably won't matter much. Otherwise, it's enormously important and sure beats channel-surfing the day away in your trailer. Want to teach the kids to swim in the pool? Looking for boat or bike rentals? Prefer a more natural vacation consisting of hikes, cross-country skiing, or bird watching? Every campground has its specialties—it's just a matter of matching them up with your preferences.

ROAD SCHOLAR

Reservations help eliminate surprises upon arrival. Double-check in advance the aspects of the stay that are important to you—for example, that the swimming pool is open. Be advised that some recreation and facilities are seasonal. Make needs known, such as a campsite overlooking the water or one near the bathroom. Reconfirm required hook-ups (water, electric, sewer, and so on) and a pull-through site, if needed.

Campground Extras

Most of us bask in enough goodies onboard our RVs and do not have to rely on a campground for a bathroom, a shower, or potato chips from the camp store. However, such aspects are important to some, especially those traveling in smaller trailers, truck campers, and camper vans where floorplans are tight. If hot showers or sewer hook-ups will make all the difference between a good stay and a sour experience, make sure the park has them. Furthermore, if little extras such as a laundry room, planned activities for the kids, internet access, full hook-ups, and cable TV are vital, use them to narrow your search for the perfect campground.

Finding Mr. Right

With more than 16,000 campgrounds in the United States and countless available campsites, you will likely find plenty of great places to stay. But how, you may ask, do you find the best of the best, those parks most suitable for you and your crew? Never fear—there are plenty of ways to accomplish such a daunting task.

Campground Directory

Simply the fastest and most comprehensive way to match up campgrounds with customers, a quality campground directory is a major asset in the life of any RVer. Well-known versions produced by *Woodall's* and *Trailer Life* provide detailed listings of the majority of private campgrounds in the land. Armed with a thorough ratings system from trained evaluators who personally inspect each park, these books deliver timely information on the level of development of facilities and of each location. A good directory is an impartial source of information and ranks high among the best $25 a camper could ever spend.

Internet

Twenty years ago, the typical campground employed a rudimentary power grid, relied on a lone pay phone to help travelers stay in touch, and hadn't the faintest clue what a slide-out was. How things have changed—and for the better. That same park today probably boasts a sophisticated phone system, an internet-friendly setup, and its own website. And who knows what the next decade will bring? Moon teleportation and jetpack rentals, perhaps. The internet affords many park owners a relatively cost-effective advertising source and the opportunity to lure potential customers from the web. Spend a few minutes surfing for suitable accommodations, using your search engine *du jour* to locate prospects. Most parks can now be found on the web and most likely allow customers to make reservations and chat with owners via email. Although this selection method is a free and relatively easy process, it won't help you locate less internet-savvy campgrounds, thus limiting your choices somewhat.

Tourism Agencies

The folks down at the Chamber of Commerce and other tourism agencies love to hear from vacationers. In fact, it's a big part of what they do, to give you the warm fuzzies about their community and attractions. Contact tourism offices in the area you want to visit for a list of names and numbers of local campgrounds. Give these PR mavens enough notice, and they'll bury you in enough tourism and information packets for a lifetime of bonfires.

Word of Mouth

As we've all been told, listening is a skill, and one that never fails to pay off when chatting with fellow RVers. Eventually, the conversation turns to campgrounds. Soon after, the hyperbole starts flying about that free little federal park next to the ocean or the New England resort with the 250-foot water slide. RVers are as opinionated about where they stay as they are about what they drive, so expect lively discord about places to stay—and the ones to avoid. The next time your itinerary leads you into uncharted territory, open up your ears, go online, and ask around—you may just find a can't-miss recommendation.

Setting Up Camp

Over the course of countless RV adventures, you will undoubtedly discover all sorts of interesting places to camp. And no two places are ever the same. It's not like checking into a Holiday Inn or other hotel chain where you know exactly how it will be before you even get there. For many, this great unknown is one of the best things about RVing. Snorkeling off the shore of that Florida Keys campground. Bass fishing at that Indiana state park. The conquering views from that little spot within the Colorado Rockies where few travelers dare to tread. The choices, the variety, the uniqueness of each make every trip an adventure.

Checking In

Hopefully you've made the campsite reservations well in advance (remember, summer and holiday weekends fill up fast) and explained exactly what you require—full hook-ups, a pull-through site, a shady spot, and so on. This should eliminate any surprises at check-in or a bitter case of the "No vacancy blues," the ultimate momentum-buster. At the entry point of every campground—no matter how big or small—is a place to check in—a campground office, a ranger booth, or a camp store where the owner mans the cash register. This is your first and best opportunity to get the lay of the land and learn what the place offers, what the area has to offer, and what the rules or restrictions are for campers. After that, they're probably going to want some money, too, usually paid in advance.

> **ONE FOR THE ROAD**
>
> Many campgrounds facilitate late-night check-in. Most provide a slot and perhaps envelopes or registration cards—you fill them out and put them in the slot with your cash or check. Others instruct campers to choose a site and pay in the morning. If there are no instructions, most RVers can just park in an empty site that meets their needs and take care of business the next day.

The campground office acts as a sort of nerve center. This is the best spot to get answers on nearly anything, get change for the laundry room, or just learn where to find the best steak joint within 20 miles. Be sure to grab a map of the premises, highlighting facilities, recreation, and the like. I'll never forget the nice owner who, after check-in, hopped on his bike, led me to my campsite, connected me to all the hook-ups, and came back with firewood later. I've even heard of a few places that are more than happy to back in your rig and do the setup chores for you. Don't expect this level of service everyplace, but it's nice when you get it.

A Site for Sore Eyes

There she sits, a well-landscaped, grassy campsite on level terrain. Or perhaps it's a level (level is good!) concrete slab set among some tall trees producing wonderful shade. If you're lucky, the spot is overlooking the water or the mountains, or carved out of the deep woods for a remote feeling. Campsites differ tremendously, with terrain, views, and proximity to key facilities always up for grabs. The one thing they all have in common, however, is that each requires one last bit of driving ability to match up the vehicle with the hook-ups. Backing into position is called for in most scenarios. Take your time and do it right. Have your co-pilot get out and help you ease the rig where it needs to go, close to hook-ups and not butted up against the camper next door. Obviously, a pull-through site eliminates any "reverse anxiety" because they're designed for you to drive right through and into position.

Initiate Docking Sequence

The first order of business when pulling or backing in is to decide where you want the RV to end up. The proximity of hook-ups, amount of shade or sunlight, and obstacles to be avoided (such as picnic tables, low-hanging branches, and campfire rings) all factor into this decision. Be especially careful to allow enough space when settled to deploy slide-out(s) and awnings, which can add a couple of feet here and there. For those pulling cars behind their motorhome, this is a good time to separate the two vehicles and remove the tow bar/dolly from the equation. Remember, never attempt a backup with either of these two devices in place (see Chapter 13 for the details). When the motorhome is in place, pull the secondary vehicle in behind; it now serves as the primary transportation.

ONE FOR THE ROAD

Dirt sites quickly devolve into a muddy mess after a rain, which may cause jacks and leveling systems to sink and become catawampus. A hardy board under each "leg" should do the trick to halt any submergence. Just be sure to incorporate the same-size board for all sides, to keep things even-Steven.

On the Level

The back-in or pull-through was uneventful (the best kind), the RV sits near the vital hook-ups, and there's plenty of room for the slide-outs and awnings to stretch out. Before we pop the champagne, is the RV level? As mentioned in Chapter 10, an RV's refrigerator works properly only when the unit is level (or mostly level).

Most motorhomes and high-end towables are outfitted with some kind of leveler to forgo the frustration of moving the entire vehicle over and over into a level plane. As with most things in life, such equipment is as nice and effortless to operate as your wallet will allow. Pricier RVs might feature a built-in leveling system, which does the work for you. The push-button varieties are the best and most expensive—just activate the device (usually near the driver's seat) and enjoy the show as the RV shakes and shimmies its way to the right horizontal plane.

Towable owners often rely on the budget-friendly, bright yellow interlocking leveling blocks that look like giant Legos. Use these lightweight, stacking blocks to prop up one set of wheels that need to be raised for leveling. Once the trailer is level from side to side, add wheel blocks (chocks) behind the towable tires, especially in the case of a slope or muddy conditions, to prevent any unnecessary roll when it is disconnected from the tow vehicle. With wheel chocks in place, now it's safe to unhitch the tow vehicle. Note: it's a good idea not to unhitch the trailer from the tow vehicle until you're confident that the towable is where it needs to be. Now it's time to level front to rear. Use the tongue jack to level the trailer from front to rear. When the trailer is level side to side and front to rear, lower the stabilizer jacks (if equipped) to help stabilize any movement felt inside the trailer as you move about. You can also use blocks of wood instead of commercial leveling blocks.

Hook-Ups

With the RV parked and level, you're ready to set up shop—er, camp. But before baiting up the fishing poles or sticking that pot roast in the oven, it's best to power up the rig's onboard systems, the core of most everything you'll want to do inside. Chances are, the kids will attempt to sneak away for some quick fun, but get them involved in the setup process, too. The sooner you're done, the sooner the leisure begins for everyone. Start with the hook-ups. The procedure varies based on the number of utilities offered in your site; full hook-ups require more steps than a more primitive site.

Locate the campsite's various utilities in question. (You should have done this when pulling in so the rig is nice and close and all the cords reach.) A tall metal box houses the electrical outlet and cable TV (if offered); the water faucet should be nearby, sticking out of the ground. You might need to scour the earth a little bit to locate the sewer drain, which is sometimes hidden among tall grass, weeds, or leaves. All these hook-ups should be relatively easy to find and may be tucked back slightly in the site to prevent any unnecessary run-ins with RVs. Still, stay alert so you don't back over them when pulling in.

Electric

I still like to begin with the electrical hook-up (better known as shore power), giving the electrical appliances some needed juice and the batteries a head start in recharging. As evidenced in Chapter 9, which covered electrical systems, this step is, to coin a phrase, "as easy as falling in love." Plug in the RV's electric power cord to the campsite's electrical outlet at the pedestal. These days, most campsites offer 30-amp power, a good thing because this is probably what your RV was built for. Fifty-amp power is becoming increasingly popular for bigger rigs with more doodads. Consider a campsite with anything less than 30 amps (15 or 20 amps) a trip back into yesteryear. These paltry levels can struggle to adequately power today's RVs, forcing you to tone down your electrical usage onboard.

An adapter is necessary in the event of a mismatch (for instance, a 30-amp power cord and a 20-amp electrical outlet). It's a good idea to have an adapter to fit each of the four kinds of outlets typically offered (15, 20, 30, 50 amps); otherwise, you won't be able to facilitate the connection. Check the site's power flow with a polarity tester first (again, see Chapter 9) to reveal any potentially faulty wiring that could damage appliances. Contact the manager if there's a problem, and request another site. If all systems are go, plug in and enjoy a steady supply of electrical juice.

Fresh Water

The nice thing about onboard fresh water tanks is that you can always rely on your own reserves. A flip of the water pump, and it's water time. Of course, you can always go with the campground's supply. It's up to you. Attach the fresh water hose from the city-water inlet on the side of the RV to the campsite's water outlet. As previously stated, using an inline water pressure regulator is good insurance when connecting to an outside water source. Some campgrounds may have unrestricted pressures, which can damage internal fittings. I also strongly advise a quality water filter or filtration system to screen out bacteria, molds, and other contemptibles. Most water is perfectly fine. However, give the water a taste—or find some other guinea pig—before you complete the hook-up.

You turn the handle and the water is flowing. As long as you're hooked up to the campsite's water source, no water pump is required to propel the water through the pipes. If a shower or other hot-water need is in your future, now's a good time to activate the water heater to heat up a batch. (It might take 30 minutes to an hour, depending on the size of the appliance.) Just make sure the heater is filled before activation because operating it without water in its tank can harm the unit. Open all the hot water faucets first, to make sure water is fully flowing. If this is the case, you know the heater is filled and safe to light.

LP Gas

It doesn't get much easier than this. Go outside, turn on the flow of propane at the container, and you're ready to go. Return to the vehicle and set the refrigera-tor to propane or 120-volt. (See Chapter 10 to determine which setting you might prefer.) The remaining LP appliances—stove, oven, and/or water heater—are ready to go (although lighting a pilot flame or activating the ignition cycle may first be necessary). It's not uncommon with a new batch of LP for some air to infiltrate the lines, making it difficult to light some appliances at first. This is also likely after periods of extended nonuse. In such an event, ignite the stove burners for a minute or so to purge any air out of the system, and then try to light the remaining appliances. The lines should quickly clear, and you shouldn't have any more problems.

Sewer

Unless the wastewater tanks resemble your cousin Al after an all-you-can-eat buffet (full), I suggest connecting to the sewer drain only when ready to empty— best performed at the end of the stay. (This may not be practical for longer stays, requiring multiple tank purges.) This gives you one less hose to trip over at night when carrying that plate of hamburgers and prevents the temptation to empty the tanks as you go, a no-no that can cause clogged pipes and tanks, as covered in our discussion of plumbing systems in Chapter 11. When it's time to dump, put on some disposable rubber gloves and attach the sewer hose from the connection underneath the RV to the (hopefully) nearby drain. Follow the dumping procedures outlined in Chapter 11.

PULL OVER

You're packing 25 feet of electric cord and a seemingly endless pile of fresh water hose, and sewer, phone, and/or cable TV connections are snaking their way through the campsite. With all these potential hazards underfoot, how does one circumvent a nasty fall? Avoid them altogether by establishing a path away from hook-ups. Coil extra hose and store underneath the RV. Brightly colored hoses work best for avoiding nighttime encounters. Wrapping cords in reflective or glow-in-the-dark tape is never a bad idea, either.

TV Options

Why, oh why would you want to go on vacation and miss wrestling? Of course you wouldn't, which is why cable TV is a nice perk. It's not offered everyplace, but it is offered in most places. As with Wi-Fi service, sometimes it's free, sometimes it isn't.

And then there are those who are waaaayyy past such prehistoric entertainment as that silly cable TV. Satellite TV allows folks to hit the highways with hundreds of juicy channel offerings along for the ride, a costly but oh-so-plush extra that guarantees you'll never miss your favorite show—even when camped in Timbuktu. I'll bet even those tenting purists might be swayed to knock on the door with a bowl of hot buttered popcorn knowing the RV owner next door is the proud owner of a satellite system. Life as a dish owner isn't as expensive as you might suspect, but it does mandate a monthly service agreement and sometimes involves plunking down a nice chunk of change on the gadget itself.

ONE FOR THE ROAD

Satellite signals must be received by a satellite dish/antenna and conveyed to an onboard receiver. Some units are obvious; some are inside a bubblelike component mounted on the roof. Some are portable and can be set up at the campsite; some are permanently mounted. Some must be manually aimed at the satellite in the sky; some automatically track the satellite on the move. You can get the satellite signal nearly anywhere in the continental United States. Possible interference comes from obstructions such as overhanging trees, mountains, tall buildings, and heavy storms.

What's Next?

After hooking up, what you do now is up to you. However, you'll probably want to deploy any slide-out rooms. That's as easy as pushing a button (just remember to unlatch/remove the safety bar that helps secure the room in place). Take a walk around the RV first to make sure any extended rooms won't ding a nearby tree, picnic table, or inattentive spouse. The same principle is true before deploying the awnings, useful in manufacturing a little shade. Electric versions are replacing the overly complicated deployment methods of the past, so it probably won't take the aid of the 101st Airborne Division to get it down. The newest models know to retract when the wind starts a-blowin', so they don't rip and end up three states away—a common pitfall for the inattentive RV owner. With propane and electricity now running through your RV's veins, feel free to regulate the temperature controls inside. Otherwise, consider yourself set up and free to unpack, roam, and start living the good life.

ROAD SCHOLAR

Late-night arrivals are a noisy experience for slumbering neighbors. If you check in late, be courteous. Don't slam vehicle doors or argue with the co-pilot about who made whom back into the maple tree. Set up as quickly and quietly as possible, avoiding unnecessary lights and engine noise. Extend others the same courtesy for early morning departures.

Rules and Etiquette

Despite all the differences from one campground to another, I've found that the attitudes of guests are roughly the same. They're like-minded travelers taking control of their vacations. They're families and couples reconnecting with one another. You'll see lots of smiles, good-heartedness, and relaxation. I'll bet these are some of the very reasons you became interested in RVing in the first place. However, in the interest of your camping brethren, a few rules must be followed. Such restrictions are rarely a secret—you'll probably receive a list upon check-in or be notified via posted warnings about possible no-no's. In addition, a number of unwritten rules—campground etiquette, if you will, that uninitiated RVers might unknowingly shun—should also be observed. We'd better look at these, too.

Shhhh ... Quiet

By day, sounds of kids playing, music, laughter, and perhaps a random hard-starting engine fill the air. However, nighttime is a different matter, with self-imposed "quiet hours" taking effect. Although you might see campfires and hear light conversation going into the wee hours of the morning (guilty as charged), it's expected that you at least put the banjo and karaoke machine away.

Gone to the Dogs

There's nothing quite as irritating as a chronically barking dog. Even the cutest pooch quickly wears out his or her welcome with excessive noise—and this is a dog lover talking. Most campgrounds frown on the practice of leaving pets unattended, especially those of the loud and edgy variety. Obey leash laws, even if your canine is as gentle as Lassie and twice as well behaved. And always pick up after pets, another non-negotiable task.

Generating Ill Will

Generators are noisy. The carbon monoxide pouring through exhaust vents into the open windows of a nearby coach won't make you any friends, either. There's simply no reason to run a generator when you're connected to an electrical hookup. Save it for the next boondocking escapade. If you must run it for some reason, do so only during the day and for brief periods of time. Never operate a generator at night when folks are sleeping—they may come visit you for a candid midnight discussion.

Don't Get Fired

I wouldn't dream of camping without a campfire. It sounds almost un-American to have one without the other. However, a minority of places don't allow them— and usually have sound reasons for such. Dry climates, where fires can quickly spread and spiral out of control (parched Western states, for example), might put the brakes on any flame-inspired activity. Sure, it's a bummer, but as the old saying goes, "Them's the rules." In other cases, owners put limits on size of fires or what goes in them. Refrain from adding anything but wood—and not the green stuff snapped off from a nearby sapling. A steel fire ring, a fixture at most campsites, corrals campfires and should be used whenever available. Always make sure the fire is completely extinguished before departing, and never leave a blaze unattended.

Trashy Behavior

Economizing and organizing garbage is a test for many campers. Families make quite a lot of waste, and for some reason, RVs never seem to come equipped with garbage cans onboard. When they do, they're usually woefully small—smaller than a Smurf and half as useful. Why, I don't know. Don't let that be an excuse to ruin a nice setting with rampant litter. Items such as cigarette butts, bottle caps, and smaller debris quickly transform a rustic campground into a disappointing mess, so stay on top of the problem. Keep a garbage bag inside and another outside (best stored in an exterior compartment away from critters) to head off a messy condition before it starts. Deliver trash bags and recycling to the proper facilities.

Walking the Walk

True, the shortest distance between your campsite and the recreation room is indeed a straight line. However, don't cut through neighboring campsites to get there. This is considered bad form and equivalent to the masses traipsing through your yard at home. Respect campers by always following the roads and paths meandering through the campground. This little extra distance is good exercise and won't irk the locals.

Kids at Play

Personally, I found the two boys sneaking around the rig and hiding our supply of firewood sort of charming. I certainly did worse as a kid. Others might not enjoy your kid's merry mischief, which is why a chat with youngsters about common courtesy is probably warranted. Keep tabs on kids who may acquaint a campground's wide-open spaces with an anarchistic free-for-all. Although campgrounds are some of the safest places around, that doesn't mean children should run amok, especially in locations fraught with water, tough terrain, or wild animals. Even rustic areas are subject to vehicle traffic, and there's no shortage of cords and hoses to trip over. Keep an eye on kids at all times, and teach them to respect the rights of others.

Breaking Camp

Get in the habit of walking around the outside of the RV to look for anything amiss before take-off. How's the tire pressure? Are the slide-outs retracted? Are you still connected to any hook-ups at the campsite? I once pulled out of an RV park with the entry door wide open, half my gear unstowed, and lawn chairs sitting back by the campfire. Double-check things inside as well, paying special attention to unlatched drawers, open cabinets, and precious heirlooms that might tumble about during transit. Finally, conform the cockpit to the driver's needs. Struggling with mirrors and seat belts during rush hour traffic is asking for unnecessary trouble.

Obviously, there are a lot of things to consider before you're ready to hit the open road again. The following is a pretrip checklist, broken into seven sections, to help ensure you've got it all covered.

Engine

- ❏ Check oil
- ❏ Check washer fluid
- ❏ Check battery fluid
- ❏ Check power-steering fluid
- ❏ Check transmission fluid
- ❏ Check brake fluid
- ❏ Check battery terminals

Exterior

- ❏ Disconnect city water and stow fresh water hose
- ❏ Dump black and gray water tanks via sewer connection
- ❏ Disconnect sewer connection, stow hose, and close valves
- ❏ Disconnect and stow electric power cord
- ❏ Disconnect phone service
- ❏ Disconnect cable TV
- ❏ Turn off LP gas supply
- ❏ Inspect tires for wear and take pressure
- ❏ Secure and lock all outside storage compartments
- ❏ Check headlights, turn signals, and brake and backup lights
- ❏ Retract stabilizing jacks/stabilizing system
- ❏ Retract awning(s)
- ❏ Latch storage pods

Interior

- ❏ Stow all gear; protect fragile items
- ❏ Securely latch all drawers, cabinets, and doors
- ❏ Close windows and secure blinds
- ❏ Close roof vents

❏ Batten down larger items

❏ Position refrigerated items for travel

❏ Secure loose objects

❏ Select 12-volt power mode for refrigerator

❏ Turn off water pump

❏ Turn off water heater

❏ Turn off furnace

❏ Extinguish all pilot lights

❏ Retract slide-out(s) and check/remove surface debris

❏ Lower TV antenna

❏ Retract entry step

Cockpit

❏ Adjust side mirrors

❏ Buckle up

❏ Determine blind spots

❏ Check gauges, particularly fuel

❏ Position seat

❏ Position steering wheel

❏ Position vents and fans

❏ Retrieve maps and directions

❏ Find coins for tolls

❏ Find sunglasses

Towable Owners

❏ Hitch up trailer or towed vehicle

❏ Connect wiring

❏ Attach safety cables

❏ Set break-away switch

❏ Double-check lights

❏ Remove wheel blocks

Campsite

- ❏ Fully extinguish campfire
- ❏ Pick up trash
- ❏ Move campsite fixtures back to original positions
- ❏ Check site for forgotten items

Final Steps

- ❏ Check out, if necessary
- ❏ Visit dump station (unless dumped via sewer connection)
- ❏ Empty garbage/recyclables in dumpster
- ❏ Provide bathroom breaks for the family
- ❏ Hook up seat belts for everyone

The Least You Need to Know

- Campgrounds come in many different shapes and sizes, and it's up to you to decide what's important. Consider a quality campground directory money well spent.
- Be careful when backing into the campsite to avoid any obstacles. Have the co-pilot or a neighbor help back you in, or opt for a pull-through site instead. Park near hook-ups, being careful to gauge the impact of sun or shade, while allowing space for slide-outs and awnings to deploy.
- Set up the campsite first, beginning with electrical and fresh water hook-ups. Sewer hook-ups are best left to the end when dumping the tanks. Release the flow of LP gas from the propane containers, set the refrigerator to the appropriate setting, and activate the water heater, slide-outs, and awnings, followed by temperature controls.
- Follow the posted rules during campground stays. Respect the rights of fellow campers. Keep children and pets under control and behaved. Honor quiet hours and take steps not to disturb neighbors with excessive noise. Be courteous during late-night arrivals and early morning departures.

Roughin' It: Boondocking

In This Chapter

- Discovering the how, why, and where of boondocking
- Thriving without hook-ups
- Learning conservation tips to preserve your resources

RVers aren't exactly made of the stuff pioneers are known for—at least, not with a queen-size bed, a kitchen, and that furnace and air conditioner tandem to protect us when the going gets tough. Operating a fully insulated vehicle flowing with electricity, LP gas, and fresh water is a long way from fiddling with a broken sleeping bag zipper, a tiny portable stove, and wet socks courtesy of a leaky tent. There's no use denying it, we RVers are pretty pampered.

That's not to say, however, that we don't like to push it now and again. Although most RV travelers springboard from campground to campground, full hook-ups to full hook-ups, others prefer the road less traveled. In fact, some folks hardly want a road at all, preferring to head to parts unknown and camp only in the remotest of areas. This kind of unconventional camping is known by many names: boondocking, dry camping, or self-contained camping. Whatever term you choose, it basically entails setting up camp where no such camp exists. Good examples include staying in a deserted parking lot for the night, settling outside the in-laws' house, attending a large RV rally void of hook-ups, and camping on federal lands open to visitors but short on utilities. RVs are designed to work under these "primitive" conditions—and, as the old saying goes, "If you've got it, flaunt it!"

Why, Oh Why?

What possible reason could someone have to give up the cushy confines of a campground? Perhaps the views at the RV park pale in comparison to those offered down the road, just left of the maple tree, and down by the creek bed of that deserted property. Or maybe Grandma just insists that you park in her driveway so she can be closer to the grandchildren. Truth is, many of us were first reeled in by the nomadic lifestyle that RVing provides. We romanticized camping on a deserted beach, waking up to the sounds of the rolling surf. We pictured ourselves entrenched deep within a forest of tall pine trees, with not another person for miles. We imagined catching trout, parked streamside at the base of a majestic mountain range, with nothing but the sounds of the eagles sailing above. These are exactly the kinds of visions that seduce curious wannabes to come kick the tires at their local RV dealership. And let us not forget that the act of forging our own trail is practically an American institution, as patriotic as the hot dogs we dream about cooking at our own private retreats. People boondock for all sorts of reasons, not least of all the freedom of choice. Here's a look at some others.

The Trouble with Boondocking

Boondocking is a prickly issue. Obviously, lots of campground owners hate the practice because it takes money out of their coffers. Local ordinances sometimes prohibit such overnight parking, citing safety concerns or loss of potential revenue. Many business owners dislike squatters, although others feel that allowing campers to bunk in their parking lots is good for business. Of course, RVers will always lobby hard for their right to camp where they like.

Let There Be Peace

A good-size campground swells to several hundred—perhaps even thousands of people—on crowded weekends. Kids run about and enormous motorhomes and trailers congregate in an orderly, although sometimes crowded, fashion. A few feet away, a neighbor talks to you passionately about gas mileage. People, people everywhere. They say some of us can't see the forest for the trees. What if you can't see the forest for the satellite dishes, slide-outs, and awnings of the crowds around you at campground XYZ? Surely it's not hard to appreciate that some folks have little patience for such a congested scene. Hop in the RV, head out in the wilderness, and leave breadcrumbs to find your way out. Ah, now that's more like it.

Money for Nothing

We gladly hand over $20,000 for a decent trailer. We have no problem tapping into the kid's college fund for gas, tolls, and a round of corn dogs and curly fries for the family. But don't you dare ask us to fork over $20 a night for the privilege of parking our RV at a campground. Although even an overpriced site is usually a good deal, especially compared to conventional lodging, some travelers just won't hear of it. Piloting a recreational vehicle designed to go anywhere, complete with self-sufficient living capabilities, it's little wonder that these folks grin at the prospect of free camping. After all, why pay the campground owner when you can get the milk for free? (Okay, so I mixed my metaphors here.) Boondocking is a lot of things, but it is most definitely free in most cases and certainly a hard offer to refuse.

No Vacancy

It's still a good idea to make reservations whenever possible, especially during peak seasons, at popular destinations, or when in need of a special type of amenity (pull-through site, handicap access, and so on). But if you find yourself at the National Banjo Picker's Festival and every site within a 30-mile radius is gobbled up, put those boondocking skills to the test.

Because I Can

Daniel Boone didn't become a legend for his microwave venison and days spent channel-surfing aboard the motorhome. Lewis and Clark didn't make history by relying on their rig's GPS system to map their way across America. No one ever took a recreational vehicle up Everest, down the Nile, or across the Atlantic, but, by golly, you're gonna try. The pioneer spirit certainly is no stranger to the RV demographic, folks who want to take control of their travels and blaze a trail as unique as they are (or think they are). Follow the pack? Never. Experience the easy life found inside the confines of an RV resort? Are you kidding? Take the easy way out? Don't be silly. Forge your own trails? Ah, now you're talking.

The Path of Most Resistance

An RVer sans hook-ups is involved in a chess match of sorts against the vehicle's capabilities. Without a city-water hook-up or a natural stream nearby (as if those existed!), the fresh water supply eventually runs dry. Propane, too, has its limits, and with it goes the heat, many of the cooking capabilities, and the hot water that's so hard to live without. Generating electricity in the wild is a little easier, thanks to generators, inverters, and solar power, but these, too, depend on outside factors (fuel tanks, battery size, hide-and-seek playfulness of the sun), and some recreational vehicles aren't outfitted with such gadgetry. Those black and gray water tanks are gonna need emptying at some point, too; there's simply no getting around that.

Certainly, there are many ways to boondock. Catching a little shuteye in the back of a deserted parking lot is much different than sequestering yourself deep within a 100,000-acre forest. Parked without utilities in the driveway is an easier concept than life in the Alaskan frontier, toiling with a sinking propane supply and a lone can of beans. However, before tangling with the particulars of where, when, and how, those interested in such boondocking behavior should always satisfy the following criteria.

Is It Legal?

Contrary to the mantra of the late 1960s, the earth does not, in fact, belong to everyone. Otherwise, those in the business of building fences, security cameras, and signs shouting "Keep out" wouldn't have a day job. Although free love may still exist, a free stopover may raise the ire of a less-than-understanding business or property owner. Finding that deep-woods oasis or beachside camping haven is great, but chances are, it belongs to someone who isn't you.

Deciding where to go takes more foresight than pulling off the road to that charming little field underneath the stars. This squatter mentality will almost certainly result in Officer Friendly's nightstick tapping against the doorway at

3 A.M. Some RVers rely on stealth tactics when deciding where to hide out and camp for a few days. They find a remote location and do as little as possible to advertise the fact that they're there. All in all, it amounts to little more than free-loading. We can do better than this.

One for the Road

Our tax dollars are hard at work preserving millions of acres throughout this country through federally protected lands. The scenery is majestic. The lands are often wild and spectacular, with not a strip mall in sight. Free camping may be provided in lieu of a formal campground, hook-ups, or an abundance of rangers to service your every wish. Bureau of Land Management areas and National Wildlife refuges are two of the most common examples of such camping.

The best advice is to secure the owner's permission before you put up stakes for the night, whether it's next to a beautiful plot near a bubbling stream or behind a local Walmart, a business long tolerant of RV sleepovers (a growing number of Walmarts are prohibited from extending the invitation due to local ordinances, though).

Be specific about your intent, how long you'd like to stay, the number of passengers, and so on. Offer to pay for the privilege and/or make a purchase from the kind business owner who allowed you to stay when the area campgrounds were overbooked. If this is just an overnight stopover and there's no one around, park the rig well out of the way and leave first thing in the morning.

Is It Safe?

Even hard-core dry campers balk at situations that appear unsafe. We certainly don't advocate camping in unfamiliar parts, because it could compromise your family's safety. You just never know. Such uncertainly is especially true in isolated areas, void of other like-minded campers or any semblance of security. If you're just looking for a spot to rest heavy eyelids, a travel plaza or truck stop is the best place. Although it's probably not ideal in terms of a peaceful sleeping arrangement, consider well-lighted venues with regular traffic flow about as safe as you can find in lieu of a protected campground.

Can the Rig Handle It?

Sure, you're up for the challenge, but is your RV? The nimble qualities of a camper van, truck camper, or smaller trailer come in handy when the roads turn to paths, the terrain gets rough, and clearance issues come into full effect. Consider the fact ahead of time that there just might not be a space big enough for a wide-body motorhome with three slide-outs. Only you know where your RV can go and, after it gets there, how long it can hold out with what's onboard. Do you lack a generator or solar power? This condition definitely limits your ability to reinvigorate the electrical system when the batteries read nil. Fresh water tanks a paltry 20 gallons? Then better not schedule a two-week trek to the outback without added water reserves. That back tire plagued by a slow leak? Better fix it before conquering the Amazon.

Getting Ready for Action

As with nearly any undertaking, the success or failure of dry camping lies in the details. Before heading out into the great beyond, you'll want to consider a few things. The most important step is to ensure that the RV and the various systems (electric, LP, plumbing) are in proper working order. Failing that, make sure your emergency roadside service boasts a helicopter with a heavy-duty crane. For longer, out-of-the-way journeys, have the vehicle inspected by an RV service technician prior to departure. And if you've never dry-camped, think baby steps. Get a taste of living without hook-ups first before you test it in a hard-core environment for real. Camp at an RV park without relying on any of the hook-ups. Think of it as a dress rehearsal, to get practice working off the coach battery, fresh water tank, and water pump and try out some of the conservation practices covered in a bit. The driveway or backyard is another good place to work out the kinks. As with everything in RVing, a little practice goes a long way.

PULL OVER

Traveling with full tanks adds a shocking amount of weight (check out Chapter 14). A full fresh water tank can add hundreds of extra pounds, which is why we recommend traveling at reduced capacity. In the case of boondocking, however, you might require every drop of that 75-gallon fresh water tank. To avoid an overweight condition, lighten the load elsewhere to compensate.

All Systems Go

Before departing on your backroads adventure, make sure the fresh water tanks for drinking and cooking are full. Ditto with the propane containers so you can fire up the kitchen as soon as you park. Just the opposite for the gray and black water tanks—keep them near empty. Remember, we always want a little fluid in these tanks as the sloshing around of the water helps to self-clean them while on the road. And last but not least, make sure you have plenty of fuel. You won't likely need to charge up the coach battery because after a decent-length drive, it should be good and charged, meaning you will have some amps to play with. (Of course, this depends on how depleted it was in the first place.)

Stock Up

Prepare for a boondocking odyssey with the same objectives and planning as for any other trip. The toothbrush, prescription medicine, and clean pair of socks are as important here as anyplace else. Rely on the packing list provided in Chapter 14 to get you started, but be aware that there may not be a camp store on the premises to bail you out when you forget the can opener again. Leave room for a few other "rugged" items on your list, including supplemental canned goods, alkaline batteries, charcoal, and extra blankets. Make a stop for local firewood; in many areas, you're not allowed to bring it with you. Remember the long-handled lighters, too. If you're on the fence about buying a cell phone, a night in relative isolation might finally convince you.

Conservative Thinking

Just how long you can stay away from civilization is up to you and your willing-ness to conserve resources. Even a tiny RV, with even tinier capabilities, should have little trouble living off itself for a couple days or longer if you ration reserves carefully and don't use up all the water wetting down the Slip 'n Slide. Larger RVs, equipped with myriad power sources, gigantic tanks, and useful add-ons, can go much longer. Again, it's up to you and your level of discipline. The following tips won't hurt, either.

ROAD SCHOLAR

Holy blackout, Batman! The battery voltage is beginning to drop, and there's no generator, inverter, or solar power to save the day. Partially recharge the batteries with a turn of the ignition key and let the vehicle idle for a while. Otherwise, take the RV for a spin. A good drive can restore some of the charge, extending your dry camping that much longer.

Power Outage

The RV's electrical limitations have a major say in most matters, including the quality and duration of a shore-powerless escapade. Fortunately, the ability to generate your own electricity is, if nothing else, pretty cool. Smaller RVs and many towables are at a significant disadvantage here, usually lacking a generator to finagle more juice when the coach battery starts to wane. Consider a portable model, inverter, or solar power solution if you expect boondocking to become a regular gig. Otherwise, a miserly approach to the stored energy is the best answer.

Remember how mad your father got when you left the lights on in the bedroom? How about that blatant disregard you demonstrated for his money as you stood gawking in front of the refrigerator with the door wide open? Assume the same easily agitated approach to energy loss, and your electrical supply should go far. Turn off all lights and unnecessary devices such as the water pump, electric step, and water heater when not in use. Those amps add up. Go manual whenever possible: forgo the electric can opener for a hand crank, the electric razor for straight edge, and the blow dryer for a vigorous shake with a towel. We are roughin' it, aren't we?

By parking in the shade on a cool day and dropping the awning, you just may keep the air conditioner at bay, which is among the hungriest of the electrical hogs. Select a sunny spot to taper furnace operation during cold climes, thus saving the output of the electric fans and precious propane. Leave the big appliances at home. Do you really need to vacuum, run the power drill, or gulp down a cappuccino every morning?

Water Logged

Mr. Motorhome Owner could probably never imagine going through 100 gallons of fresh water, but how it does seem to vanish. Just ask Mr. Pop-Up

Owner, saddled with a 10-gallon tank and a bunch of thirsty kids, how popular fresh water is over a long, hot weekend. Protecting the water supply is critical. Fortunately, it's also the easiest to horde and replenish. Obviously, for those perplexed by tiny tanks, a few well-placed jugs of water never hurt. Cumbersome and weighty, yes, but good in a pinch when the natives need a round of drinks and are getting ornery. Extend the reserves with a few behavior modifications. Never leave faucets running when washing dishes and brushing teeth. The same is true for showering. Use a showerhead that you can turn on and off as you soap up to conserve water. Get in and get out.

This disciplined approach to dispensing fresh water naturally prolongs the need to empty the gray and black water tanks. If less goes in, less comes out. Mark this down in the two-birds-with-one-stone category. The only added suggestion for wastewater tanks is to use any available facilities—yes, even that scary porta-potty or outhouse.

PULL OVER

Why not just dump those tanks right here in the boonies? Come on, no one's around. Who's to know? We've all thought about it. The question is not whether you can get away with it, but why? Is this how we show gratitude for a wonderful camping environment, by submerging it in wastewater? Come on, you know better. Plus, unwanted critters and bugs may come calling.

Don't Touch That Dial

Shifting some of the cooking operations to natural methods outside is among the best ways to save propane. Substitute a smoldering campfire for the cooking range, a portable charcoal grill for the oven. Turn off the LP gas when not in use. Engage the water heater only when necessary. Go easy on the thermostat to lessen the impact of the biggest LP gas-guzzler, the furnace. Like Mom always commanded, wear a sweater and follow some of the insulation practices found in the next section to take the chill off. With all that said, propane is usually the least of your worries (unless it's below zero outside).

Cold-Weather Camping

Some folks take boondocking to the extreme, favoring an RV trip when the temperatures are ridiculous and snow has enveloped the once-grassy campsite. Winter camping is a strange phenomenon; some do it by choice, in support of seasonal activities such as cross-country skiing, snowshoeing, and snowmobiling (which aren't much fun in the summer). We can attest to winter's power as an incredibly beautiful and remote time of year to camp. Others simply find themselves the victims of an unruly weather pattern, accidental tourists stuck in a winter wonderland. Whether by choice or by fault, RVing in colder climes is certainly possible and worthwhile, although it does present some unique challenges.

> **ROAD SCHOLAR**
>
> Diesel fuel must be blended for use in cold climates, which is why that batch you bought during warmer times might yield lackluster results in freezing temperatures. Fortunately, popular truck stops or travel plazas, where the big boys fill up, should know the difference. The marketplace is also full of additives to protect diesel tanks from the gelling and icing brought on by frigid conditions.

One Cool Customer

The first question poised on your lips should be "Can my RV handle life in such temperature extremes?" Many pop-ups and lightweight travel trailers are really year-round vehicles in name only; they simply weren't built to handle hard-core winter conditions. Remember, there's a big difference between a chilly fall night and a January morning when you awake to the sounds of your own teeth chattering. Spartan insulation, thin building materials, and smallish tanks combine to leave inhabitants of less-expensive RVs pondering the location of the nearest Holiday Inn. Vehicles constructed with the year-round camper in mind—namely motorhomes and midsize or larger trailers—are the best bet for cold-weather camping and are better constructed to handle variable weather. Look for added insulation packages, enclosed underbellies to heat the tanks, and larger furnaces to keep the chill out.

For those of us who endure six months of winter every year, the goals are simple: stay warm and prevent the pipes from freezing. This is doubly true in your RV, even when hooked up to shore power at a campground with winter service.

Let There Be Heat

Finding a built-in heating system, typically a forced-air furnace, is not the problem. Every RV has one, and so will yours. Getting one powerful enough to heat the entire RV when it's 4°F outside and dropping is the challenge. Insulation is a major part of this as well (see the following section). Pay attention to your comfort level on a chilly September night. If jumping jacks are the only thing between you and hypothermia, leave the RV at home for a Minneapolis getaway in February. If you can't seem to stay warm during modest temperatures, don't expect the furnace to perform better in the grip of winter. Supplement a hard-working furnace with a space heater, and set the thermostat at a constant temperature to avoid overworking. And keep that hot cocoa coming.

> **PULL OVER**
>
> Snowdrifts can block vents and lead to a dangerous situation. A quick walk-around should reveal the status of heater and refrigerator exhaust. Keep out carbon monoxide by eliminating blockage. Snow piled on the top of slide-outs must be cleared before retracting. De-ice doors and locks when necessary to avoid a lockout.

Insulation

Despite what most of us think, extra insulation isn't just a cold-weather fighter; it pays off year-round. A well-insulated ride acts as a sort of thermos, keeping the RV warm in winter and cool in summer. Consult the manufacturer to gauge the quality of insulation (some are mum on the subject, so as not to draw comparisons to house-type insulation values). The magic "R" rating (R-5, for example) measures these levels. The higher the rating, the better.

A few interior alterations help retain warm air. Weather-strip all doors and windows to combat drafts. Seal windows in plastic, and add rugs and carpeting to trap in heat. Park in the sun to soak up the free heat whenever possible. Plug up any holes where nasty breezes could infiltrate your cozy sanctuary. And by all means, keep that door shut!

Tanks and Pipes

Ever tried to empty a frozen gray water tank? There are certainly better ways to spend an afternoon. The same is true for any of the other holding tanks, which are vulnerable to freezing—your pipes, too. RVs with exposed tanks and plumbing are prone to more problems during winter camping. One of the easiest things to do is put RV antifreeze in the wastewater tanks (*not* the fresh water tank) and keep the tanks relatively full. Fortunately, newer models are taking cold-weather operation more seriously and implementing a number of safeguards in recent designs. Nicer models offer enclosed tanks to soak in the interior's warm air. Others route heat around tanks and plumbing or insulate pipes for an extra barrier against the elements.

> **ROAD SCHOLAR**
>
> Keep tank levels up, so as not to tempt a frozen situation. Adding specially formatted RV (yes, RV) antifreeze to the wastewater tanks should prevent an icy condition from forming inside. About a quart per tank should do it. Although RV antifreeze is safe for use with your RV's plumbing system, do not add this to the fresh water tank.

Tank Capacities

The larger the various tank and propane container capacities, the happier you'll be. This is true for two reasons. First, larger and fuller holding tanks are more difficult to freeze; second, expect the furnace to work double-duty on cold days, sapping the LP supply faster than a keg at a frat party.

Icy Conditions

If you are bold enough to accept the challenge of a winter retreat, there are options to boondocking. You may just get lucky and find some campgrounds open in places where snow falls and temperatures dip below freezing. Most campgrounds stick to seasonal schedules, but a dedicated search will reveal cold-weather-friendly grounds with waiting electrical and water hook-ups.

In icy conditions, campground or not, a separate fresh water hose for winter use is a good idea. Keep it as short as possible (10 feet or so), wrap it in heat tape (available at hardware stores and such), and cover it with pipe insulation, available in 4-foot lengths from the builder supply stores. (It comes split up the middle so you can insert the hose.) An extra layer of duct tape never hurts, either. The water connection should now be doing its best mummy impression and be completely wrapped. Make sure the faucet itself and water inlet on the RV receive some TLC as well, to prevent these exposed areas from freezing when they're needed most.

A high-quality sewer hose is the only type you want working on your behalf during winter camping. Add a layer or two of insulation wrap here for good measure. Straw acts as a great buffer between it and the frozen tundra. Maintain as steep an angle for the hose connection as possible, to avoid the propensity of water or materials from settling and freezing. Leave release valves closed until you're ready to dump, following the procedures listed in Chapter 11.

The Least You Need to Know

- Camping without hook-ups, or boondocking, is a common practice among RVers seeking remote locations or during times when suitable campsites can't be found. Settings range from primitive campgrounds and some government lands to driveways, parking lots, or wherever one might stay for the night or longer.

- Camping illegally gives RVers a bad name and could raise the ire of property owners and the police. Always get permission before boondocking on unfamiliar lands. Never compromise your safety factor by parking in unfamiliar areas.

- Your RV's capabilities and your conservation practices dictate the success of any boondocking venture. The fresh water and propane supply is finite; holding tanks must eventually be emptied. RVs equipped with a generator, inverter, or solar power can generate electricity.

- Camping in cold weather, either by design or by accident, mandates steps to keep warm and protect pipes from freezing. Proper insulation and heating, as well as design elements to protect tanks and plumbing, are crucial to thrive in frigid conditions.

Playin' It Safe

In This Chapter

- Overcoming bad weather, breakdowns, and medical problems
- Avoiding crime, accidents, and potential road hazards
- Bringing must-have emergency equipment and learning safety procedures

It would certainly be remiss if I got you all fired up on the thought of life as an RV traveler without walking you through some potential pitfalls. Now take it easy, Nervous Nellie—RVing is perfectly safe. You're in good company, with millions of folks having taken the proverbial plunge before you. There's just a few things we need to chat about to keep all those would-be adventures safe. How to handle bad weather is but one example; tips for triumphing over a breakdown (your vehicle, not you) is but another. And there's a host of potentially risky scenarios to discuss in between.

Fair-Weather Fan

The ever-changing weather patterns are life's greatest sideshow. Like the bearded lady and the lobster boy at the carnival, they never cease to surprise and amaze. One day it's calm and beautiful, the next we're running for cover. We can't control it, we can't affect it, and, if your meteorologist is anything like the guy on my local station, you can hardly predict it. Unless you're camped year-round in San Diego (78°F and sunny), weather is somewhat of a crapshoot.

A great falsehood of operating a large vehicle is the belief that you're better insulated from the effects of the elements. It's simply not true. In fact, it's just the opposite. Towables can struggle mightily with big winds and wet pavement. Motorhomes require more diligence in icy conditions, and their size makes them harder to stop and maneuver out of trouble. But bad weather is bad weather, no matter what you drive. It's just a matter of knowing how to handle it.

> **ROAD SCHOLAR**
>
> A number of websites relay the most current conditions and forecasts. One of the best is www.weather.com. Simply type in the city or zip code, and up comes the status on everything Mother Nature is up to. For those on the go, check out the free weather phone apps, like AccuWeather or The Weather Channel, or scan through the local AM radio stations to uncover a news channel with constant updates.

Wind Breaker

Wind is an insidious threat, the one weather condition we can't see coming. But when it arrives, you know it, slapping the side of the RV with vicious intent. Most automobiles breeze (pun intended) right through it. Meanwhile, RVers are battling for control, because taller vehicles and trailer combos only make us a bigger and more tantalizing target. But although wind is invisible, its approach isn't. Watch the landscape for signs of unsavory updrafts—shaking tree limbs, leaning crops, and similar things are all clues that wind is on the prowl. When the winds swirl, hearken (yes, hearken) back to your driver's ed days and grip the wheel tightly at 10 and 2. Give fellow travelers—especially larger vehicles—plenty of room. Pick a lane and stay put; this is no time for your Jimmie Johnson impression. Rebuff gusts with subtle steering in that direction to compensate, but don't overdo it. If things get ugly, find an exit and fly a kite.

Stormy Monday

Nasty rain often packs a one-two punch: wet conditions matched with low visibility. Moreover, wind, thunder and lightning, and the zealous pelting of drops against the rig can all rattle the driver's confidence even further. Step one: turn on your lights, to help you both see and be seen. Add an extra cushion (no, not a pillow) between you and those other vehicles around you to allow for extra stopping time, and be doubly alert for brake lights and vehicles stopped on the shoulder. If the afternoon skies turn green and the winds pick up, put the co-pilot on tornado patrol. Things might get worse in a hurry, so start looking for shelter and a place to dock.

Snow Day

I know, avoiding the white menace is why you purchased an RV in the first place. Fair enough. But coming from someone who has attended snowy Cubs games in April and gotten hit by a blizzard in Colorado in June, I'm not sure the stuff is totally avoidable. Our warm-weather friends insulated from such winter won-derlands don't always know how to react when first confronted with it—kind of Close Encounters of the Flurried Kind. A little snow is like rain, only prettier and easier to throw at the kids across the street. Take it slow, be ultrafaithful to one lane, and opt for major highways, usually first to convalesce with Mr. Plow and his magical salt dispenser. Unplowed roads are tricky and best avoided if the snow is sticking and starting to add up. Always turn on lights and stop for the night if things get icy and dicey.

> **ROAD SCHOLAR**
>
> How do you know conditions are bad enough to pull over? Watch the pros. Semis lining the sides of the highway or congregating in truck stops are good indica-tions that the roadways have lost their friendly demeanor. If the 18-wheelers, known for their "just drive through it" attitudes, fear to tread, you should have been off the highway long ago.

And speaking of ice …. You'd do better to mess with Texas before going toe-to-toe with a slick roadway covered in ice. In a rogue's gallery of driving villains, ice is easily the worst offender. Difficult to detect, tough to negotiate, and unapolo-getically deadly under the worst circumstances, icy conditions deserve your fullest attention. Although the folks in Palm Springs may have no idea what you're talking about, any time spent in northern climes will bring you face-to-face with the stuff. Take it slow. And remember, bridges freeze first. Excessive braking is not the answer here; it only locks the wheels on a slippery dance floor. The better remedy is to allow a wide berth for fellow vehicles and to decelerate instead of applying the brakes. We like to think of decelerating as that limbo zone between accelerating and braking. Downshifting gears is also a useful maneuver to slow the RV steadily. Ice worsens at night (when temps sink), so limit travel to daylight hours and only in conditions you can safely handle.

In a Fog

Pea soup is great to eat but not so great to drive through. Most likely to occur in the early morning, fog tends to burn away as the day heats up. We often adjust our departure time accordingly. A light, low-lying batch is meddlesome but driveable. Keep the lights on (skip the ineffective high beams), keep the speeds low, and watch those around you like a hawk. If you can't tell if that's a semi-truck or a horse and buggy in front of you, it's time to find a place to sit this one out.

Disaster Plan

The truly big hitters—hurricanes, tornadoes, earthquakes—require slightly different coping tricks, but all have one thing in common: you don't want to drive through 'em. In any event, an RV isn't where you want to be. Even inside a locked rig, sitting in the bathtub with blankets over your heads, you and your family are unbelievably vulnerable. Say *adios* to your vehicle and find real shelter—a basement for tornadoes, somewhere away from structures during earthquakes, and as far away as possible from that 100-foot wave that may accompany a deadly hurricane. Disaster plans are taken seriously, and local governments may order evacuations.

The Accidental Tourist

I remember the older gent who proudly exclaimed that he had never been in an accident. This was no simple feat, considering his some 50 years of driving. However, after letting the group praise him accordingly, his wife leaned in and said, "Yeah, but he's caused a hundred of them." Unfortunately, the world is full of so-so drivers. Some are downright awful, seemingly aiming their vehicles like heat-seeking missiles rather than driving them. As a whole, RVers continually earn praise for their abilities behind the wheel. Accidents throughout this segment are wonderfully low, thanks mostly to mature operators heeding their limitations. However, the rest of the world is not always as skilled. Accidents happen, and sometimes, despite our Herculean efforts, we're stuck in the crossfire. Here's what to do.

PULL OVER

Parking on the shoulder during times of low visibility is like painting a bull's-eye on your back. In the event of a roadside breakdown, pull off as far as possible. Activate hazard lights, and set up flares and reflectors to warn on-comers. Vacate the RV and get away from the road. Contact roadside assistance immediately; a dangerous circumstance such as this may merit a call to 911.

Watch Yourself

Protecting the people involved in the accident is job one—yes, even the guy who rammed into you. Safeguarding the involved parties takes two forms: treating those in the accident and making sure you don't add to the number by involving any oncoming traffic. Don't press injured passengers to move unless there's a risk of fire, explosion, or danger from other vehicles—further movement could add to their injuries. Treat yourself first; if you're okay, move on and ascertain the status of passengers. If everyone can walk and is okay, get them away from the scene. Call 911 and explain the situation. Do your best to provide the location, and await authorities.

Don't Be a Hero

Some people believe it's your duty to "secure the area" after such an occurrence. However, scurrying around a fast-moving highway, setting up flares and reflectors after an accident, is an easy way to end up getting hit by another vehicle. Take these steps only if it's safe to do so. Frankly, your crew is the primary responsibility, so stay with them and await authorities. The police may want to investigate the scene, so it might be best to leave it alone. For accidents of the fender-bender variety, in which the damage is minimal, get vehicles off the thoroughfare and onto the shoulders or to another out-of-the-way area.

Motion Sickness

No, I'm not talking about that queasy feeling you get after two baskets of fried calamari. You're on your own with that. However, the RV might need more than a few antacids to get righted in case of a roadside breakdown, another of life's annoying little adventures. Maybe it's a wobbly tire, a glowing "E" on the fuel gauge, or an overheated state brought on by August in Death Valley. No matter the cause, your vehicle isn't going to stand for it another minute. Find somewhere to pull over, and do so quickly. And when the spouse and children look at you with those worrisome expressions, be cool. You know just what to do.

Okay, that's a big lie. You have no idea what to do. Changing a motorhome's tire is a tough, dirty job. A dead battery 50 miles from the nearest service station shakes the confidence of any soul. Worse yet, maybe the rig just went dead on you, succumbing to a malady beyond your range of expertise. Is that a coyote in the background? Are those vultures circling above? Is the sun setting on your last ray of hope? Now what?

ROAD SCHOLAR

The good news is that most breakdowns are preventable. The worn tread on the now flat tire was trying to tell you something. Running the tank to empty is taking a chance in a gas guzzler. Routine maintenance both curtails and corrects mechanical problems. Don't be stingy with service procedures, or you may find yourself stewing about it while waiting for the tow truck.

Circle the Wagons

Again, a sizable tow vehicle/trailer combination sticks out when disabled along the side of the road. A motorhome is no small thing, either. If safe to do so, warn oncoming traffic by setting up reflector triangles and/or flares (skip it if oil or gas leaks are present) to direct them to other, safer lanes. If you can fix the problem, then get fixing. A blaze-orange vest or other reflective clothing (don't worry about appearing on the worst-dressed list) heightens one's visibility when tinkering about. Keep passengers off the road and away from the scene, just in case.

Road Worrier

Assuming you can't cure what ails your sick rig, someone has to come and play doctor. Hopefully, you'll take my advice and sign up for a comprehensive roadside assistance service, where help is just a toll-free number away. If you decided to skip it and save a few bucks, you're the next contestant on Dial-a-Date. Break out your mobile phone and call around for assistance. More easily remedied problems, such as running out of gas or dealing with a dead battery, can usually be handled by the local service station. RV-specific setbacks—tires, towing, and mechanical maladies—require some advanced assistance. Get on the phone and find an RV service station with towing capabilities. Otherwise, it's time to use that secondary vehicle. What secondary vehicle, you ask?

We've preached the benefits of enlisting the tow vehicle or auxiliary auto as a bailout in case of trouble. Here's where it really pays off. If the trailer has a bum tire, the tow vehicle stands ready to shuttle passengers into town or directly to the nearest tire store. Motorhome acting funny? That dutiful secondary vehicle you've been pulling behind is more than just a pretty face; it's there to save the day and provide reliable transit to wherever you need to go.

Mr. Fix-It

Want to see an unscrupulous mechanic cry for joy? Show up on the lot with your RV pulled behind a tow truck. If you don't like their inflated prices or dubious track record, well, it's their way or the highway—and you've already done the highway. Like the song goes, "Breaking down is hard to do." You're at the mercy of an unknown service center, with both your home and your transportation up on blocks. Not anyone's best moment, to say the least.

Enrolling in a roadside assistance club offers consumers at least some protection. In theory, only reputable technicians and businesses comprise the service network. Shoddy repairs and con artists reflect badly on the club, so—again, in theory—such contemptibles are hopefully weeded out. When deciding what service center to do the work, try calling the factory that built your RV. They can help you locate the nearest technician who does work on your type of unit. Go online or use your smartphone to look up RV service centers. Campground directories may also have information about nearby service centers.

Camping Calamities

Unlike you and the kids, safety never takes a vacation. Care must be taken even when the destination is reached, whether it's preventing falls in the shower, overcoming a grease fire in the galley, or thwarting that squirrel with a mean attitude hopping around the campsite. At the risk of sounding like an alarmist, a surprising number of RV calamities occur when happily parked at the campground. Why? Who knows. Perhaps our guards are down, or maybe the outdoors really is a place where only the strong survive. Whatever the reason, it doesn't mean we should go willingly to the emergency room. Here's how to nip potential problems in the bud.

Pride Goeth Before the Fall

Hide-and-seek with the kids is going well until—boom—you trip over the fresh water hose. You throw open the entry door to take the dog for an early morning walk and—crash—there's no entryway step there to greet you. Setting foot on a rubber roof covered with early morning dew results in … well, I'm sure you can use your imagination here. Either someone's doing their best Three Stooges routine or you need a visit from the Safety Patrol. It may sound like a little thing, but falls inside the RV and around the campsite account for numerous traveler follies—and injuries. This problem is exacerbated for those who don't get around as well as they used to and within vehicles jam-packed with passengers, running around in a sort of daze.

Counter slippery areas such as the entryway, steps, ladder, rooftop, and shower/bathtub with nonskid mats. If it's a decent drop between the RV and the ground, add a platform step (available in both electric and manual versions, although usually included with the RV purchase) to smooth this transition. Get in the habit of looking down to see if it's deployed (an onboard power failure may leave the automatic step retracted when you're counting on it). Handrails along the inside and outside of the entryway are a must; another in the bathtub/shower is also a brainy idea. Inspect the campsite for trouble spots. Pick up loose items around the campsite, which take on a landmine persona when you're stumbling around in near darkness. Curl extra hose and cords under the RV, away from traffic areas.

It's important to announce where you put the ground spike to tie out the dog, to avoid tripping on that puppy. Discourage running, keep walkways clear, and award an extra s'more for the safest camper.

ONE FOR THE ROAD

Some well-placed reflector tape can virtually eliminate most causes of nighttime falls. Wrap a few lengths over the plugged-in cords, over that water hose that's just looking to grab an ankle, or along the base of an unlit entry step to avoid a rapid, late-night descent.

Medical Emergencies

Top on my "Things Not to Do" list is getting sick or hurt away from home. A quick poll of the room might suggest many of us share the same concern. Obviously, the fluctuating state of our health-care system, matched with the particulars of one's insurance carrier, makes this a difficult subject to tackle, to say the least. Running to the emergency room with a pain in your chest without contacting your primary doctor first might mean the bill is yours to absorb. It can—and does—happen all the time. Because my advice may run counter to the procedures outlined by the insurance company, let me just say this: your health is the most important thing. If you're in a serious medical emergency, I don't advise waiting around for an HMO to say it's okay to visit that doctor who falls "out of the network."

Finding a doctor for allergies that won't go away or a dentist for a tooth that doesn't like ice cream as much as you while away from home is a challenge. You may have to rely on the advice of a total stranger. For emergencies, the local ER is the place to go. If needed, get an ambulance to take you there. Otherwise, there are urgent care facilities available and many Walgreens stores now offer Take Care Clinics right inside the store. If you can wait to receive medical care from your doctor at home, that's also an option. It's important, however, to be honest in assessing an emergency condition. Don't delay in getting medical care when it's necessary.

Don't leave home without the contact information for both your primary doctor and your insurance company. Pack additional medications for longer trips. Using national chain pharmacies makes refills on the road that much easier. If a medical condition leaves you incapacitated, can your spouse or co-pilot drive the RV back home? Travelers constantly relegated to the passenger seat may struggle when it's finally time to drive the big rig or trailer. Sharing the driving duties keeps both parties fresh and prevents you from becoming stranded if the main driver gets hurt or sick.

ONE FOR THE ROAD

How does one handle getting medical care away from home? In a nonemergency, ask your doctor. Because the insurance company ultimately has a role in paying the tab, get their input if you're unsure whether you're covered. What procedures does your insurance carrier require? Must you first get a referral from a doctor? Can you choose your own provider and get reimbursed in full? What is and isn't deemed an emergency? As always, it's best to get the answers before a medical problem arises. This is especially true when traveling out of the country.

Sound the Alarm

Ask anyone who has smelled LP gas in his rig to describe the odor, and you'll get a number of responses: overcooked onions, garlic, bad eggs, or the first dish your roommate made in college. Although its presence is indeed a stinky one, we should be thankful LP has any smell at all, because liquid petroleum is naturally odorless. The lousy aroma was added to give our noses a chance to catch this airy intruder in the event of a leak. An installed LP gas detector, standard in all RVs, does that one better by sounding the alarm upon detection. As previously noted, many RVers say they notice a faint whiff of LP just before the container goes empty or right after a fill-up.

Carbon monoxide is known as the "silent killer" for a reason. Virtually undetectable without a monitoring device, this gas is colorless and odorless and strikes without warning. Fortunately, a CO detector (another mandated feature) stands ready to alert us of any signs of infiltration, whether caused by a leak, a clogged vent, or a camper next door aiming his generator your way. Onboard smoke alarms often suggest the obvious—that the drapes are on fire—but are important protection nonetheless.

At the first bell, buzzer, or shriek of an onboard detector, make plans to scatter. In some cases, it's a false alarm, but don't bet on it. False alarms can trigger when spraying aerosol cans inside the trailer. Our RV alarm went off recently while I was applying a new type of continuous spray sunscreen. Even a potent dog fart can make the alarm sound. Some RVers report a faint smell of propane upon receiving a new batch or after long periods of storage, and this can cause the alarm to go off as well.

Gas leaks aren't worth waiting around for. Get everyone to safety, get out of the RV, and then concoct an appropriate plan of action. Let the houseplants and Mother's crystal fend for themselves. Leave the door open to ventilate the interior. Don't create a flame or spark, as it could ignite LP gas into the world's biggest bonfire. Turn off the propane supply at the container (some LP gas detectors automatically shut down the tanks). Ventilate, ventilate, ventilate. Do not return until the alarm shuts off. Turn off any and all appliances and systems related to the problem—you don't want a repeat performance. If the source of the leak is unknown, have the rig inspected by a professional.

PULL OVER

Never run the generator as you sleep. Although there are several candidates for a possible carbon monoxide leak, generators rank highest among them—particularly antiquated models. Of course, the culprit may not be your own, but someone's close by. It's possible to suffer secondhand effects from the camper's generator next door, usually triggered when wind blows exhaust back into the rig. Keep windows near the generator's position closed (yours and the neighbors') to avoid this blow-back effect.

House Warming

You don't need to reroll footage of the *Hindenburg* to see how quickly fire can spread. An RV with propane and gasoline/diesel running through its veins doesn't lack fuel for the proverbial fire, which is why you probably shouldn't stick around to battle a formidable blaze. My personal mantra? If the fire is bigger (and meaner) than you, run. Grab the passengers and pets, and get away—as far as possible, in case of an explosion. Do your neighbors a favor and give them a lifesaving heads-up as well. The overhead smoke detector watches over you as you sleep—if you hear its piercing scream, chances are, smoke has filled the interior. Repeat the same drill as above—hightail it out of there if the fire is taking over. An onboard fire extinguisher is a must-have.

RVers should adopt a serious attitude to any sort of flame, controlled or otherwise, onboard: "Fire bad!" Leave the torched shish-kabob recipe at home. As mentioned routinely in Chapter 10, being on the go with flowing propane containers puts you at further risk. Be sure to extinguish pilot lights and shut off the propane supply while on the go, especially when filling up at the gas pump. Store a fire extinguisher both inside and outside the vehicle to squelch possible blazes. Devise a series of escape routes inside, and review them with passengers. In some cases, the best way might be through an emergency exit, a window, or a side door.

> **ONE FOR THE ROAD**
>
> RV code mandates an "alternative means of egress," or another door or hatch on the opposite side of the entry door, on the roof, or rear window. Older RVs were designed with a wider roof vent or a hinged rear window to allow escape. Check the workability of these devices annually. Newer coaches usually come equipped with a driver's side door to satisfy this requirement.

Where the Wild Things Are

Prevent furry campsite invaders by putting away all food and garbage at night. Take special precautions when camping in parks unknown, such as in the middle of bear country. Don't let children or pets wander off alone where they could find trouble. Always make your presence known, whether on-site or when walking a secluded path, to avoid startling or antagonizing anything with sharp teeth and a short temper. Boondocking in such an environment can be a risky proposition.

Bugs are a more insidious threat. How do you think they got the name "pests"? A few well-placed mosquitoes aboard the motorhome or an ant trail leading that watermelon from the icebox out through the front door is a real headache. And because you're not looking for any hitchhikers, get rid of these tag-alongs now before they become like family. Create an impenetrable barrier around the RV by spraying bug spray around the perimeter. (A ring of Ajax is another popular option against ants.) Spray bugs and set traps onboard if they begin to congregate like Greenpeace at a nuclear power plant.

A clean and orderly campsite and interior also makes for a less attractive target. Don't let trash build up, keep dishes washed and counters clean, and don't park in the middle of Ant Colony, USA. At the first sign of serious infestation, launch a thorough search-and-destroy campaign. A deep-down cleaning—yes, even in the scary closets and under the sink—and adequate spraying should tame the problem. If problems persist, enlist the aid of a professional exterminator.

Trouble at Home

The pop-up trailer with three kids, a dog, and a pair of goldfish onboard might not be that alluring of a target to criminals, but the five-bedroom colonial house you left behind with two cars in the garage and priceless art on the walls is. Peace of mind on the road starts with taking the necessary precautions before you leave. The goal here is to make your home look like you never left, a clever ruse performed by taking a few simple steps. Do your best Fort Knox imitation. Lock all doors and windows, and pull the shades/curtains to prevent clear views into your home—and its contents—by prowlers. Next, tie up loose ends. Enlist a friend or neighbor to pick up mail and the morning paper. (They can water the plants and feed the iguana while they're there.)

A scattering of on-again, off-again lights, perpetrated by an installed timer, should keep anyone casing the joint guessing. And no matter how bad you want to gloat, don't change the phone message to one proclaiming the family's vacation plans. My parents always included one final step before we left on vacation, and that was to call the police. We'd state that we'd be away from home for the week and ask if they wouldn't mind driving by and checking up on things once in a while. Did our local constable step up patrols or camp out in our driveway? Who knows, but I always liked the idea of the coppers staking out my comic collection in my absence.

Here's a checklist of important equipment to have in your RV.

Emergency Equipment

- ❏ Mobile phone
- ❏ Important phone numbers (insurance, roadside assistance, doctor, and so on)
- ❏ Road flares
- ❏ Reflective triangles
- ❏ Fire extinguishers
- ❏ Child safety seats
- ❏ Air bags
- ❏ LP gas detector
- ❏ Carbon monoxide detector
- ❏ Smoke alarm
- ❏ First-aid kit
- ❏ Jumper cables
- ❏ Spare keys
- ❏ Flashlight
- ❏ Extra prescription medications
- ❏ Spare tire
- ❏ Basic tool kit
- ❏ Reflective tape
- ❏ Ice and/or heat packs
- ❏ Extra batteries
- ❏ Spare LP regulator

The Least You Need to Know

- In bad weather, take it slow, give those vehicles around you plenty of space, stay visible, and know when to stop and find a place to sit it out.
- Alert, rested, and prepared drivers are more likely to avoid accidents. However, in the event of a collision, the most important aspect is the well-being of those involved.
- A comprehensive roadside assistance program is the best defense against breakdowns.

Resources

RV and Camping Phone Applications

4RoadService: Fifth-wheel (or third or fourth) go flat in the middle of Wyoming? This app helps locate the closest repair, towing, or tire service from the comfort of your RV. Your phone is connected directly to the servers and fetches your closest service provider.

iPhone—Free (will have a nominal fee when the full version is released)

AccuWeather: Updated every hour, AccuWeather give you interactive Google maps and weather in 23 languages.

iPhone and Android—Free

Allstays Rest Stops Plus: With more than 2,800 listings searchable by amenities (need a bathroom, a place for Fido to run around, or Wi-Fi to check email?), this app maps out welcome centers, service plazas, and rest stops near your location.

iPhone and Android—Fee

Allstays RV Dumps: Is your go-to dump station paved over or closed for the season? Been boondocking for a week and need to lighten the load? RV Dumps checks your location and displays on a map up to 150 locations of its more than 12,000 listings.

iPhone and Android—Fee

AllTrails: View photos, read reviews, and find maps of more than 40,000 high-quality trail guides. Whether you're interested in a 2-mile loop trail for hiking or a nearby body of water to drop your kayak, this free app lets you find one nearest your current location.

iPhone and Android—Free

Camp Finder: Get access to more than 14,000 campgrounds and RV parks across the United States. Easy to use, with a cool feature that lets you read fellow campers' and RVers' reviews, as well as share your own.

iPhone and Android—Fee

DishPointer Augmented Reality: Can't live without reruns of *Seinfeld*? Finding the best spot for your dish has never been easier. Point your phone toward the sky and see where the satellites are on the screen, and whether anything is blocking their line of sight (like trees).

iPhone and Android—Fee

GasBuddy: Those pennies add up when you have a 75-gallon tank! GasBuddy locates gas stations near your current location and lists their current gas prices.

Android, iPhone, and Windows—Free

Geocaching: A great family activity, geocaching resembles a treasure hunt. This app allows you to view the location of the geocaches (small, hidden containers) on a map, use its GPS device to track it down, and even post photos of your find.

iPhone and Android—Fee

iExit Interstate Exit Guide: When no other burger will do but one from In-N-Out Burger, this app is for you! iExit tells you what restaurants, hotels, coffee shops, and so on are coming up in real time while driving on the interstate. You can select which chain you're looking for (mocha caramel latte, anyone?) and which upcoming exit has it.

iPhone and Android—Fee

National Park Field Guides: Need help identifying that bird that just flew by? Curious to know whether the 6-foot-long snake slithering under your RV is poisonous? The National Park Field Guides app arms you with information on the wildlife of 50 National Parks, along with directions, hours, fees, and phone numbers.

iPhone—Free

OhRanger! Parkfinder: Mom wants to birdwatch, Grandpa wants to fish, and the kids are eager to go caving. How to satisfy them all? This app makes it easy to find the parks nearest you with listings of activities you want to do.

iPhone—Free

(Android version coming soon)

RV Checklist: Forget the days of scavenging through the garbage looking for the piece of scrap paper with your "what to bring" or "departing from a site" checklists. This app organizes your various checklists and comes populated with some routine tasks to get you started.

iPhone—Fee

Trip Advisor: Everything you love about the website now comes in a phone app. You'll find millions of reviews by fellow travelers of restaurants, attractions, and hotels (in case your RV becomes plagued by thousands of lady bugs—don't ask!).

iPhone and Android—Free

The Weather Channel: Are 75 mph winds coming your way? Better retract the awning! The Weather Channel app keeps you informed of weather conditions wherever you are.

iPhone and Android—Free

Woodall's RV & Camping Copilot: From the leader in campground directories, this iPhone app gives users the ability to search campgrounds by location and gives extensive information, such as amenities, services, and recreation. An added bonus: Woodall's exclusive 5W/5W rating system.

iPhone—Free

RV/Camping Clubs

Camping World President's Club
1-800-626-3636
www.campingworld.com/pc

Escapees
1-888-757-2582
www.escapees.com

Explorer RV Club
1-800-999-0819
www.explorer-rvclub.com

Family Campers and RVers (FCRV)
1-800-245-9755
www.fcrv.org

Family Motor Coach Association (FMCA)
513-474-3622
www.fmca.com

The Good Sam Club
1-800-234-3450
www.goodsamclub.com

Handicapped Travel Club
714-524-2700
www.handicappedtravelclub.com

Loners on Wheels, Inc.
1-866-LOW-CLUB (1-866-569-2582)
www.lonersonwheels.com

North America Camping Club
1-866-885-6222
www.campnacc.com

Passport America
1-800-681-6810
www.passportamerica.com

RVing Women
1-888-55-RVing (1-888-557-8464)
www.rvingwomen.org

Campground Clubs/Franchises/Associations

Coast to Coast Resorts
1-800-368-5721
www.coastresorts.com

Kampgrounds of America (KOA)
406-248-7444, 1-888-562-0000
www.koa.com

National Association of RV Parks and Campgrounds (ARVC)
1-800-395-2267
www.gocampingamerica.com

Outdoor Resorts of America
1-800-541-2582
www.outdoor-resorts.com

Thousand Trails
1-888-453-4391
www.thousandtrails.com

Yogi Bear's Jellystone Park Camp-Resorts
1-800-558-2954
www.campjellystone.com

Federal Campgrounds/Properties

Bureau of Land Management (BLM)
202-208-3801
www.blm.gov

National Park Service
202-208-4747
www.nps.gov

Recreation.Gov (Explore America)
1-877-444-6777
www.recreation.gov

U.S. Army Corps of Engineers
www.usace.army.mil

U.S. National Forest Camping Guide
www.forestcamping.com

USDA Forest Service
202-205-1706
www.fs.fed.us

RV Rentals

Cruise America
1-800-671-8042
www.cruiseamerica.com

El Monte RV
1-888-337-2214
www.elmonterv.com

Recreational Vehicle Rental Association (RVRA)
1-800-336-0355, 1-888-467-8464
www.rvra.org

RV Dealer Association

Recreation Vehicle Dealers Association (RVDA)
1-800-336-0355, 703-591-7130
www.rvda.org

RV Education

Road Scholar/Elderhostel
617-426-7788, 1-800-454-5768
www.roadscholar.org

RV Education 101
www.rveducation101.com
www.rvconsumer.com
www.rvuniversity.com

RV Industry Associations

Go RVing Canada
www.gorving.ca

GoRVing
1-888-GO-RVING (1-888-467-8464)
www.gorving.com

Recreation Vehicle Industry Association (RVIA)
703-620-6003
www.rvia.org

Recreational Park Trailer Industry Association
770-251-2672
www.rptia.org

Driving Instruction

RV Driving School
530-878-0111
www.rvschool.com

RV Caravans and Tour Providers

Adventure Caravans
1-800-872-7897
www.adventurecaravans.com

Camping World President's Club Tours
1-800-626-0042
www.campingworldrvtours.com

Fantasy RV Tours & Creative World Travel
1-800-952-8496
www.fantasyrvtours.com

Good Sam Club Tours
1-800-664-9145
www.goodsamclub.com

Publications

Camping Life
1-800-786-2721
www.campinglife.com

Coast to Coast
1-800-368-5721
www.coastresorts.com

Escapees
1-888-757-2582
www.escapees.com

Family Motor Coaching
513-474-3622
www.fmca.com

Highways
1-800-234-3450
www.goodsamclub.com/highways

MotorHome
1-800-678-1201
www.motorhomemagazine.com

Pop Up Times
www.popuptimes.com

Rand McNally Road Atlas
1-800-678-7263
www.randmcnally.com

RV Education Newsletter
http://rveducation101.com/email

RV Gazette
1-800-999-0819
www.explorer-rvclub.com

RV Lifestyle Magazine
905-844-8218
www.rvlifemag.com

RV Times
1-250-642-1916
www.rvtimes.ca

RV View
1-800-616-2267
www.rvview.com

RV Women
1-888-557-8464
www.rvingwomen.org

Trailer Life
1-800-825-6861
www.trailerlife.com

Woodall's Regional Publications
1-800-323-9076
www.woodalls.com

Workamper News
501-362-2637
www.workkamper.com

RV/Camping Websites

About camping: www.camping.about.com

Explore America: www.recreation.gov

Gateway to RV information: www.rvnetlinx.com

Great outdoors recreation pages: www.gorp.com

National forest camping: www.forestcamping.com

New RVers: www.newrver.com

RV advice: www.rvadvice.com

RV classifieds: www.rvclassified.com, www.rvtrader.com, www.rvtraderonline.com

RV clubs, forums, and blogs: www.rvclub.com

RV dealer location and RV sales: www.rvamerica.com

RV education: www.rveducation101.com, www.rvconsumer.com, www.rvuniversity.com

RV forum and blog: www.rv.net

RV information: www.rvusa.com

RV lifestyle: www.fulltiming-america.com

RV maintenance: www.rvdoctor.com

RV ratings and RV consumer group: www.rv.org

RV safety: www.rvsafety.com

RVers website: www.rversonline.org

Used RV sales: www.motorhomesused.com

Work for RVers: www.workersonwheels.com

Glossary

12-volt DC electrical system   Onboard electrical system powering 12-volt appliances via the coach and engine batteries.

120-volt AC electrical system   *See* shore power.

adult-oriented park   Campground that tailors its activities and recreation to adults only.

aftermarket   Segment of the industry that provides products and services available to all RVers after the initial purchase of an RV.

alternator   Engine-mounted device that produces 12-volt DC electricity for battery charging and other 12-volt functions while the engine is running.

ammeter   Device that measures an RV's total power draw, in amps.

antisway device   Accessory designed to stabilize and restrict motion between a tow vehicle and a travel trailer.

automotive battery   Power source for starting the RV's or tow vehicle's engine and running 12-volt dashboard equipment.

auxiliary vehicle   *See* towed vehicle.

backup monitoring system   Combination rear-mounted camera and in-cockpit display monitor, designed to aid the driver in backing up a larger RV.

ball mount   Connection point between the trailer and the tow vehicle; the ball mount slides into the receiver hitch and is pinned in place.

basement model   RV with a separate storage section between the chassis and the floor of the interior space.

black water   Water and waste materials predominantly from the RV's toilet.

black water holding tank   Tank where black water is deposited and stored until it's later emptied.

boondocking   Camping without hook-ups of any kind (electric, sewer, or fresh water). Also known as dry camping or self-contained camping.

bounce-aways   For use with truck campers. Shocklike devices attached to the truck below the cab-over section to reduce turbulence while in transit.

brake controller   Device mounted within a tow vehicle to activate the trailer's brakes independently or in conjunction with the tow vehicle brakes.

break-away switch   Pin-activated safety device mounted near the trailer's tongue that automatically activates the braking system, in case of separation from the tow vehicle.

cab   Another name for the driver's area or cockpit.

cab-over area   Inhabitable space built over the cockpit of some recreational vehicles. Found on Class C vehicles and truck campers.

camper van   *See* Class B.

campground directory   Resource guide providing evaluations and comprehensive listing information of private campgrounds.

campsite   Plot of land where RVs park within a campground. Usually comes equipped with various hook-ups.

caravan   Group of vehicles traveling together.

catalytic heater   Wall-mounted or portable heater that uses a mix of propane and oxygen to warm the interior.

Class A   Motorhomes built on a specially designed chassis, ranging in size from 25 to 45 feet. Can be gas or diesel powered.

Class B   Also known as camper vans. These smaller, fully self-contained motorhomes share the same chassis and sizes as most traditional vans.

Class C   Also known as mini-motorhomes. Smaller motorhomes built on a traditional van chassis, with a specially manufactured frame added later. Sizes generally range from 20 to 32 feet.

Class I hitch   Weight-carrying hitch for trailers weighing up to 2,000 pounds.

Class II hitch   Weight-carrying hitch for trailers weighing up to 3,500 pounds.

Class III hitch   Weight-distributing hitch for trailers weighing up to 5,000 pounds.

Class IV hitch   Weight-distributing hitch for trailers weighing up to 10,000 pounds.

Class V hitch   Weight-distributing hitch for trailers weighing up to 15,000 pounds.

clearance   Distance between a vehicle's exterior height and possible obstructions, such as an overpass.

coach power   Also known as the auxiliary battery system. It powers the majority of 12-volt DC equipment onboard an RV, excluding functions controlled by the automotive battery.

conversion bus   Also known as a custom-made bus or coach. Deluxe RVs made from a typical bus shell, with sizes between 40 and 45 feet.

conversion vehicle   Any vehicle undergoing a dramatic alteration to its chassis or interior. Examples include modified heavy-duty haulers and van conversions.

converter   Transforms 120-volt AC into usable 12-volt DC electricity for use onboard an RV.

coupler   Apparatus located at the forward-most point of the trailer's tongue, connecting to the tow vehicle's ball mount.

deep-cycle battery   Also known as a marine-style battery or coach battery. Stores and supplies power for the RV's 12-volt electrical system.

diesel pusher   Motorhome powered by a rear-mounted diesel engine, equipped to propel rather than pull larger vehicles. Generally found in motorhomes exceeding 34 feet.

dinette conversion   Table and two bench seats that transform into a sleeping area.

dinghy vehicle   Also known as an auxiliary vehicle, toad, or towed vehicle. Nautical term used to describe a car or truck pulled behind a motorhome via a tow bar, dolly, or small trailer.

direct spark ignition (DSI)   Method of electrically controlling the LP combustion cycles in RV appliances, eliminating the need for a pilot light.

dry camping   *See* boondocking.

dry weight   The weight of the RV unloaded. *See also* unloaded vehicle weight (UVW).

electric hook-up   Connection made from the RV to an outside 120-volt electrical outlet, common at most campsites.

electrical connector   Electrically connects the RV to the tow vehicle to operate running lamps, turn signals, trailer brakes, and other 12-volt functions. For use with truck campers, fifth-wheels, and conventional travel trailers.

engine power   Twelve-volt DC power generated from the RV or tow vehicle's engine.

fifth-wheel   Trailer that relies on a fifth-wheel hitch mounted within the bed of a truck, most evident by its gooseneck design. The largest of all towable RVs—up to 40 feet in length.

fold-down camper   Also known as a pop-up or folding trailer. These are the smallest towable RVs, known for their boxy shape in transit. Sides expand and must be deployed upon arrival at destination, usually via a hand crank or push-button activation.

fold-down truck camper   Truck camper that lies flat in transit and must be deployed, usually by use of a hand crank, after the destination is reached.

forced-air furnace   Onboard heating source utilizing a fan to blow heated air throughout the ducts of the RV's interior.

fresh water hook-up   Connection made from the RV to an outside fresh water source, common at most campsites.

fresh water storage tank   Where fresh water is stored during transit until ready for use.

fresh water system   Clean water running from all faucets, including sinks and showers, as well as the water heater; also used to maintain the toilet's water level.

full hook-up   Campsite with water, electrical, and sewer connections. Some campgrounds also include cable TV, but this may be an additional charge.

full-timer   An RVer who lives and travels year-round in his or her RV.

galley   Another name for the RV's kitchen.

generator   Device driven by an internal combustion engine that produces 120-volt AC electricity for RV use when other power sources are not available.

Global Positioning System (GPS)   Onboard device capable of pinpointing a vehicle's exact location; provides navigational functions.

gooseneck   Area of a fifth-wheel trailer that fits into the bed of a pickup truck or conversion vehicle to make a connection for towing.

gray water   Used water from an RV's sinks and tub/shower.

gray water holding tank   Tank where gray water is deposited and stored until it's later emptied.

gross axle weight (GAW)   Amount of weight each axle can safely support.

gross combined weight rating (GCWR)   Used for towing combinations. The rating applies to the maximum weight limit for the tow vehicle, the towed object, and all passengers, cargo, and liquids inside each vehicle.

gross vehicle weight rating (GVWR)   Also known as the wet weight. The maximum weight limit of an RV, including all gear, passengers, and liquids.

hitch   Device that facilitates the connection between a tow vehicle and a towable.

hitch receiver   Part of the hitch that's bolted or welded to the frame of a tow vehicle.

hitch weight   Also known as the tongue weight. Specified by towable manufacturers, this is the recommended weight to rest on the hitch for greater stability.

hook-up   Term used to describe a situation in which an RV relies on outside utilities, such as electricity, water, sewer, cable TV, or phone.

hybrid trailer   Also known as a hybrid, this small, lightweight towable features expandable bunks to provide more bedding options.

hydronic heat   Onboard heating source that uses circulating water instead of air for radiant and semiconvected heat and for instantaneous water on demand.

inverter   Opposite of a converter. Inverters turn 12-volt DC power into 120-volt AC power for use in running typical RV appliances and devices.

isolator   Maintains battery separation between automotive and coach batteries, to prevent one from taxing the reserves of the other.

jackknife   Serious condition in which the tow vehicle ends up perpendicular to the trailer.

kingpin   Portion of the fifth-wheel trailer that slides and locks into the truck-mounted fifth-wheel hitch.

leveling jack   Manually or electronically deployed apparatus used to level and stabilize an RV after the destination is reached.

lightweight travel trailer   Trailer that usually weighs less than 5,000 to 6,000 pounds (unloaded). Sizes rarely exceed 25 feet.

load equalizing hitch   *See* weight-distributing hitch.

locking pin   Also known as the safety pin. Secures the connection between the kingpin and the fifth-wheel hitch for added safety.

LP gas   Also known as liquid petroleum or propane. Fuels many of the appliances onboard an RV.

marine-style toilet   Similar to that found in airplanes, a toilet that operates via floor pedals or a flush mechanism.

membership campground   RV park belonging to a larger private network, where members receive discounted stays.

mini-motorhome   *See* Class C.

mobile home   Small dwelling with limited mobility designed for stationary living.

modem-friendly   *See* Wi-Fi.

monitor panel   Interior display unit that provides important information about the various levels of the RV's onboard systems, including tank levels and battery voltage.

motorhome   Motorized recreational vehicle built on a special or traditional chassis. Includes Class A, B, and C vehicles.

motorized RV   Also known as a self-propelled RV. A recreational vehicle that relies on its own engine for mobility. Includes motorhomes, camper vans, and truck campers.

net carrying capacity (NCC)   Maximum amount of weight in the form of passengers, cargo, and fluids that an RV can safely transport.

park model   Residential-style structure, capable of being towed but designed to be set up in one location for greater lengths of time.

patio-hauler   *See* sport-utility trailer (SUT).

pickup camper   *See* truck camper.

polarity tester   Device designed to test 120-volt AC receptacles to determine proper wiring and output.

pop-up   *See* fold-down camper.

primitive site   Campsite predominantly known to feature electric and water hook-ups only. Term also may describe campsites with no hook-ups.

propane   *See* LP gas.

pull-through site   Campsite with access from more than one direction, allowing RVs to drive through the site, thereby avoiding backing up.

rally   Large get-together of RVers, often associated with a specific type or brand of RV or travel club.

rear bumper extensions   For use with truck campers. May be needed so the truck's license plate is visible from underneath the camper.

recreational vehicle (RV)   Motorized or towable vehicle that provides a place to sleep, basic cooking functions, and livable space.

regulator, LP   Also known as a two-stage regulator. An adjustable device that regulates the fluctuating container pressures, delivering an even flow of fuel to all LP appliances.

RV show   Gathering of the latest recreational vehicles and RV-related products and services for sale.

safety chains   Vital towing attachment that prevents the trailer from veering off in case of separation during transit.

seasonal   A person who stays in a campground long term, usually at least a month, but most likely a season or more.

seasonal site Campsite reserved for longer-term tenants, those willing to stay at least a month or possibly year-round.

sewer Connection made from the RV to an outside septic system, common at most campsites.

shore power Also known as the 120-volt AC electrical system. A term used when receiving electricity from an AC outlet, such as those found at most campsites.

site *See* campsite.

slide-out room Section of an RV's interior that expands several feet outward at the touch of a button, thus creating more space for those onboard.

snowbird RVer who heads off to warm-weather climates to avoid the winter months.

sofa conversion Also known as a pull-out sofa bed.

solar panel Apparatus installed on some RVs' roofs, to capture the sun's energy and transform it to usable 12-volt power.

solar power Uses the sun's energy as a power source.

sport-utility trailer (SUT) Also known as patio-haulers or toy box models. Towable RV with a ramp and special cargo space for smaller motorized vehicles such as jet skis, motorcycles, and snowmobiles.

spring bar Also known as the tension bar. Part of the hitch designed to properly disperse the weight among the axles.

suspension coverage Type of insurance that allows policyholders to cancel or reduce vehicle coverage during periods of dormancy, including storage.

sway bar *See* antisway device.

tie-downs For use with truck campers. Attachments that secure and fasten a camper to the bed or frame of a truck.

toad *See* towed vehicle.

tongue Two diverging frame members that form the trailer's A-frame, for use in towing.

tongue weight *See* hitch weight.

tow bar   Device used to connect a secondary vehicle behind a motorhome.

tow dolly   Designed to tow a secondary vehicle behind a motorhome, with two of its tires off the ground and two tires riding on the pavement.

tow rating   Listed in pounds; measures the maximum weight a vehicle can safely tow.

tow vehicle   Vehicle responsible for transporting a towable RV.

towable   Any recreational vehicle that relies on a primary vehicle to tow it.

towed vehicle   Also known as a dinghy, auxiliary, or toad vehicle. A secondary vehicle that is pulled behind a motorhome for easier transport when the destination is reached.

travel trailer   Most common towable RV, with sizes ranging from 20 to 40 feet. Subclass is the lightweight travel trailer.

truck camper   Hard-sided camper affixed to the cargo area of a pickup truck.

unloaded vehicle weight (UVW)   Also known as the dry weight. Actual weight of the RV, without passengers, cargo, or liquids.

voltage meter   Also known as a voltmeter. Used to measure the exact AC voltage at the campsite's electrical pedestal.

walk-around   Final check of the RV before departing. Inspection includes the interior and exterior of the vehicle, as well as a possible check of the surrounding area.

water pressure regulator   Device that maintains even water pressure when hooked up to a water outlet.

water pump   Device designed to force water from the fresh water storage tank through the pipes of the RV.

weight-carrying hitch   Hitch configuration in which the tow vehicle's back bumper and axles bear the majority of the towable's weight. Best reserved for towables weighing less than 3,500 pounds.

weight-distributing hitch   Type of hitch attached to the frame of the tow vehicle; disperses the towable's weight to the vehicle's axles.

wet weight   *See* gross vehicle weight rating (GVWR).

Wi-Fi   A service that allows the public to connect to the internet via a wireless hotspot or access point. Commonly found in many locations throughout the United States, like campgrounds, eateries, and coffee shops.

wide-body   Any recreational vehicle wider than 96 inches, with 102 inches being the most common measurement.

winterizing   Taking steps to prepare an RV for storage or extended periods of nonuse.

goose neckCan'T go from car To Trailer

Index

Numbers

12-volt DC (direct current)
  automotive systems, 160-161
  coach power, 161-163

A

accessories
  aftermarket, 53
  antisway device, 53
  driving, 268-270
  electrical systems, 175-176
  towable RVs, 52-53
  truck campers, 43
accidents
  rental RVs, 138
  safety tips, 322-324
aftermarket accessories, 53
alarms, 328-329
alternators, 161
amenities
  selecting RVs, 84
  wish lists, 114
antifreeze, winterizing process, 206-207
antisway device, 53
appliances
  inspection criteria, 108
  LP gas powered, 178-181

B

backing-up tips, 265-267
ball mounts (hitches), 226-227
bars (tow bars), 236-238
basement model RVs, 27
bathrooms
  fresh water systems, 195-196
  livability tests, 102
  supplies, packing tips, 252
batteries
  automotive, 161
  charging, 173
  deep-cycle battery, 162-163
  isolators, 163
  winterizing process, 208-209
benefits
  boondocking, 306-308
  motorized RVs, 18-19
  towable RVs, 48-50

ASME (American Society of Mechanical Engineers) LP containers, 183
automotive battery, 161
awnings, 104-105
axles, GAW (gross axle weight), 246

Better Business Bureau AUTO LINE, 154-155
black water holding tanks
  cleaning, 202
  dump stations, 199-201
  purging, 197
  sewer hook-ups, 198-199
blackouts, 174
boondocking
  benefits, 306-308
  cold-weather camping, 314-317
  legalities, 308-309
  pretrip suggestions, 310-311
  resource conservation tips, 311-313
  RV capabilities, 310
  safety tips, 309
brake controllers, 230
braking
  conventional trailers, 230
  tips, 262-263
  towing behind motorhomes, 240-241
break-away switches (conventional trailers), 231-232
breakdowns, safety tips, 324-325
breaking camp (pretrip checklist), 301-304